Best
of the
Best

Best of the Best

THE BEST RECIPES FROM THE BEST COOKBOOKS OF THE YEAR

FOOD&WINE BOOKS

American Express Publishing Corporation
New York

Editor in Chief: Judith Hill
Art Director: Nina Scerbo
Managing Editor: Terri Mauro
Project Editor: Judith Sutton
Assistant Editor: Laura Russell
Editorial Assistant: Evette Manners
Art Assistant: Leslie Andersen
Cover Designer: Iris Jeromnimon
Production Manager: Yvette Williams-Braxton

Vice President, Consumer Marketing: Mark V. Stanich
Vice President, Books and Information Services: John Stoops
Marketing Director: Mary V. Cooney
Marketing/Promotion Manager: Roni Stein
Operations Manager: Doreen Camardi
Business Manager: Joanne Ragazzo

AMERICAN EXPRESS PUBLISHING CORPORATION
©1998 American Express Publishing Corporation

ISBN 0-916103-44-7

Published by American Express Publishing Corporation
1120 Avenue of the Americas, New York, New York 10036
Manufactured in the United States of America

Contents

Best of the Best—Defined 6

chapter 1 · Chefs' Cookbooks 8

chapter 2 · Italian and Mediterranean Cooking 90

chapter 3 · Best-Sellers 156

chapter 4 · Vegetarian and Healthy Cooking 198

chapter 5 · Special Topics 232

Acknowledgements 298

Publishers 303

Recipes by Course 306

Index 309

Best of the Best — Defined

What's in this book

Over a thousand cookbooks came out this year. We read them, we tested and tasted recipes, we checked sales statistics. Eventually, we winnowed the field to the thirty-five that we, the editors of FOOD & WINE Books, consider to be the most popular and the most deserving cookbooks of the year. We found the most interesting, tastiest recipes in those chosen thirty-five—the best of the best—and offer them to you here as a delicious sampling.

The organization into categories was dictated by the best books themselves, and thus the categories will change each year depending on the content of the chosen books. The divisions are often telling in themselves. For example, there were not nearly as many over-the-top rich, rich, rich dessert books this year as in recent years, not even enough to warrant their own category, but we see a huge drop-off in low-fat books, too. Could it be that the trend is to relatively sane eating?

So that you can get a real feeling for the books, we have printed each recipe exactly as it appears in its own book, and we duplicated the layout of the pages, the photographs, and the illustrations as closely as we could. The cover of each book, some highlights, and an explanation of why we selected it precedes each set of recipes.

What's not

- We have not included culinary reference books or textbooks.
- No books that were published exclusively as paperbacks were considered.
- Books published outside the United States were excluded.
- We included no book that failed our test-kitchen trial by tasting.

JUDITH HILL
Editor in Chief
FOOD & WINE Books

Editor's Choice Awards

During the year, as we lived with these cookbooks, favorites emerged.
So now, we're pleased to present the Editor's Choice Awards—our picks for the tippy-top of the best:

Best Book of the Year

Marcella Cucina (PAGE 92)

AUTHOR:
Marcella Hazan

PUBLISHER:
HarperCollins Publishers, Inc.

Most Luscious Recipe

Chocolate Bread Pudding with
Spiced Cream (PAGE 45)

FROM
Emeril's Creole Christmas

AUTHOR:
Emeril Lagasse

PUBLISHER:
William Morrow and Company, Inc.

Easiest to Cook From

*The Good Housekeeping Step-by-Step
Cookbook* (PAGE 164)

EDITOR:
Susan Westmoreland

PUBLISHER:
Hearst Books

Most Fun to Read

Cookwise (PAGE 294)

AUTHOR:
Shirley O. Corriher

PUBLISHER:
William Morrow and Company, Inc.

Nicest to Look At

*Alfred Portale's Gotham Bar and
Grill Cookbook* (PAGE 16)

AUTHOR:
Alfred Portale

PUBLISHER:
Doubleday

Chapter 1
Chefs' Cookbooks

The decades-long transformation of the chef from kitchen drudge to acclaimed celebrity continues apace. More and more chefs have their own TV programs; they're popping up on mainstream talk shows and making personal appearances; and they're all writing cookbooks—many of which are surprisingly practical for the home cook. These form the largest specific category of our best-of-the-year picks.

■ **THE FOOD OF CAMPANILE** BY MARK PEEL AND NANCY SILVERTON

Garlic Soup 12

Black Cod with Brown Butter Sauce and Fresh Herbs 13

Roasted Beet Salad with Horseradish Vinaigrette 14

■ **ALFRED PORTALE'S GOTHAM BAR AND GRILL COOKBOOK** BY ALFRED PORTALE

Ginger Crème Brûlée with Warm Plum and Raspberry Compote 18

Fettuccine with Lobster Bolognese Sauce 21

Tomato, Basil, and Fresh Ricotta Sandwich with Tapenade 24

Duck Breast, Caramelized Endive, Sweet Potatoes, and Green Peppercorn Sauce 27

■ **COOKING WITH TOO HOT TAMALES** BY MARY SUE MILLIKEN AND SUSAN FENIGER

Salmon Baked in Salsa Verde 32

Wrapped Spicy Snapper 33

Roasted Chicken with a Papaya Glaze 35

Black Jalapeño Salsa 36

■ **EMERIL'S CREOLE CHRISTMAS** BY EMERIL LAGASSE

Quail and Smoked Sausage Christmas Gumbo 41

Sugarcane Baked Ham with Spiced Apples and Pears 42

Chocolate Bread Pudding with Spiced Cream 45

■ **THE NEW MAKING OF A COOK: The Art, Techniques, and Science of Good Cooking**
BY MADELEINE KAMMAN

Chunky Summer Tomato Soup 48

Ragout of Peas and Artichokes 48

Steamed Mountain-Style Trout Fillets 50

Butterflied Leg of Lamb in Citrus Marinade 51

■ **AMERICAN BRASSERIE: 180 Simple, Robust Recipes Inspired by the Rustic Foods of France, Italy, and America** BY RICK TRAMONTO AND GALE GAND

Roquefort and Pear Salad with Grapes and Spiced Pecans 56

Orange-Ricotta Gnocchi with Broccoli Rabe 58

Tramonto's Escarole, Sausage, and White Bean Stew 64

Plum Crostata 65

■ **PIERRE FRANEY COOKS WITH HIS FRIENDS: With Recipes from Top Chefs in France, Spain, Italy, Switzerland, Germany, Belgium & the Netherlands** BY PIERRE FRANEY

Grilled Tuna with Capers and Tomato Sauce 69

Sautéed Chicken with Wine and Herbs 70

Medallions of Lamb with Basil 71

■ **MATTHEW KENNEY'S MEDITERRANEAN COOKING: Great Flavors for the American Kitchen** BY MATTHEW KENNEY

Fennel Salad with Clementines and Moroccan Olives 74

Pan-Roasted Cod with Provençal Fava Bean Ragout 77

Loin of Venison in Black Pepper-Pomegranate Marinade 79

■ **DEATH BY CHOCOLATE COOKIES** BY MARCEL DESAULNIERS

Chocolate Crackups 83

Chocolate Boulders 84

Chocolate Drop Shortcakes 87

Almighty Chocolate Divinity 88

MARK PEEL & NANCY SILVERTON

THE FOOD OF
CAMPANILE

Recipes from the famed Los Angeles restaurant

Mark Peel and Nancy Silverton, the husband-and-wife, chef-and-baker team behind Campanile and the adjacent La Brea Bakery

■ WHY THEY WROTE IT
"The purpose of this book is not to document the latest fashion in food, or to dazzle people with food based on a school of architecture, but to illustrate that everyone, with a little concentration and passion, can prepare flavorful and deeply satisfying food."

■ WHY IT MADE OUR LIST
Though many chefs' books purport to be written for the home cook, this one embraces that mission most enthusiastically, patiently explaining not only how to recreate Campanile's Mediterranean-inspired specialties but how to blanch a vegetable, how to select fresh produce, how to use a pasta machine, even how to develop a sense of taste. The dishes are do-able but not dull, the text considerate but not condescending.

FROM THE BOOK

■ ADVICE ON ADJUSTING RECIPES TO YOUR TASTE
"You might push too far sometimes and ruin something. Just try not to do it when you've got a dozen well-cocktailed guests seated in the dining room expecting the Meal of all Meals."

■ CHAPTERS
Cooking and Eating ▪ Equipment ▪ Appetizers ▪ Salads ▪ Soups ▪ Pastas, Risottos, and Polenta ▪ Main Courses ▪ Stocks ▪ Sauces ▪ Vegetables ▪ Desserts

■ PREVIOUS CREDITS
Silverton wrote about her breads in *Breads from La Brea Bakery*; in *Mark Peel and Nancy Silverton at Home*, the pair presented recipes for the simple food they like to cook with their three children.

■ SPECIFICS
310 pages, 157 recipes, 34 black-and-white photographs, $35. Published by Villard Books.

Garlic Soup

THIS is an easy and quick soup to make. It is garlicky, but in a refined and understated way, as the garlic is tempered by the cooking and sweetened by the light caramelization of the other vegetables. Rapini, also called broccoli rabe, adds a slightly bitter counterpoint to the sweet richness of the soup.

¼ cup plus 1 tablespoon vegetable oil

2 large brown onions (2 pounds), peeled and coarsely chopped

3 celery stalks (12 ounces), trimmed and coarsely chopped

1 large carrot (4 ounces), trimmed, peeled, and coarsely chopped

1 large parsnip (3 ounces), trimmed, peeled, and coarsely chopped

10 cups chicken stock or vegetable stock

2 russet potatoes (1¼ pounds), peeled and cut into chunks

4 large heads (1 pound) garlic, cut in half horizontally

Bouquet garni (5 sprigs Italian parsley, 3 sprigs thyme, 1 sprig rosemary)

Kosher salt

Freshly cracked black pepper

1 bunch rapini (8 ounces)

Extra-virgin olive oil

Have ready

The chicken stock or vegetable stock, warm, in a medium saucepan over low heat

IN a large stockpot, over medium-high heat, preheat ¼ cup of vegetable oil. Sauté the onions, celery, carrot, and parsnip until the vegetables are lightly colored, about 10 minutes. Stir the vegetables frequently to prevent uneven browning. Pour in the warm stock. Add the potatoes, garlic, and bouquet garni, and gently simmer until the vegetables are softened, about 1 hour. It is important that the garlic be soft enough to puree smoothly.

Remove the bouquet garni and puree the soup, in batches, using a food mill or blender. Using a coarse-mesh, stainless-steel strainer, strain into a clean stockpot and correct the seasoning to taste with kosher salt and black pepper. Keep warm over low heat until needed, or allow to cool and refrigerate, covered, for up to 3 days.

Using a sharp knife, cut off the top 2 inches of each rapini stalk, reserving the tops and discarding the remaining portion. In a medium sauté pan, over high heat, preheat 1 tablespoon vegetable oil to smoking. Sauté the rapini tops until lightly browned, about 2 minutes. Season the rapini with about ¼ teaspoon of kosher salt.

Warm the soup over low heat if necessary. Ladle about 8 ounces into each large, warm soup plate. Add a few sprigs of seared rapini and a drizzle of extra-virgin olive oil to each portion, and serve immediately.

Black Cod with Brown Butter Sauce and Fresh Herbs

Serves 4

BLACK cod is a West Coast fish. It is white fleshed and very tender. The toasty, nutlike flavor of the brown butter is a wonderful complement to the mild flavor of the black cod. The fish sautés well but is difficult to grill, so this quick preparation is ideal. The fish has a number of small bones, but they are all in a line down the center of the fillet. The best technique to remove the bones is to simply eat half the fillet, then scrape the bones away with your fork and finish eating. This recipe works well with other types of fish, such as rock cod or a true cod from the East Coast.

Four 6-ounce black cod fillets, skin removed
Kosher salt
Freshly cracked black pepper
Unbleached all-purpose flour for dusting
2 tablespoons vegetable oil
1 bunch chives cut 1 inch long (½ cup)
1 bunch fresh Italian parsley, stemmed (1 cup)
1 bunch fresh chervil, stemmed (½ cup)
5 sprigs fresh dill, stemmed (⅓ cup)
1 bunch fresh tarragon, stemmed (⅓ cup)
1 stick (4 ounces) unsalted butter
1 large shallot, peeled, trimmed, and minced
    (1 tablespoon)
Juice of 1 lemon

PREHEAT the oven to 400 degrees,

Lightly season the black cod fillets with kosher salt and black pepper, Then lightly dust the fillets in flour, and shake off any excess flour.

In a large, ovenproof cast-iron skillet, over medium-high heat, preheat the vegetable oil until just smoking. Sear the fillets on the side that was connected to the bone until lightly browned, about 5 minutes. Using a wide stainless-steel spatula, turn the fillets over, and transfer to the oven to cook for about 5 minutes more.

In a large mixing bowl, toss together the parsley, chervil, dill, tarragon, and chives.

To serve, divide the herb salad equally among 4 large, warm plates. In a small saucepan, over medium heat, melt and brown, not blacken, the butter, about 3 to 4 minutes. Remove the pan from the heat. Add the shallot and the fresh lemon juice. Adjust the seasoning to taste with kosher salt and black pepper. On each plate, place a fillet next to each portion of herb salad, and splash the brown butter sauce over the salad and the fillet. Serve immediately.

Roasted Beet Salad with Horseradish Vinaigrette

Serves 6

I never liked beets until we made this salad; it was something about the color that put me off. In this recipe, the beets are roasted to bring out a sweet, earthy, and concentrated flavor. It was the flavor that overcame my resistance to beets. We serve this when the horseradish and beets are in their prime, as part of an antipasto platter, or as a fall salad all by itself. This salad is a perfect first course before a roasted meat dinner.

Sometimes fresh horseradish root from the supermarket is not strong enough in flavor. If that is the case, add a little of the bottled horseradish to fortify the vinaigrette. If horseradish root is not available, increase the amount of bottled horseradish by ¼ cup. Try to find a good bottled horseradish, one made with only horseradish and vinegar. Regardless of the type of horseradish used, the greens should have real presence of flavor, to complement the strong horseradish.

Salad

2 pounds (2 bunches) red beets
1 teaspoon kosher salt
⅛ teaspoon freshly cracked black pepper
5 sprigs fresh thyme, whole leaves only
    (2 teaspoons)
¼ cup extra-virgin olive oil
½ large red onion (6 ounces), cut into very
    thin slices
¼ cup chopped fresh Italian parsley
½ cup arugula leaves, watercress, or other
    greens, for garnish

Horseradish Vinaigrette

About 6 ounces horseradish root
½ cup vegetable oil
¼ cup apple cider vinegar
3 tablespoons chopped fresh Italian parsley
½ teaspoon freshly cracked black pepper
2 to 4 tablespoons prepared white horseradish
    (optional)

PREHEAT the oven to 400 degrees.

To make the salad: Wash the beets and trim the ends. Place the beets in a large mixing bowl and toss with kosher salt, black pepper, thyme, and extra-virgin olive oil, coating all the beets well. Place the beets on a large baking pan in 1 layer, cover the pan with aluminum foil, and roast for about 1 hour. Uncover and roast about 10 minutes longer, or until the beets are tender. Remove them from the oven and allow to cool to room temperature. When the beets are cool, the skins will slip off easily by hand. After you have done this, cut them into 4 to 6 wedges and transfer to a large mixing bowl.

To make the vinaigrette: While the beets are roasting, wash the horseradish. Using a vegetable peeler, peel the horseradish. Remove any discolored portions, and then, using a grater, shred the horseradish to yield about ½ cup. In a medium mixing bowl, combine the fresh horseradish, vegetable oil, vinegar, parsley, and black pepper, adding prepared horseradish to taste if desired. Mix the vinaigrette well and reserve.

Toss the vinaigrette, red onion, and the beets, and correct the seasoning to taste with kosher salt and black pepper.

Mound the beets in the center of a large platter. Sprinkle them with the chopped parsley and surround them with the leaves of arugula, or greens of your choice, and serve immediately.

Alfred Portale's Gotham Bar and Grill Cookbook

■ **AUTHOR**

Alfred Portale, the Gotham Bar and Grill chef known for his "architectural cuisine"

■ **WHY HE WROTE IT**

"Many people make the same dish every time they entertain, returning continually to the recipes they know and have mastered . . . . I'd like to help you overcome the 'Dinner Party Cycle' by giving you the tools to develop your own expanded repertoire—sharing the product of the time *I've* spent learning and creating. Since I believe the best way to teach is by example, I hope this book will provide some instructive examples to follow."

■ **WHY IT MADE OUR LIST**

His dishes are pretty spectacular. And if they aren't all easy to execute, it's a treat just to see them; this is a cookbook that could double as a coffee-table book. We don't know how many folks are going to want to try these gravity-defying arrangements at home, but Portale does thoughtfully include an "everyday" presentation for the more complicated constructions. With make-ahead advice, tip boxes, variations, and recipes broken down into simpler components (that are often worth making all by themselves), the delectable recipes become surprisingly accessible.

■ **CHAPTERS**

Gotham Bar and Grill: The Making of a Restaurant ▪ How to Use This Book ▪ A Few Gotham Basics ▪ Starters, Salads, and Small Meals ▪ Soups and Sandwiches ▪ Pasta and Risotto ▪ Fish and Shellfish ▪ Poultry, Game Birds, and Rabbit ▪ Meats and Game ▪ Desserts

■ **SPECIFICS**

384 pages, 110 main recipes, approximately 90 color photographs and 70 black-and-white photographs, $45. Published by Doubleday.

FROM THE BOOK

■ **SALT TALK**

"The right amount of salt can make or break a dish . . . . In general, though, I find home cooks rarely cook with enough salt. Most people would be shocked at the amount of salt used in professional kitchens, where we season every component of a dish carefully, and then combine them."

Ginger Crème Brûlée with Warm Plum and Raspberry Compote

MAKES 8 SERVINGS

THOUGH THE CRÈME brûlée and the fruit compote are served in separate containers at the Gotham, they are meant to be eaten together, or at least in alternating mouthfuls. The tart sweetness of the fruit cuts the richness of the cream, while the ginger, plum, and raspberry all leave ghosts of flavor with each bite, dazzling the palate with bright sensations.

Thinking Ahead: The custards and the compote may be prepared as much as 1 day in advance, covered, and refrigerated. Caramelize the custards right before serving.

Special Equipment: eight 6-ounce ovenproof ramekins

CRÈME BRÛLÉE

4 cups heavy cream

$1/2$ cup chopped fresh ginger

12 large egg yolks

1 cup sugar

Position a rack in the center of the oven and preheat to 325° F. Place the ramekins in a large baking pan.

In a medium saucepan, bring the cream and ginger to a simmer over medium heat. Reduce the heat to very low and simmer gently for 30 minutes.

In a medium bowl, whisk the egg yolks and sugar. Gradually whisk in the cream. Strain through a wire sieve into a bowl, and discard the ginger. Place the baking dish with the ramekins in the oven, and carefully ladle or pour the mixture into the ramekins. Using a teaspoon, skim off any foam that forms on the surface of the custards.

Pour enough hot water into the baking pan to come $1/2$ inch up the sides of the ramekins. Bake until the custards seem firm (the centers will be slightly loose), 40 to 50 minutes. Remove from the water bath and cool completely. Cover each ramekin with plastic wrap and refrigerate until ready to serve.

WARM PLUM AND BERRY COMPOTE

2 tablespoons unsalted butter

3 ripe dark-skinned black or Santa Rosa plums, pitted and cut into sixths

2 to 3 tablespoons sugar, depending on the sweetness of the plums

¹/₄ cup fresh orange juice

¹/₂ pint fresh raspberries

In a medium saucepan, heat the butter over medium-low heat. Add the plums and sugar. Cook, stirring occasionally, until the plums begin to release their juices, 3 to 4 minutes. Add the orange juice and bring to a boil over high heat. Cook until the orange juice is slightly thickened, about 2 minutes. Remove from the heat and fold in the raspberries. Spoon the warm compote into small serving dishes.

ASSEMBLY

¹/₃ cup packed light brown sugar (see Sidebar)

Position a broiler rack about 6 inches from the source of heat and preheat the broiler. Rub the brown sugar through a wire sieve to cover each custard with a dusting of the sugar. Put the ramekins on a baking sheet and broil, watching carefully to avoid scorching, until the brown sugar has caramelized, 1 to 2 minutes. On a large plate, place a crème brûlée and a small dish of the compote.

For the best, thinnest sugar crust, rub the brown sugar through a wire sieve onto a baking sheet and spread it out. Let stand overnight to dry.

At the Gotham, our pastry chefs prefer to glaze the crème brûlée with a hand-held propane torch, available for relatively little cost at hardware stores. Wave the ignited flame in a circular pattern about 2 inches above each brown sugar–dusted custard, and let the flame melt the sugar, which will only take a few seconds.

Fettuccine **with**
Lobster Bolognese Sauce

MAKES 6 TO 8 APPETIZER OR 4 MAIN-COURSE SERVINGS

WHEN I BEGAN MY career at the Gotham in 1985, I became one of the first young American chefs who were riffing on time-honored dishes, revamping them in ways that people had never imagined. This dish was one such departure that I've always felt played a part in our earning the first of four three-star reviews from *The New York Times.* Before we introduced this dish, bolognese sauce had always been made with ground meats like veal, pork, and chicken livers, and finished with cream. This was never altered. When designing the Gotham's menu, I wanted to be sure to include a number of pastas. Maybe it's just my Italian heritage, but at the time I felt American restaurants never made enough room on their rosters for this pasta.

Using some creative license, I put a spin on the concept of bolognese and devised this decadent sauce, loaded with lobster, cream, and herbs. It's thick enough to coat a flat noodle like fettuccine. It also offers a *small* economy as three lobsters will feed four hungry adults.

Thinking Ahead: The sauce may be prepared as much as 8 hours in advance, cooled, covered, and refrigerated.

LOBSTER BOLOGNESE SAUCE

10 quarts water

$^3/_4$ cup white wine

3 (1- to 1$^1/_4$-pound) live lobsters

2 tablespoons olive oil

1 medium onion, chopped

$^1/_2$ medium carrot, chopped

$^1/_2$ small celery rib, chopped

4 garlic cloves, sliced

5 sprigs flat-leaf parsley

1 dried bay leaf

3 tablespoons tomato paste

$^1/_4$ cup Cognac or brandy

6 cups White Chicken Stock (page 23), or as needed

1 cup heavy cream

Coarse salt and cayenne to taste

Using a large stockpot, bring the salted water and $^1/_4$ cup of the wine to a boil over high heat. In batches, if necessary, add the lobsters and cover. Cook for 5 minutes. (The lobsters will be only partially cooked.) Drain the lobsters, place them in a bowl, and set aside until cool enough to handle.

Working over a bowl to catch the juices, twist the lobster bodies away from the tails; reserve the bodies. Saving as much of the juice as possible while working, crack the lobster tails and claws. Remove the meat and cut it into $^3/_4$-inch dice. Transfer the meat to a bowl, cover with plastic wrap, and refrigerate. Coarsely chop the lobster shells.

In a large stockpot, heat the oil over medium heat. Add the onion, carrot, celery, garlic, parsley sprigs, and bay leaf. Cover and cook, stirring occasionally, until the vegetables soften, about 10 minutes. Stir in the tomato paste. Add the lobster shells and bodies and cook, stirring often, for 2 minutes. Add the Cognac and reduce by half, about 2 minutes. Add the remaining wine and reduce by half, about 3 minutes. Add the reserved lobster juices and enough stock to barely cover the ingredients. Bring to a boil over high heat, skimming off any foam that rises to the surface. Reduce the heat to low and simmer until well flavored, about 45 minutes. Strain into a large bowl, pressing hard on the solids to extract as much flavor as possible, then discard the solids. (If making in advance, cool, cover, and refrigerate.)

In a large saucepan, bring the lobster stock to a boil over high heat and reduce it to 1 cup, about 30 minutes. Add the cream, return to a boil, and cook until the sauce thickens slightly, about 5 minutes. Taste and season carefully with salt and cayenne.

ASSEMBLY

1 pound fresh or dried fettuccine

2 tablespoons unsalted butter, cut into eight pieces

1 tablespoon finely chopped fresh flat-leaf parsley

2 teaspoons finely chopped fresh tarragon

10 basil leaves, cut into chiffonade*

10 sprigs chervil

Bring a large pot of salted water to a boil over high heat. Add the fettuccine and cook until al dente, 2 to 3 minutes for fresh, 8 to 10 minutes for dried. Drain and return the pasta to the pot.

If necessary, reheat the lobster sauce over low heat and stir in the butter a piece at a time. Add the lobster meat and cook just to heat through, about 2 minutes. Stir in the parsley, tarragon, and basil. Add the warm lobster sauce to the pasta and toss well.

Serve in warmed pasta bowls, garnishing each serving with the chervil sprigs.

*"Chiffonade" is a term for thin strips of herbs. Large herb leaves, such as basil or sage, are stacked, rolled lengthwise into a cylinder, and cut into very thin (1/16 inch) "ribbons."

Variations: Just about any flat noodle will work in this dish. If you have a preference for tagliarini, pappardelle, or another pasta, you should experiment and determine which works best for you.

White Chicken Stock

MAKES ABOUT 2½ QUARTS

Thinking Ahead: The stock may be prepared up to 4 days in advance, cooled, covered, and refrigerated; or it may be frozen for up to 3 months.

THIS IS THE MOST **useful stock to have on hand at all times.**

6 pounds chicken bones, coarsely chopped (substitute wings if bones or carcasses are unavailable)

4 quarts cold water, or as needed

1 large onion, chopped

1 small carrot, coarsely chopped

1 small celery rib, coarsely chopped

1 head garlic, halved crosswise

2 sprigs thyme

2 sprigs flat-leaf parsley

1 teaspoon whole black peppercorns

1 dried bay leaf

Place the chicken in a large stockpot, and add the cold water to cover by 2 inches. Bring to a boil over medium-high heat, skimming off any foam that rises to the surface. Add the remaining ingredients. Reduce the heat to low and simmer uncovered gently for at least 6 hours or overnight.

Strain the stock into a large bowl, and cool completely. Skim off and discard the clear yellow fat that rises to the surface. Or, refrigerate the stock until the fat chills, about 4 hours, then scrape it off with a large spoon.

To make a simple herb sauce, boil 3 cups White Chicken Stock until reduced by half and intensely flavored. Swirl in 2 or 3 tablespoons unsalted butter to enrich the sauce and give it some body. Season with salt and pepper, and add whatever finely chopped herbs you wish.

I specify dried imported bay leaves for this book. I always prefer fresh herbs, but fresh bay leaves are an exception—they have a medicinal flavor that I don't like. (I also use dried oregano for some dishes, as it has a different, somewhat more pronounced Mediterranean flavor than fresh.)

Tomato, Basil, and Fresh Ricotta Sandwich with Tapenade

MAKES 4 SANDWICHES

8 large slices crusty sourdough or Italian bread, lightly toasted

1/2 cup Tapenade (page 26)

2 large ripe beefsteak tomatoes, thickly sliced

2 tablespoons extra-virgin olive oil

Coarse salt and freshly ground white pepper to taste

1/2 cup fresh ricotta cheese

12 large basil leaves

To make each sandwich, spread 1 toasted bread slice with 2 tablespoons of tapenade. Cover with a few overlapping tomato slices, drizzle with olive oil, then season with salt and pepper. Spread with 2 tablespoons of the fresh ricotta, season again with salt and pepper, then top with 3 basil leaves. Top with another slice of toasted bread, then cut in half with a serrated knife.

Variations: Make this into an open-faced sandwich, and serve it with a bouquet of dressed salad greens.

Substitute Roquefort cheese for the ricotta, and leave out the tapenade.

THIS SANDWICH illustrates how much pleasure can be created with just a few drastically different ingredients. Juicy beefsteak tomatoes and fragrant basil leaves set against the bracing taste of tapenade and cool ricotta cheese—all within the confines of toasted bread. Each bite teases the tastebuds for a long, expectant moment before all the ingredients begin to register. Don't even think about making this sandwich outside of August or September, when tomatoes are at their juiciest, plumpest peak. This sandwich is a great indulgence to bring to the beach, especially since it actually gets better after the flavors have had some time to blend.

Tapenade

MAKES ABOUT ³/₄ CUP

THIS THICK OLIVE PASTE
with anchovies and capers
makes a great spread for
sandwiches and hors
d'oeuvres.

2 whole salt-packed anchovies

1 cup pitted niçoise or kalamata olives

2 teaspoons capers, rinsed

1 teaspoon fresh lemon juice

1 teaspoon Cognac or brandy

1 small garlic clove, minced

Freshly ground white pepper to taste

Place the anchovies in a small bowl and cover with cold water. Let stand for 10 minutes to remove the salt. Drain. Using a small knife, lift the anchovy fillets from their bones.

In a food processor fitted with the metal blade or blender, pulse the anchovy fillets with the remaining ingredients until coarsely chopped. Transfer to a small bowl and mix well. Serve at room temperature.

Salt-packed anchovies are found at Italian and Mediterranean grocers. They are superior to oil-packed canned anchovies. If necessary, substitute 2 oil-packed anchovy fillets for each whole salt-packed anchovy.

Duck Breast, Caramelized Endive, Sweet Potatoes, and Green Peppercorn Sauce

MAKES 4 SERVINGS

DUCK WITH GREEN peppercorn sauce was an old idea, even 20 years ago when I started cooking, but it is a sauce I still use from time to time with excellent results. The flavors and colors of this dish—rare duck breast, caramelized endive, and orange sweet potatoes (flavored with maple syrup), are an ideal autumn combination. While most Americans don't think of endive when trying to settle on a vegetable, it's remarkably easy to prepare and is the perfect accompaniment in dishes like this one, where the slightly bitter flavor contrasts the other components.

Thinking Ahead: The sweet potato puree may be made up to 1 hour in advance and kept warm. The green peppercorn sauce may also be prepared up to 1 day in advance, covered, and refrigerated.

SWEET POTATO PUREE

4 large sweet potatoes (2 pounds total), pierced with a fork

4 tablespoons unsalted butter

1 tablespoon Grade B maple syrup (if Grade B is unavailable, use Grade A)

Coarse salt and freshly ground white pepper to taste

Preheat the oven to 400° F. Bake the sweet potatoes until tender, about 1 hour. When cool enough to handle, peel and place the flesh in a medium saucepan. Add the butter and maple syrup. Mash the potatoes over very low heat until they are smooth and the butter is incorporated, about 1 minute. Season with salt and pepper. Keep warm by placing the saucepan in a skillet of simmering water over low heat.

DUCK

4 (10-ounce) Muscovy duck breasts, wing tips removed

Coarse salt and freshly ground white pepper

Trim away any excess skin and fat from the duck. Using a sharp knife, score the skin lightly in a crosshatch pattern, but do not cut into the flesh. Season the duck breasts with salt and pepper. Place in a large cold nonstick sauté pan and set over medium-high heat. Cook until the skin is beautifully browned and crisp, about 10 minutes. Turn and cook until medium-rare, about 3 minutes. Transfer the duck to a plate and cover loosely with aluminum foil to keep warm. Let rest for 5 minutes before slicing.

ASSEMBLY

4 Belgian endives

1 tablespoon olive oil

Green Peppercorn Sauce (recipe follows)

Heat a tablespoon of olive oil in a sauté pan. Sauté endives cut side down until nicely caramelized. Turn endives and keep warm over low heat. Cut each duck breast into $1/4$-inch slices. Slip the knife blade under a sliced breast, and transfer it to the bottom half of a warmed dinner plate, fanning out the slices. At the "ten o'clock" position, place a spoonful of warmed sweet potato puree. Fold back a few of the outside leaves, and place the endive in the "two o'clock" position. Spoon the sauce around the edge of the plate and serve.

Variations: In seasons other than fall, substitute mashed potatoes or creamy polenta for the sweet potato puree.

Green Peppercorn Sauce

MAKES ABOUT 1 CUP

1 tablespoon canola oil

1 tablespoon finely chopped shallot

1 garlic clove, finely chopped

$1^{1}/_{2}$ teaspoons brine-packed green peppercorns, drained and rinsed

1 cup dry red wine, preferably Cabernet Sauvignon

1 cup brown chicken stock

$1/2$ cup water

2 tablespoons unsalted butter

Coarse salt and freshly ground white pepper to taste

TRY THIS SAUCE WITH grilled steak. Be sure to use the green peppercorns packed in brine, not dried green peppercorns, which are better used for grinding.

In a medium saucepan, heat the oil over medium heat. Add the shallot and cook, stirring often, until it's lightly browned, about 2 minutes. Add the garlic and half the green peppercorns and cook until the garlic is fragrant, about 1 minute. Pour in the wine and bring to a boil over high heat. Cook until the wine is reduced to a syrup, about 10 minutes.

Add the stock and water and cook until well flavored and reduced to 1 cup, about 10 minutes. Strain the sauce into a small saucepan. Whisk in the butter, 1 tablespoon at a time. Stir in the remaining green peppercorns and season with salt and pepper.

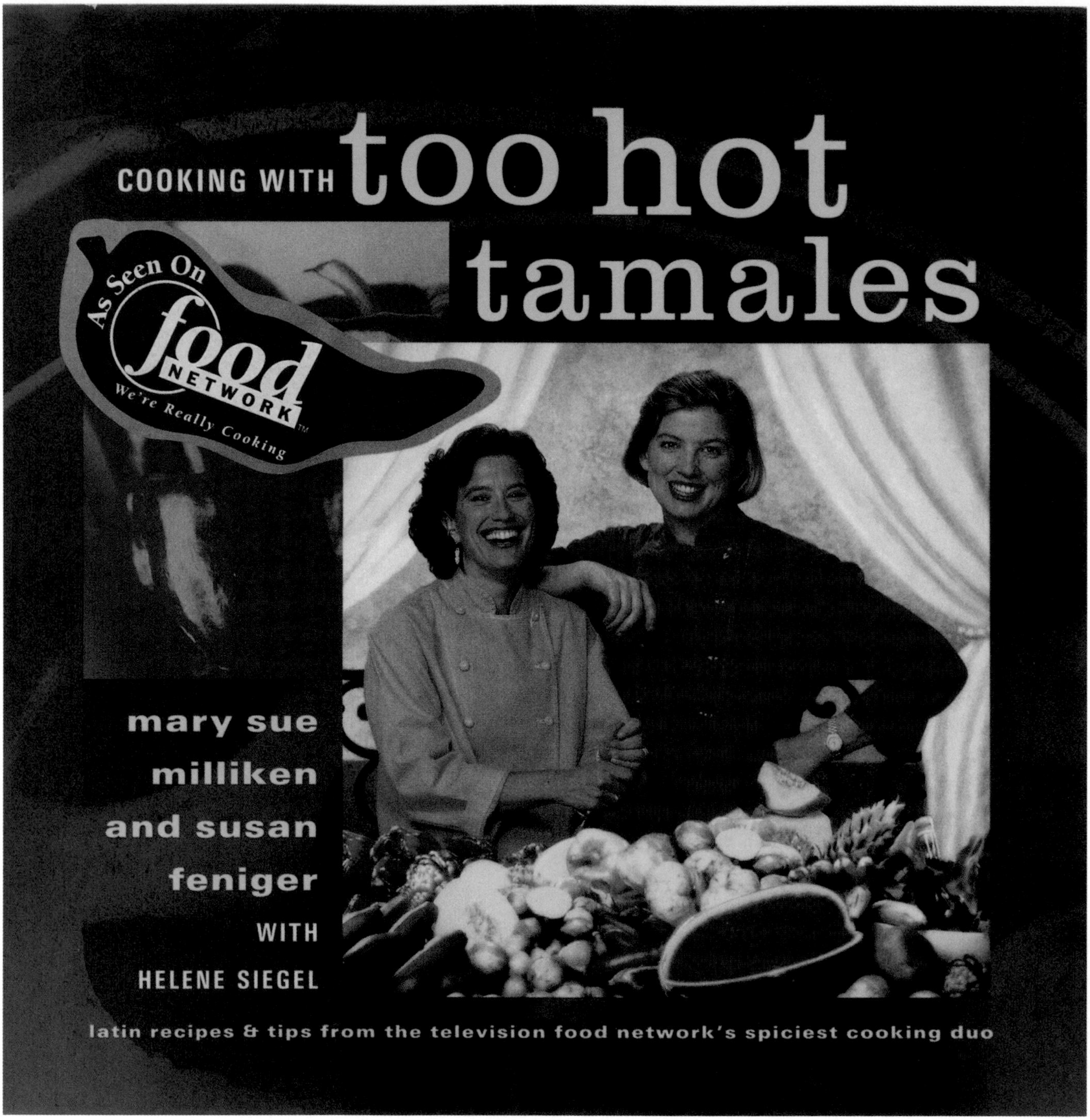

COOKING WITH **too hot tamales**

As Seen On
food NETWORK™
We're Really Cooking

mary sue milliken and susan feniger

WITH

HELENE SIEGEL

latin recipes & tips from the television food network's spiciest cooking duo

TV Food Network stars Mary Sue Milliken and Susan Feniger, with their regular co-writer, Helene Siegel

■ WHY THEY WROTE IT

As a companion to their popular food-network series, *Too Hot Tamales*.

■ WHY IT MADE OUR LIST

With a whimsical design, lots of photos of the pair in action, and chatty little boxes and introductions that bring to mind their on-screen repartee, this book does a great job of capturing the spirit of the TV series. The Latin-inspired recipes are very fine, too, delicious, uncomplicated, and vibrantly flavored. Chiles are, of course, very much in evidence; there's plenty of heat in this kitchen.

■ CHAPTERS

Cocktail Hour: Snacks, Great Salsas, Cocktails (with and without the booze) ▪ Little Treasures ▪ Latin Soups ▪ Salads ▪ Main Courses: from the Coop, from the Sea, from the Field, from the Range ▪ Sides ▪ Desserts ▪ Brunch

FROM THE BOOK

■ DINING ADVICE

"Chewing on bones is every eater's inalienable right, and if you've given it up in favor of more refined eating, all the more reason now to cook up some messy ribs or a whole chicken and gnaw on some bones."

■ PREVIOUS CREDITS

The duo's first cookbook, *City Cuisine*, was a collection of recipes from their first Los Angeles restaurant, City; their current restaurant, Border Grill, was featured in *Mesa Mexicana*.

■ SPECIFICS

226 pages, 164 recipes, approximately 75 black-and-white photographs, $22. Published by William Morrow and Company, Inc.

salmon baked in salsa verde

6 (4-ounce) salmon fillets

coarse salt and freshly ground
    black pepper

Salsa Verde

2 garlic cloves

1 poblano chile, stemmed,
    seeded, and chopped

$1/2$ bunch cilantro, leaves only,
    chopped

$1/2$ bunch Italian parsley,
    leaves only, chopped

6 scallions, white and light
    green parts only, chopped

3 Roma tomatoes, cored,
    seeded, and chopped

$1/3$ cup water

2 tablespoons fruity olive oil

1 tablespoon white wine
    vinegar

2 teaspoons dried oregano

1 teaspoon coarse salt

lemon wedges, for serving

Roasting the fish in its sauce integrates the flavors in the pan, and the cook is saved the bother of making a separate sauce.

Preheat the oven to 350°F. Season the fish all over with salt and pepper and place in an oiled baking dish.

To make the salsa, combine all of the ingredients in a blender or food processor and puree.

Pour the salsa over the fish and bake 8 to 12 minutes, until the thickest part of the fish is cooked through. Serve hot with lemon wedges and the salsa spooned on top.

Serves 6

wrapped spicy snapper

1 (8-ounce) package dried
    corn husks

4 ancho chiles, wiped clean,
    lightly toasted, stemmed,
    and seeded

½ cup white vinegar

½ cup warm water

1 tablespoon cumin seeds

2 teaspoons dried oregano,
    crumbled

2 teaspoons dried thyme,
    crumbled

2 teaspoons coarse salt

1 teaspoon freshly ground
    black pepper

4 garlic cloves, peeled

2 tablespoons olive oil

1½ pounds skinless whitefish
    fillets, such as snapper or
    sea bass

Garnishes

1 small onion, finely chopped

½ bunch cilantro, leaves only,
    finely chopped

2 serrano chiles, stemmed,
    seeded, and thinly sliced

2 limes, quartered

Wrapped foods are an excellent choice for dinner parties since they add an immediate element of fun. Wrapping the fish in corn husks before grilling seals in all of the juices and seasonings so that the fish steams in the fragrant liquid. While the fire is still hot, wrap some corn tortillas in foil and heat through on the grill to serve with the fish.

Place the corn husks in a saucepan with enough water to cover. Tamp down the husks with a plate to completely submerge them and simmer about 10 minutes. Remove from the heat and let stand, in the water, a few hours, until pliable.

Meanwhile, place the toasted anchos in a bowl. Add the vinegar and warm water and soak about 20 minutes. Drain, reserving the soaking liquid, and transfer to a blender. Add the cumin, oregano, thyme, salt, pepper, garlic, and olive oil. Puree, adding just enough of the soaking liquid to make a smooth paste.

Cut the fish into 3 × 1-inch pieces. Place in a glass or ceramic bowl, add the ancho chile paste, and toss to coat evenly. Cover and refrigerate 30 minutes to 1 hour.

Choose enough of the largest and most pliable corn husks, patching them together as necessary, to make 12 sheets for wrapping the fish. Drain the corn husks on paper towels. Make 6 ties by tearing a few of the remaining husks into strips. Divide the fish into 6 portions.

Arrange 6 corn husk sheets on a work counter. Place a portion of fish on the wider end of each. Fold over the sides and then the ends to enclose. Lay the wrapped fish seam side down on top of a second corn husk sheet and wrap again to enclose thoroughly. Tie each packet twice around the width with a husk strip to seal. The wrapped fish may be held in the refrigerator until ready to cook.

Preheat the grill or heat a large griddle over medium-high heat. Place the packets on the grill or griddle and cook, turning frequently, about 12 minutes, or until the husks start to dry out and color a bit. Open one to check for doneness.

To serve, cut the ties and carefully unwrap and remove the outer layer of husks. Set each on a serving plate, and carefully open the remaining husks. Pass the onion, cilantro, chiles, and limes.

Serves 6

hot tip

COOL AND DARK IS ESSENTIAL

A cool dark storage area in your kitchen is essential for properly storing most fruits, garlic, onions, potatoes, yams, and eggplant. Be sure to keep potatoes out of sunlight, since that is what promotes that green tinge under the skin which must be removed before eating.

roasted chicken with a papaya glaze

1 (3-pound) chicken

coarse salt and freshly ground
   black pepper

1 orange, quartered

1/2 onion, chunked

4 garlic cloves, crushed

1 cup orange juice

1/4 cup olive oil

1/4 cup packed light brown
   sugar

2 shallots, halved

2 bay leaves

Papaya Glaze

2 tablespoons Dijon mustard

2 garlic cloves, sliced

1 ripe papaya, halved, peeled,
   and seeded, one half diced,
   for garnish

1 tablespoon chopped fresh
   thyme

1/2 teaspoon coarse salt

1/4 teaspoon freshly ground
   black pepper

1 tablespoon cold unsalted
   butter

Roasting the chicken breast side down first makes the juices run into the breast, keeping it extra-moist. The bird also gets an extra dollop of moistness and flavor from papaya, which contains an enzyme called papain that acts as a natural meat tenderizer.

Rinse the chicken and pat dry with paper towels. Rub the cavity with salt and pepper. Stuff with the orange, onion, and garlic. Rub the outside with 1 teaspoon salt and 1/2 teaspoon pepper and place in a baking dish just large enough to hold it.

In a blender or a food processor, combine the orange juice, olive oil, brown sugar, and shallots. Process until the shallots are finely minced. Pour over the chicken, crumble the bay leaves over the top, and cover tightly with plastic wrap. Marinate in the refrigerator at least 3 hours, preferably overnight, spooning the marinade over the chicken occasionally.

Preheat the oven to 375°F.

Transfer the chicken to a rack in a roasting pan, breast side down, reserving marinade. Roast the chicken 20 minutes. Prepare the papaya glaze. Pour the marinade into a food processor and add the mustard, garlic, the papaya half, the thyme, salt, and pepper. Process until smooth. Divide the glaze in half. Use half to baste the chicken; reserve the other half for the sauce.

Turn the chicken breast side up and baste with the glaze. Roast 50 to 60 minutes longer, basting every 20 minutes, until golden brown. Transfer to a serving platter, cover with foil, and keep warm at the back of the stove.

To make the sauce, drain the fat from the pan. Add the reserved papaya mixture and place over medium heat. Bring to a simmer, scraping the pan. Whisk in the butter and diced papaya. Transfer to a sauceboat and pass at the table.

Serves 4

black jalapeño salsa

2 (½-inch-thick) slices
  red onion

4 garlic cloves, peeled

2 teaspoons dried Mexican
  oregano

¼ cup olive oil

12 jalapeño chiles, stemmed,
  seeded, and halved

3 Anaheim chiles, stemmed,
  seeded, and halved

juice of 2 limes

½ teaspoon coarse salt

If you love chiles as we do, do not miss the opportunity to taste a truly chile-infused sauce. Make it in the summer, when the farmers' market is selling jalapeños by the bagful and you are planning on grilling some steaks. Jalapeños and beef are a natural combination.

Heat a cast-iron skillet over high heat; add the onion slices and char, separating them into rings. Remove from the pan. Toast the garlic until it begins to brown in spots, then add the oregano, cook for a minute, and remove from the pan.

Add the olive oil to the skillet and sear the chiles, turning until evenly charred.

Transfer the chiles, with the onion, garlic, and oregano, to a food processor. Add the remaining ingredients and pulse until finely chopped; for a finer paste, add ½ cup water and process until smooth. Store in a plastic container in the refrigerator 2 to 3 days.

Makes about 1½ cups

hot tip

CHILES, CHILES, AND MORE CHILES

It didn't take long for us, especially Susan, to fall in love with chiles, and we suggest you dive right in and get to know them better. Chiles are no more difficult to work with than any other vegetable or fruit and they deliver a great deal of sparkle to your foods for very little cost.

We often specify a range when calling for chiles and sometimes consider the seeds and veins optional. All you really need to know is that most of the heat is stored in the inner membranes, so if what you want is chile flavor without too much heat, scoop out the seeds and veins. (You know what to do if heat is what you are after.) Because a chile's heat will vary according to season, we like to break open a chile and carefully taste it to determine fire power.

Always shop for chiles by appearance rather than name, since that can vary according to the region of the country. Usually, the smaller the chile, the hotter the pepper.

Dried chiles, particularly some of our favorites like anchos and chipotles, are available these days at specialty shops and by mail order. Go ahead and buy a bunch once you find a good source. They can be stored, sealed in a plastic bag, in the freezer for a long time.

Emeril's Creole Christmas

EMERIL LAGASSE
WITH MARCELLE BIENVENU

Famed New Orleans chef and TV Food Network favorite Emeril Lagasse, with food historian Marcelle Bienvenue

■ WHY HE WROTE IT
"If you can't come over to my house, you'll be able to fix these and a whole lot more fantastic dishes at yours. It's my holiday wish that the recipes in these pages become part of your holiday tradition."

■ WHY IT MADE OUR LIST
His TV Food Network popularity has made the sight of Lagasse cooking, schmoozing, and "kicking things up a notch" almost inescapable. His menus here are like his personality—exuberant and unrestrained. Lots of caviar and truffles. Lots of dishes, lots of courses, lots and lots of items on the page-long shopping lists. It may be a bit much for some, but you can find some luscious year-round additions to your repertoire by picking and choosing from the menus or sampling from the chapter of holiday favorites.

FROM THE BOOK

■ DINING PHILOSOPHY
"I like to be surrounded by the people I love and enjoy a good meal—well, maybe not just a good one, more like an incredible one."

■ CHAPTERS
Christmas Eve Dinner for Ten ▪ Emeril's Christmas Day Brunch Buffet ▪ New Orleans New Year's Eve Dinner ▪ New Year's Day Supper Family Style ▪ Chef's Holiday Favorites ▪ Emeril's Stocking Stuffers

■ PREVIOUS CREDITS
Lagasse served up Acadian fare in *Louisiana Real & Rustic* and recipes from his restaurants in *Emeril's New New Orleans Cooking*.

■ SPECIFICS
162 pages, 84 recipes, approximately 85 color photographs, $22. Published by William Morrow and Company, Inc.

Quail and Smoked Sausage Christmas Gumbo

MAKES 8 TO 10 SERVINGS

¾ cup vegetable oil
1 cup bleached all-purpose flour
2 cups chopped yellow onions
1 cup seeded and chopped green bell
  peppers
½ cup chopped celery
1 teaspoon salt
1 teaspoon cayenne
3 bay leaves
4 quail, about 3½ ounces each,
  breastbones removed
2 teaspoons minced garlic
8 cups chicken stock
1 pound smoked sausage, cut crosswise
  into ¼-inch-thick slices
½ cup chopped green onions (scallions),
  green parts only
2 tablespoons finely chopped fresh
  parsley leaves

Stocking Tip ■ When making the roux, it is important that the oil-and-flour mixture be stirred constantly to keep it from burning.

Combine the oil and flour in a large nonstick saucepan over medium heat. Cook, stirring constantly, until the roux mixture is dark brown, the color of chocolate, 30 to 35 minutes.

Add the onions, peppers, celery, salt, cayenne, and bay leaves. Cook the vegetables, stirring often, until they are soft and tender, about 10 minutes.

Add the quail and garlic. Cook for about 5 minutes, turning the quail in the roux to coat evenly. Add the stock and sausage. Bring the mixture to a boil, then reduce the heat to medium-low, and simmer, uncovered, until the quail are very tender, about 1 hour.

Skim off any fat that rises to the surface of the gumbo and discard. Remove the bay leaves. Stir in the green onions and parsley. Serve immediately with steamed white rice.

SUGARCANE BAKED HAM WITH SPICED APPLES AND PEARS

MAKES 10 TO 12 SERVINGS

Stocking Tips ■ The sugarcane swizzle sticks used here are sold in some specialty markets. Packaged sugarcane stalks (usually imported from Hawaii) are available in some specialty produce markets. These have to be stripped of their outer skin to expose the white flesh, which can then be cut into sticks or strips. If neither of these products is available in your area, don't worry. This ham, basted with a glaze, is quite delicious even without the sticks. ■ If there is any leftover ham, use it for making sandwiches.

12 sugarcane swizzle sticks, each cut into about 3-inch pieces
1 hickory smoked ham, spiral sliced, 8 to 10 pounds (no bone, water added, cooked)
1 recipe Spiced Glaze (below)
1½ pounds (about 4) Granny Smith apples
1½ pounds (about 4) Bartlett pears

Preheat the oven to 350°F.

Line a shallow baking pan with parchment or waxed paper.

Insert the sugarcane sticks into the ham at 3- to 4-inch intervals. Tie the ham, using kitchen twine, at two-inch intervals horizontally and vertically to keep it together. Place on a wire rack in the baking pan. Brush the entire ham with the glaze, coating it evenly.

Wash, core, and halve the fruit. Place all around the ham. Baste the ham a second time and baste the fruit with the glaze. Bake for 45 minutes. Baste the ham and fruit again. Bake another 45 minutes. Remove the ham from the oven and let it rest for 5 minutes. Remove and discard the string and swizzle sticks.

Serve the apples and pears on a platter with the ham. Serve everything warm or at room temperature.

SPICED GLAZE

MAKES 2½ CUPS

1 cup firmly packed light brown sugar
1 cup Steen's 100% Pure Cane Syrup
½ cup dark molasses
½ cup dark corn syrup
⅛ teaspoon freshly grated nutmeg
¼ teaspoon ground cloves
⅛ teaspoon ground allspice
½ teaspoon ground cinnamon
1 teaspoon dry mustard
¼ cup water

Combine the sugar, cane syrup, molasses, corn syrup, nutmeg, cloves, allspice, and cinnamon in a medium-size bowl and mix well. In another bowl, dissolve the mustard in the water, then add to the spice mixture. Blend well.

Use immediately or store in an airtight container in the refrigerator until ready to use. Will keep for 2 weeks.

CHOCOLATE BREAD PUDDING WITH SPICED CREAM

1 teaspoon unsalted butter
4 large eggs
1 cup firmly packed light brown sugar
½ teaspoon ground cinnamon
⅛ teaspoon freshly grated nutmeg
1 teaspoon pure vanilla extract
1 cup semisweet chocolate chips, melted
¼ cup Grand Marnier or other orange-
    flavored liqueur
2 cups half-and-half
8 slices day-old white bread, crusts
    removed and cut into ½-inch cubes
    (about 4 cups)
2 cups semisweet chocolate chips
Spiced Cream (below)

Preheat the oven to 350°F.

Grease a 6-cup (9¼ × 5¼ × 2¾-inch) loaf pan with the butter.

Whisk the eggs, sugar, cinnamon, nutmeg, vanilla, melted chocolate, and Grand Marnier together in a large mixing bowl until very smooth. Add the half-and-half and mix well. Add the bread and let the mixture sit for 30 minutes, stirring occasionally.

Pour half of the mixture into the prepared pan. Sprinkle the top with the unmelted chocolate chips. Pour the remaining bread mixture over the chocolate chips. Bake until the pudding is set in the center, about 55 minutes. Let cool for 5 minutes.

To serve, cut the pudding into 1-inch-thick slices. Top with the spiced cream.

SPICED CREAM

1 quart heavy cream
¼ cup granulated sugar
½ teaspoon ground cinnamon
¼ teaspoon freshly grated nutmeg

Beat the cream with an electric mixer on high speed in a large mixing bowl for about 2 minutes. Add the sugar, cinnamon, and nutmeg and beat again until the mixture thickens and forms stiff peaks, another 1 to 2 minutes.

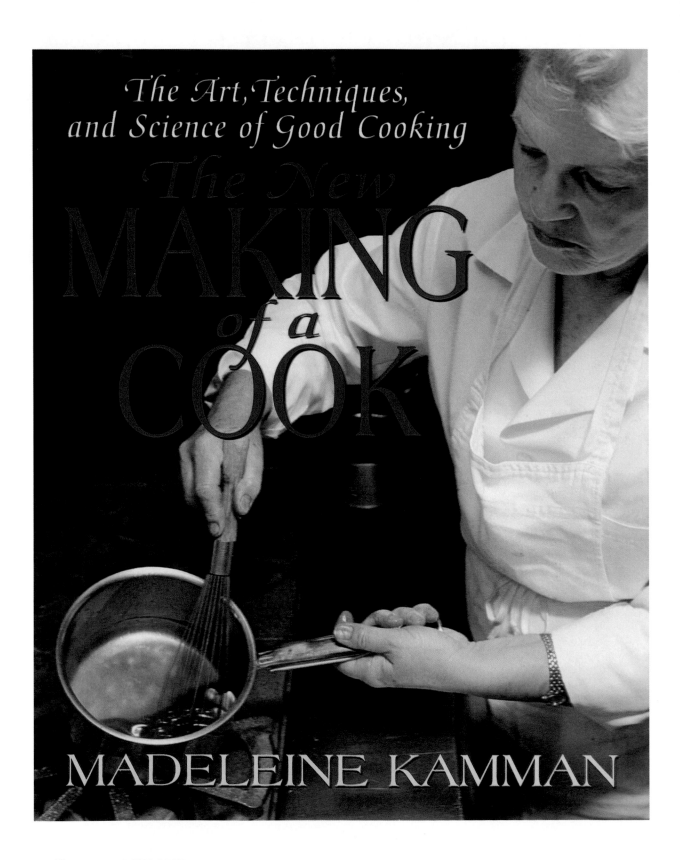

The Art, Techniques,
and Science of Good Cooking

The New
MAKING
of a
COOK

MADELEINE KAMMAN

Chef and cooking teacher extraordinaire Madeleine Kamman, author of the 1971 original

". . . I realized that the first edition contained quite a few imperfections, and that, like all young cooks with a passion, I had given in to the 'passion' first and then only to reasoning. I simply had written it too soon, when I still thought I knew so much."

More a rewrite than a revision, this version has over twice the pages of the original and almost none of the same recipes. It's an exhaustive encyclopedia of techniques and classic formulas, sure to be the important reference for future chefs that the earlier edition has been for current ones. With additions like time-saving tips and easier variations on the more involved recipes, it should be an inspiration for home cooks, too.

Tools of the Trade: Kitchen Equipment and How to Use It ▪ Good Ingredients for Good Dishes ▪ A Wine Primer for Cooks ▪ Miracles in a Shell: The Techniques of Egg Cookery ▪ Happy Marriages: Vegetable Broths, Meat Stocks and Consommés, and All Types of Mixed Vegetable and Meat Soups ▪ A Multinational Society: Sauces from All Over the World ▪ Colors on Your Plate: Cooking Vegetables ▪ Grains, Legumes, and Pasta ▪ Of River, Lake, and Sea Critters: All Manner of Cooking and Preparing Fish ▪ All Manner of Cooking Meats ▪ Fruit and the Cook ▪ Cooks in the Bakery

1,228 pages, more than 650 recipes, 200 line drawings, $40. Published by William Morrow and Company, Inc.

FROM THE BOOK

■ HER PORTRAIT OF A BORN COOK

"There are born cooks, people of great imagination and taste, who can start dancing at the stove with any ingredient and end up putting masterpieces on the dinner table. They do it without apparent effort, not a piece of paper, book, or recipe in sight, enlisting the mere help of what I have called for years in my classrooms 'the Holy Trinity' of the kitchen: the brain, the heart, and the hands."

For the cook's convenience, the recipes have each been coded with three letters: FFR represents a full-fat recipe containing saturated fats in the form of butter, cream, bacon fat, lard and/or duck fat; FCR represents a fat-controlled recipe in which the fat used is an unsaturated oil; LFR represents a recipe containing only a small amount of fat; and NFR is a recipe with only a very small percentage of fat.

Chunky Summer Tomato Soup

FCR — 6 SERVINGS

¼ pound dried **Great Northern beans**, soaked overnight in 6 to 8 cups water

6 cups cold water

Small bouquet garni of 1 bay leaf, 1 sprig fresh thyme, and 10 parsley stems

Salt

Pepper from the mill

1 tablespoon olive or other unsaturated oil of your choice

3 large cloves garlic, finely chopped

2 large leeks, white part only, well washed and finely chopped

12 large sun-ripened tomatoes, peeled, seeded, and cut into chunks

2 tablespoons chopped fresh parsley leaves

¼ pound cheese of your choice (optional), grated

All gardens and farmers' markets across the United States offer, come late summer, the wonderfully ripe and warm tomatoes that we all fancy. Here is how to use those that may have a spot of overripeness here or there. To make this soup faster, you can heat a can of cannellini beans in 3 cups of water seasoned with the bouquet garni, then add the tomatoes. The choice of cheese is yours; use any of the Gruyère- or cheddar-type cheeses, Parmigiano-Reggiano, or Pecorino.

Drain and sort the soaked beans, then cover them with 4 cups of the water; bring slowly to a boil with the bouquet garni, then add salt and pepper to your taste and cook until the beans are three quarters done, 35 to 40 minutes.

Heat the olive oil in a large saucepan, then add two thirds of the garlic and sauté over medium-high heat until beige. Add the leeks and sauté until wilted. Add the chunky tomatoes and sauté until their juices start running into the pan. Finally, add the cooked beans, their broth, and the remaining water and simmer together, uncovered, until the mixture tastes good, about another 40 minutes. Correct the final seasoning. If the soup turns too thick, lighten with boiling salted water or the hot broth of your choice.

Just before serving, chop the remaining garlic and parsley together and add to the soup. Serve with a loaf of crusty bread and pass the grated cheese in a bowl for family and guests to help themselves as they wish.

Ragout of Peas and Artichokes

FCR — 6 SERVINGS

2 tablespoons pure olive oil

Two 10-ounce packages frozen artichoke hearts thawed, or 18 fresh artichoke bottoms, chokes removed

For the proper taste, both the vegetables must be overcooked. You must trim the harder leaves from the artichokes. The amount

I dime-size piece lemon rind

1½ tablespoons chopped fresh tarragon leaves

2 tablespoons Pure Vegetable Broth or Secondary Stock (recipes follow)
   or broth of your choice

Salt

Pepper from the mill

One 10-ounce package frozen baby peas (without butter sauce)

1½ teaspoons chopped fresh Italian parsley leaves

1½ teaspoons chopped fresh mint leaves

Heat the olive oil; add the artichokes, lemon rind, tarragon, and stock and season with salt and pepper. Cover the pot tightly and cook 10 minutes over low heat. Defrost the peas under cold running water, drain well, and mix with the artichokes. Toss well, cover again, and continue cooking until the vegetables are very tender, 10 to 15 minutes. Remove the lemon rind and correct the final seasoning. Add the parsley and mint and serve rapidly.

of stock needed will depend on the size of the artichokes used. And unfortunately frozen baby peas are still the best unless you grow your own. Excellent for chicken cutlets and veal chops or scaloppine.

Pure Vegetable Broth

NFR— 5 QUARTS

1½ pounds carrots, cut up

2 pounds medium-size yellow onions, cut up

3 bunches scallions, chopped

10 leeks, white and light green parts, well washed and sliced into ¼-inch slivers

1 celery rib from the center of the heart

5 quarts cold water

Large bouquet garni of parsley stems, 1 bay leaf, and 1 sprig fresh thyme

Salt

Wash and drain all the vegetables well. Put them in a large stockpot. Cover with the cold water and slowly bring to a boil; skim if necessary, then add the bouquet garni and simmer until the volume of liquid is reduced to 8 cups and the broth tastes good, about 1½ hours. Strain through a conical strainer lined with cheesecloth. Salt to taste.

Microwaving is not recommended for vegetable broth if you want to obtain the deep taste and flavor that comes from vegetables that have cooked at some length. This is a personal opinion, though; please use your microwave if you prefer and do not mind the lighter texture and taste.

Store in the refrigerator for up to 1 week or freeze for up to 2 months in 16-ounce (2-cup) freezer containers at home or in 32-ounce (1-quart) containers in restaurant operations.

This recipe may be multiplied by two, four, six, etc. It is the famous bouillon de légumes, *the French nectar of health, cure for the* crise de foie, *a general malaise across the French nation caused by overindulgence in great food at an occasional celebration dinner, after weeks, even months, of generally frugal meals.*

Note that this is a neutral basic stock which can be used for all ethnic cuisines. You can add whatever other vegetables you feel like tasting in such a stock: more celery, for example; the tops of red, green, or yellow bell peppers; any hot pepper; and, of course, tomatoes. I have avoided all these to keep the stock from having any ethnic tendencies.

Secondary Stock

A LIGHTER WHITE VEAL
AND POULTRY STOCK

FFR — VARIABLE YIELD

This stock corresponds roughly to what was called a rémuage in the old days, when, after the freshly finished stock had been poured away, one filled the pot with water again and cooked again. Only it is cleaner in look and taste, because already cooked meats and bones are not indiscriminately used.

You will discard old vegetables and bones, keeping only those large blocks of gelatin to be found between the floating ribs and any piece of meat that still appears moist, instead of being fully stringy.

There is no list of ingredients for secondary stock; you make it up with whatever scraps you have stored in your freezer. Take to the habit of saving: uncooked chicken carcasses, uncooked duck carcasses, game birds, quail carcasses, veal chop bones, small scraps of veal, etc. Poultry giblets are fine also, with the exception of livers which will turn the stock gray and can be used to better advantage in other preparations.

Do not brown duck or other poultry carcasses; the stock will not taste as good if you do, for these bones are small and lose a lot of their taste-giving properties as they brown. If you do not believe me, try both browning the carcasses and not browning them and compare both tastes; notice also the very small amount of glaze left in the roasting pan once you are finished roasting the carcasses.

Add new soup vegetables, such as two large yellow onions, a very small carrot, as many leeks as you can afford, a medium-size bouquet garni. Cover the stock with enough water to cover all the meats and vegetables, plus 2 inches. Bring to a boil, turn down to a simmer, and skim well during the first hour of cooking, then simmer until the stock tastes good; it will take at least 2 hours. You will have to taste to know when the stock is done, for its taste and length of cooking will again depend on the amount of nutrients contained in the meats you used. Cool, strain, defat, and store the stock. The color of this stock is more white than dark, even if it contains duck and a bit of lean beef.

Steamed Mountain-Style Trout Fillets

FFR — 6 SERVINGS

A good recipe for those wonderful Rocky Mountain trout fillets. This can be served either as a light dinner course or a first course for a more substantial company dinner.

I pound thin-sliced bacon

12 boneless trout fillets

Salt

Pepper from the mill

3 tablespoons peeled and coarsely chopped hazelnuts

6 tablespoons chopped fresh chervil leaves

12 light green escarole leaves, blanched in boiling salted water 1 minute and cooled
   completely

Large bouquet garni

1 medium-size yellow onion, coarsely chopped

2 cloves garlic, coarsely chopped

1 shallot, very finely chopped

2 tablespoons wine vinegar of your choice

¼ cup hazelnut, walnut, or corn oil

½ pound baby frisée salad leaves

12 nasturtium leaves and flowers (optional only if not available)

SUGGESTED WINE: *A light red Zinfandel, a Beaujolais-Villages, a Mondeuse from the French Alps, or a Bourgogne Aligoté*

Render the bacon slices slowly until crisp in a large skillet. Pat them dry of all fat and crumble into small pieces.

Pat the trout fillets dry with a wad of paper towels lightly impregnated with a bit of oil. Salt and pepper them. Mix together 3 tablespoons of the crumbled bacon, the chopped hazelnuts, and ¼ cup of the chopped chervil. Sprinkle an equal amount of the mixture over what was the bone side of each fillet. Roll each fillet upon itself so the bacon and nuts are inside and wrap in one blanched leaf of the escarole.

Lightly oil the steamer basket and add the trout packages. Fill the bottom of the steamer one half of the way with water and add the bouquet garni, onion, and garlic. Bring to a boil, then reduce the heat to medium and simmer 10 minutes, uncovered, before you begin to steam the trout. Steam the fillets 8 minutes. Remove from the heat and keep warm, covered, over the water. Strain ½ cup of the steaming water into a small saucepan.

Reduce the steaming water to 2 tablespoons over high heat, then add the chopped shallot, vinegar, oil, and salt and pepper to taste and homogenize well. Add the remaining 2 tablespoons of chervil.

Toss the salad leaves with half the dressing; open the packages of fish with a pair of scissors, opening the greens around the fillets; arrange the fish and salad on serving plates, each one decorated with two nasturtium flowers and their leaves. Spoon the remainder of the dressing over the fillets.

Butterflied Leg of Lamb in Citrus Marinade

FFR to FCR—6 to 8 servings

Oriental-style marinade

Grated rind of 1 orange

Juice of 5 large navel oranges

2 cloves garlic, coarsely crushed

One ¼-inch-thick slice fresh ginger, peeled and coarsely chopped

SUGGESTED WINE: *An opulent Pinot Noir, well-rounded Cabernet Sauvignon, or the first-growth Beaujolais known as Fleurie, or an Italian Barolo*

2 tablespoons fresh lemon juice

3 tablespoons dark soy sauce

3 tablespoons hoisin sauce

1 whole leg of lamb, 6 to 7 pounds

Salt

Pepper from the mill

In a small stainless steel saucepan mix together the orange rind and juice, garlic, and ginger and reduce to ⅓ cup over medium heat. Strain out the rind and ginger, then add the lemon juice, and soy and hoisin sauces. Mix well.

Completely strip the meat of all fell and underlying fat. Remove all the bones and flatten the leg completely, patting it out to an even thickness. Place the leg on a stainless steel rack set over a sheet pan; brush with a thin layer of the marinade. Let marinate refrigerated for 2 hours; bring back to room temperature 30 minutes before cooking.

Preheat the coals to glowing red. Stick a piece of lamb fat on the prongs of a long-handled fork and rub it over the hot grill. Grill the leg 5 minutes on each side 4 to 5 inches from the coals. Raise the grilling rack to 8 inches above the coals and cook until the internal temperature reads 125°F, a few more minutes on each side. Remove from the heat leaving the thermometer in the meat, salt and pepper immediately on both sides, and let rest until the thermometer reads 130° to 135°F (USDA 145° to 160°F). Slice into thin slices, salt and pepper the slices, and serve promptly.

TO BONE AND DETAIL A LEG OF LAMB Use only a well-aged leg on which the fell looks somewhat dry and parchmentlike. Remove the fell, its thin layer of underlying fat, and the silverskin covering the different muscles of the leg all at once by sliding your blade under each of them, at a 10-degree angle to prevent removing too much of the muscle meat.

1. If the leg is to be roasted whole:

    Gently pass a finger between the two muscles clearly visible on the top part of the leg until you see a large walnut-size piece of fat appear; pull it out. This nugget of fat surrounds the so-called eye of the pope, which is a lymph node. If you cut through the nugget of fat, you will see the darker pink node. Pat the two muscles back together after removal.

    Now turn the leg over. You will see a blotchy red region. This is where the femoral artery has been cut; 75 percent of the time it will still contain some bright red liquid. Take a large wad of paper towels and push about 1 inch above the opening to drain all the liquid into the paper towels.

2. If the leg is to be "butterflied":

    Butterflying means boning the leg of lamb so it can lie flat with an approximately even thickness of all its muscles. This is easily done by first separating the meat from the thigh bone, then separating the meat from the shank bone. If you are butterflying, you can wait to remove the "eye of

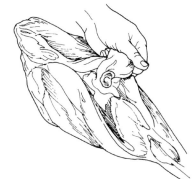

Removing the eye of the pope from a leg of lamb

the pope" when you cut the meat from the bones. Leave both of the shank muscles on, as they roast deliciously. The so-called heart of the leg is a tight, round ball-like muscle thicker than the other muscles. Snip it open with the tip of your blade until it is of the same thickness as the other muscles.

3. If the leg is to be roasted for a restaurant à la carte menu or catered dinners or for a special dinner party at home:

Roasting a whole leg on the bone is often not a favorite for à la carte service because it is difficult to keep all the muscles of the leg fresh tasting and juicy throughout the serving and carving of many portions. But since a well-aged leg is an excellent tasting cut, and more affordable than loins and racks of lamb, here is a practical way to obtain fresh slices and enough meat to prepare a small sauce.

Bone the leg entirely; lay it flat on the board cut side down. Remove both the upper and the lower shank muscle; set both aside. Following the very visible dividing line between the two major top muscles, separate the leg into two parts. Roll each into a smaller roast and tie each well at ⅓-inch intervals and into a round shape. One will be larger and serve up to five portions, while the second will serve only three. After you have roasted the rolls and removed the ties, you will see that each roast will separate into individual muscles. Cut each and every muscle individually *across the grain* into thin slices, or scaloppine; serve three- to four-slice portions, depending on the size of the muscle.

With the shank muscles you can prepare excellent stews for home and bistro-style meals. To entertain at home, in catering preparations, or in classy restaurant-style food presentation, use those shank muscles to prepare an essence of lamb which can serve as a sauce.

Once the two small roasts have been carved for service there will be some small amount of leftover outer cuts; they will taste excellent in lamb salads or for an everyday meal blended with risotto, a grain, or a pasta and freshly stir-fried vegetables.

Cut the roasts apart along the line described by the knife

Butterflied leg of lamb with whole shank muscle beside the knife handle

AMERICAN BRASSERIE

180 Simple,

Robust Recipes Inspired

by the Rustic Foods of

France, Italy, and

America

Rick Tramonto and Gale Gand
with Julia Moskin
Photography by Tim Turner

Rick Tramonto and Gale Gand, the husband-and-wife, chef-and-pastry-chef team behind Chicago's Brasserie T, with writer Julia Moskin

■ WHY THEY WROTE IT

"We know that when you've gone to the trouble of cooking, you want a dish whose flavors and textures please and soothe you. Our goal in developing the menu for Brasserie T was to come up with a group of dishes we—and our customers—could choose from *every single day* and always feel happy and satisfied. The same principle applies to this book."

■ WHY IT MADE OUR LIST

Simple, stylish, satisfying food is what we all want to make these days. And here it is, based on tried-and-true Italian, French, and American dishes. A traditional French brasserie is similar to an American brew pub, though with much better food, and the book appropriately has beer as well as wine choices for many dishes, and a quite interesting history of beer itself. To which we say, Cheers!

FROM THE BOOK

■ BRASSERIE DEFINED

"In Paris today a brasserie is any restaurant where the beer is on tap and the menu is large and flexible . . . . The beer-soaked heritage of brasseries doesn't mean that you don't drink wine at a brasserie—everyone does. In fact, you can eat and drink just about anything you want at a brasserie. That's what we like about them."

■ CHAPTERS

Salads and Appetizers ▪ Soups and Chowders ▪ Pizzas ▪ Breads and Sandwiches ▪ Pastas, Risotti, and Grains ▪ Main Courses ▪ Weekend Cooking ▪ Side Dishes ▪ Cheese Plates ▪ Desserts ▪ Cookies ▪ Ice Cream and Cool Drinks ▪ Brasserie Basics

■ SPECIFICS

334 pages, 183 recipes, 24 color photographs, $32.50. Published by Macmillan.

Roquefort and Pear Salad
with Grapes and Spiced Pecans

SERVES 4 TO 6

❧

All the Roquefort cheese in the world is aged in the limestone caves of Roquefort-sur-Soulzon, in a rocky region of south-central France that we visited in 1982. When the round cheeses arrive at the caves, they are creamy white and firm, giving no indication of the miraculous changes that are about to take place. The damp, fragrant air in these caves contains a particular blend of microorganisms that enter the cheese through precisely thirty-six carefully pierced holes, which results in the sharp, blue-green-veined cheese we love.

As we entered the caves for the first time, we were astonished by the sight of thousands of wheels of Roquefort stacked up to the necks of the workers who, dressed all in white, are responsible for piercing, brushing, salting, and turning the cheeses during the three-month ripening process. As the cheeses become strong and ripe, they are removed, and new ones come to take their place, in a carefully calibrated procedure that has constantly revived itself over centuries. The caves have never been empty since a long-ago shepherd discovered the miraculous effect the air had on a forgotten cheese sandwich—or so the legend goes.

We love the combination of earthy, salty Roquefort cheese and crisp, sweet pears so much that we built an entire salad around it, bringing in red grapes to back up the fruitiness of the pears and toasted pecans to enhance the nuttiness of the cheese.

1) Make the spiced pecans: preheat the oven to 350°F. In a mixing bowl, combine the cayenne, cumin, and brown sugar. Add the oil and mix thoroughly. Add the pecans and toss until thoroughly coated. Spread the pecans out on a baking sheet and bake for 15 to 20 minutes, watching carefully to make sure the nuts do not burn. Stir the pecans halfway through the cooking. When toasty, remove from the oven and set aside to cool. (The pecans can be made up to 2 days ahead and kept in an airtight container.)

2) In a large salad bowl, combine the pecans, salad greens, beans, pears, grapes, and drained onion rings. Add about half of the vinaigrette and toss thoroughly. Sprinkle salt and pepper over the top of the salad.

3) Crumble the Roquefort over the salad with your fingers, or chop it with a knife and sprinkle it over. Sprinkle the chives over the top of the salad.

4) Toss at the table and serve, passing the remaining dressing separately.

A NUTTY BROWN OR DARK ALE WOULD WORK WELL WITH THIS COMBINATION OF SWEET AND SALTY INGREDIENTS.

For the spiced pecans:

1/4 teaspoon cayenne pepper

1/4 teaspoon ground cumin

1 tablespoon light brown sugar

2 teaspoons olive oil

1 cup pecan halves

For the salad:

8 ounces mixed salad greens (mesclun) or a mixture of at least 3 lettuces such as red leaf, romaine, endive, radicchio, arugula, frisée, watercress, and Boston

6 ounces haricots verts or string beans, blanched in boiling salted water until crisp-tender, then rinsed under cold water until cool

2 ripe but firm pears, cored and sliced lengthwise 1/4 inch thick

8 ounces seedless red grapes, stemmed

1/2 small red onion, sliced into thin rings and soaked in cold water or wine vinegar

1 recipe Apple-Walnut Vinaigrette (below)

Kosher salt and freshly ground black pepper

6 ounces Roquefort cheese, chilled

1 tablespoon chopped chives

Apple-Walnut Vinaigrette

MAKES ABOUT 1 CUP

In a blender or food processor, combine the apple chunks and shallot and process until smooth. Add the vinegar and sugar and blend. Add the oils and blend until creamy. Add salt and pepper to taste and pulse to combine. Use immediately or refrigerate in a tightly closed jar. Shake well before using.

1/2 Granny Smith or other tart apple, peeled, cored, and cut into chunks

1 shallot, peeled

1/4 cup cider vinegar

1 teaspoon sugar

1/3 cup walnut oil

2/3 cup canola or light olive oil

Kosher salt and freshly ground black pepper

Orange-Ricotta Gnocchi with Broccoli Rabe

SERVES 6 TO 8

For a textbook definition of "family-style," the place to go is a popular restaurant outside Verona called Al Ponte. This friendly restaurant has served the same four pastas—meat-stuffed tortellini, spinach-stuffed ravioli, tagliatelle alla bolognese, and light gnocchi—for as long as anyone can remember. All of them are perfectly made. The pasta course at Al Ponte consists of just as much as you want of each kind of pasta (no need to make the agonizing choice); your hostess comes around with a smile and a heaping platter to ask if anyone wants more. "Yes, please. . ."

Gnocchi not only have a name that's hard to pronounce, but they have the reputation of being difficult to make. Well, here's how to pronounce the word: "nyaw-kee," spoken quickly and with the accent on the first syllable. And here's how to make the dish: with potatoes for moisture, ricotta cheese for light texture, and orange zest for flavor. It's hard to go wrong—if you can make mashed potatoes, you can make gnocchi.

For the gnocchi:

8 ounces Yukon Gold or other boiling potatoes (not Idahos or new potatoes), peeled and cut into 1-inch chunks

3^1/4 cups all-purpose flour

2 large eggs, lightly beaten

^{1}/2 cup ricotta cheese

^{1}/2 cup freshly grated Parmesan cheese

Grated zest of 1 orange

Pinch of freshly grated nutmeg

1 tablespoon plus ^{1}/4 teaspoon kosher salt

1) Put the potatoes in a saucepan, cover with cold salted water, and bring to a boil. Cook until very tender, about 20 minutes. Drain, return the potatoes to the pot, and shake them over medium heat for 30 seconds to dry them out. Mash smooth in the pot or transfer to the bowl of a mixer with a paddle attachment and mash until very smooth. Set aside to cool.

2) Meanwhile, begin the sauce: in a pot of boiling salted water, blanch the broccoli rabe for 2 minutes to remove the bitterness (it will finish cooking later in the recipe). Fill a bowl with ice cubes and cover with cold water. Lift the broccoli rabe out of the boiling water and plunge it into the ice water to stop the cooking. Drain, chop into 1-inch lengths, and set aside.

3) Make the gnocchi: line a large baking sheet with wax paper.

4) Mound the flour on a clean work surface. Make a large well in the center and pour the eggs into it. Working with your hands, gradually and gently work the potatoes and then the ricotta into the eggs. Sprinkle this mixture with the Parmesan, orange zest, nutmeg, 1/4 teaspoon salt, and pepper.

5) Working in circles, gradually expand the well by incorporating the flour into the potato-ricotta mixture. By the time you get to the outermost rim of flour, you should have a workable dough. Knead the whole thing together until smooth and soft, almost sticky.

6) Pull off a handful of dough and roll it between your hands to form a snake about 1/2 inch thick. Cut the snake with a sharp knife into 3/4-inch lengths and transfer to the lined baking sheet. If you like, use your fingers to gently roll each gnocchi against the back of a fork, creating the typical ridged pattern. (This helps them cook evenly and hold the sauce.) Repeat with the remaining dough.

7) Heat a gallon of water to boiling with the remaining salt and olive oil in a large covered pot.

8) Make the sauce: heat the oil in a skillet over medium-high heat. Reduce the heat to medium, add the onion and garlic, and cook 2 minutes, until softened. Add the broccoli rabe and cook, stirring, 5 minutes. Stir in the orange juice and stock and simmer until reduced by half, 8 to 10 minutes.

9) Meanwhile, cook the gnocchi: in batches of 2 dozen or so, drop the gnocchi into the boiling water and let them cook just until they float to the surface. Remove them with a slotted spoon and transfer them to the simmering stock.

10) Add the tomatoes, Parmesan, basil, and butter. Stir and simmer 3 minutes.

11) Stir in the orange segments.

12) Serve sprinkled with toasted almonds, if desired, and parsley.

2 pinches freshly ground black pepper
1 tablespoon olive oil

For the sauce:
8 ounces broccoli rabe
2 tablespoons olive oil
1 medium onion, chopped
4 garlic cloves, minced
Juice of 1 orange
4 cups chicken stock
2 plum tomatoes, diced
1/4 cup freshly grated Parmesan cheese
6 leaves basil, finely chopped
2 tablespoons unsalted butter
1 orange, peeled and cut into segments

To finish the dish:
2 tablespoons slivered almonds, toasted (optional)
1 tablespoon finely chopped fresh parsley

A TART TOCAI FROM
ITALY'S FRIULI REGION—
NO RELATION TO SWEET
HUNGARIAN TOKAJI—
IS PERFECT HERE.

Roquefort and Pear Salad
with Grapes and Spiced Pecans

*Orange-Ricotta Gnocchi
with Broccoli Rabe*

Tramonto's Escarole,
Sausage, and White Bean Stew

Plum Crostata

Tramonto's Escarole, Sausage, and White Bean Stew

SERVES 4 TO 6

✺

Juicy sausages and bitter greens are a natural combination—and with creamy white beans added, they're one of our favorite one-pot dinners. This wonderful family-style stew can be made well in advance; it reheats beautifully over a low flame. It also freezes well, but as always, taste for salt and pepper before serving. Be sure to serve some crusty bread alongside to mop up the savory liquid at the bottom of the bowl. Thanks, Mom.

1 teaspoon olive oil

8 ounces bulk Italian sausage, sweet and/or hot, broken into 1-inch chunks

5 large garlic cloves, minced

$^1/_2$ teaspoon red pepper flakes, or to taste

1 head escarole, leaves washed, dried, and chopped into 2-inch pieces

3 cups cooked or canned white beans

3 cups chicken stock or low-sodium canned chicken broth

4 tablespoons ($^1/_2$ stick) unsalted butter

$^1/_2$ cup freshly grated Parmesan cheese or a combination of Parmesan and Romano

2 plum tomatoes, diced

2 tablespoons chopped fresh parsley

Kosher salt and freshly ground black pepper

Extra-virgin olive oil

Parmesan cheese, shaved or grated

1) In a large deep skillet, heat the olive oil and cook the sausage pieces over medium-high heat until they begin to brown, about 10 minutes.

2) Add the garlic and pepper flakes to the skillet and sauté over medium-high heat just until the garlic softens, about 2 minutes. Add the escarole and cook, stirring, until wilted, about 2 minutes.

3) Add the beans and cook, stirring, 1 minute. Add the stock and bring to a gentle boil.

4) Add the butter, cheese, tomatoes, and half of the parsley. Mix to combine and cook until the mixture is heated through and the butter is melted. Add salt and pepper to taste.

5) Serve in heated bowls, sprinkled with the remaining herbs and drizzled with a bit of olive oil. Use a vegetable peeler to shave curls of Parmesan over each bowl or sprinkle each bowl with grated cheese.

TRY A BRIGHT, YOUNG DOLCETTO OR A RUSTIC RED FROM SOUTHERN ITALY.

Plum Crostata

Under the name of tarte aux quetsches, plum tart is a favorite dessert all over Alsace, especially in the fall when the purply-blue quetsch (pronounced "kwetch") plums come into season. A heavenly eau-de-vie is also made from the ripe fruits, which we know as Italian prune plums. This crostata is easier to make than any tart, since no custard is required: just sound fruit and good jam. The recipe can be doubled; it can also be made in any shape you like and with any soft fruits: peaches and berries are especially good.

1) Make the dough: in the bowl of a mixer, blend the flour, sugar, and lemon zest at low speed. Add the butter and continue blending at low speed until the mixture is coarse and sandy-looking. Add the egg mixture and blend just until the mixture comes together. Form into a ball, wrap with plastic wrap, and refrigerate at least 1 hour.

2) Preheat the oven to 375°F. Line a baking sheet with parchment paper.

3) On a floured surface, roll the dough out to a rough circle about 14 inches in diameter. Transfer it to the baking sheet. All around the edge of the dough, fold in the outer 1/2 inch to form a rough, "rustic" edge for the tart.

4) Using a rubber spatula, gently spread the jam over the bottom of the tart. Then arrange the plum wedges in concentric circles over the jam. Dot with the raspberries and drizzle with the honey.

5) With a pastry brush, brush the tart edge with the milk. Sprinkle with the coarse sugar.

6) Bake until the fruit is tender and the underside of the tart is lightly browned, 25 to 30 minutes.

For the dough:

2 cups all-purpose flour

1/2 cup sugar

Finely chopped zest of 1 lemon

1 cup (2 sticks) cold unsalted butter, cut into pieces

1 large egg plus 1 large egg yolk, whisked together

For the filling:

2 tablespoons raspberry jam

6 to 8 ripe but firm plums, pitted and cut into wedges

1 cup raspberries, fresh or frozen

1 tablespoon honey

2 tablespoons whole milk

1 tablespoon coarse, turbinado, or "raw" sugar

BELGIAN WHITE BEER, WITH ITS ORANGEY FLAVOR, WOULD DRINK WELL WITH THIS BRIGHT, FRUITY DESSERT.

MATCH WITH AN EXOTIC BLACK MUSCAT FROM CALIFORNIA OR AUSTRALIA.

PIERRE FRANEY
COOKS WITH HIS FRIENDS

PIERRE FRANEY
WITH CLAUDIA FRANEY JENSEN
PHOTOGRAPHS BY MARTIN BRIGDALE AND JEAN CAZALS

The late Pierre Franey, best known as the "60-Minute Gourmet," with his daughter, Claudia Franey Jensen

■ **WHY HE WROTE IT**

As a companion to his fifth PBS series, *Pierre Franey's Cooking in Europe*.

■ **WHY IT MADE OUR LIST**

"In this book," writes Franey, "I bring you a sampling of recipes from today's top European chefs." And really, what more is there to say than that? There are plenty of Franey's own recipes here, too, and they're generally quicker than his friends'. All in all, this lavishly illustrated volume stands as a fitting tribute to the popular and personable chef.

■ **CHAPTERS**

Pierre Franey with . . . Paul Bocuse ▪ Michel Guérard ▪ Juan-Mari & Elena Arzak ▪ Ferran Adrià, Antonio Bellés, & Gary Danko ▪ Bruna & Nadia Santini ▪ Paola & Maurizio Cavazzini ▪ Frédy Girardet ▪ Harald Wohlfahrt, Claus-Peter Lümpp & Peter Müller ▪ Roger Souvereyns ▪ Pierre Wynants ▪ Maartje Boudeling ▪ Marc Meneau

FROM THE BOOK

■ **CULINARY REVELATION**

"Two years ago, after finishing my successful 'Cooking in France' series for public television, I felt a real desire to make a television series visiting some of the best chefs in Europe. After all, France is not the only country where one can eat well!"

■ **SPECIFICS**

214 pages, 111 recipes, approximately 95 color photographs, $22. Published by Artisan.

GRILLED TUNA WITH CAPERS AND TOMATO SAUCE

YIELD: 4 SERVINGS

I always enjoy going to fish markets and deciding what to cook that day. This way I can pick what fish looks most fresh to me. The fish market in Barcelona was wonderful, with an amazing array of seafood. The tuna I bought was very fresh, and I cooked it with a light sauce of capers and tomatoes. The tomatoes, purchased in the same market, caught my eye because they were so red and fresh-looking.

4 center cut tuna steaks (about 4-5 ounces each)

2 tablespoons olive oil

Salt and freshly ground pepper, to taste

¼ teaspoon hot red pepper flakes

4 sprigs fresh thyme, coarsely chopped, or 1 teaspoon dried

⅓ cup drained capers

4 small, ripe plum tomatoes, cored and cut into small cubes

1 tablespoon fresh lemon juice

4 tablespoons chopped fresh basil or parsley

1. Prepare a charcoal grill or preheat the broiler.

2. Place the tuna on a flat dish and spoon 1 tablespoon oil over it. Sprinkle with salt and pepper, red pepper flakes, and thyme, and spread well into the steaks. Cover with plastic wrap and let stand at least 15 minutes before grilling.

3. Heat the remaining tablespoon olive oil in a small skillet. Add the capers and cook briefly over medium-high heat. Add the tomatoes, salt and pepper, and lemon juice, and cook for about 5 minutes. Keep warm.

4. If using a grill, rub the rack lightly with olive oil. Place the fish on the grill and cook for 3 minutes, then turn and cook for another 3 minutes for rare. If you wish the fish to be more well done, cook longer on each side. If broiling, place in pan and broil for 6 minutes for rare, turning once.

5. Remove the fish and cut it into thin diagonal slices. To serve, divide the tomatoes among 4 warm plates. Place the tuna slices on top and sprinkle with basil or parsley.

SAUTÉED CHICKEN WITH WINE AND HERBS

YIELD: 4 SERVINGS

This is one of my favorite chicken recipes, one I learned as an apprentice cook in Paris. I have been making it ever since. But now I make it using olive oil and less butter. Also, I use the cooked garlic cloves to help bind the sauce at the end and to give it more flavor.

1 small chicken (3-3½ pounds), cut into serving pieces
Salt and freshly ground black pepper, to taste
1 tablespoon olive oil
2 garlic cloves, unpeeled
2 sprigs fresh thyme, or ½ teaspoon dried
1 large bay leaf
⅓ cup dry white wine
1 tablespoon butter

1. Sprinkle the chicken with salt and pepper. To facilitate cooking, make a gash on each thigh opposite the skin side.

2. Heat 1 tablespoon olive oil in a large, heavy skillet. When quite hot, add the chicken pieces, skin side down. Do not add the liver. Cook 5-7 minutes, or until golden brown, moving the pieces around to keep them from sticking. Turn the pieces, and add the garlic, thyme, and bay leaf.

3. Add the liver and reduce the heat. Cook chicken over moderate heat, turning the pieces so they cook evenly, for 17-18 minutes.

4. Remove the chicken to a warm platter, leaving the herbs in the pan. Carefully pour off the fat from the pan. Return the pan to the heat and add the wine. Cook over high heat, stirring to dissolve brown particles that cling to the pan, until the wine is reduced by half. Add ⅓ cup water and bring to a boil, then reduce by about half.

5. Swirl in the butter. With a fork, squash the garlic cloves to squeeze out the softened insides. Remove the skins and blend the garlic puree with the sauce. Add the chicken pieces and any juices that have accumulated. Check for seasoning, remove the bay leaf, and serve.

MEDALLIONS OF LAMB WITH BASIL

YIELD: 4 SERVINGS

Lamb has a lower fat content than beef and the outer fat can be easily removed. When cooking these medallions, it is very important to sear the meat quickly on all sides. They can be served with sautéed potatoes or any kind of vegetable.

2 boned loins or racks of lamb (about 1½ pounds), all fat removed
4 ripe plum tomatoes (about 1 pound)
2 tablespoons olive oil
2 teaspoons finely chopped garlic
¼ cup chopped fresh basil
Salt and freshly ground pepper, to taste
1 teaspoon ground cumin
2 sprigs fresh thyme, or ½ teaspoon dried
2 tablespoons finely chopped shallots
3 tablespoons coarsely chopped basil or parsley

1. Cut the lamb into 12 pieces of equal size. Pound them lightly with a meat pounder or mallet.

2. Drop the tomatoes into a pot of boiling water for 10 seconds. Remove and let cool. When the tomatoes have cooled, remove the skins, core them, and cut into ¼-inch chunks. There should be about 1½ cups.

3. Heat 1 tablespoon olive oil in a large saucepan over medium-high heat. Add the garlic and cook briefly until soft but not brown. Add the tomatoes, basil, salt, and pepper. Stir, lower heat, and simmer for 5 minutes. Keep warm.

4. Blend salt and pepper to taste with the cumin and sprinkle over the lamb medallions.

5. Heat 1 tablespoon of olive oil in a nonstick skillet large enough to hold the pieces in one layer. Add the lamb and the thyme. Brown the lamb quickly on all sides and cook over relatively high heat, about 2 minutes on each side for rare or longer if desired. Remove the lamb to a warm platter.

6. In the same pan, add the shallots and cook briefly, stirring until wilted. Add the tomato mixture and any meat juices that have accumulated in the platter and blend well.

7. To serve, divide the tomato sauce evenly among 4 plates. Place 3 pieces of lamb over the sauce on each plate and garnish with chopped basil or parsley.

matthew kenney's
mediterranean cooking

great
flavors
for the
american
kitchen

•

by
matthew
kenney
and
sam gugino

•

photographs
by
paul
franz-moore

Hot New York chef Matthew Kenney, owner of Matthew's, Mezze, and Monzù, with wine writer Sam Gugino

■ WHY HE WROTE IT

"Ultimately, what I've tried to accomplish in this book is to bring the flavors of the Mediterranean Rim to you as simply and as easily as possible while still maintaining their authenticity . . . . Don't keep it on the shelf just for weekends. I want you to use it as often as you can. Think of it not as a bible but as a map to help you on your own culinary explorations."

FROM THE BOOK

■ QUOTABLE QUOTE

"When made well, risotto acts like a symphony, combining the music of many instruments into one clear and delicious composition."

■ WHY IT MADE OUR LIST

Kenney's own culinary explorations led him to Moroccan, Egyptian, and a variety of farther-flung Mediterranean cuisines as well as the usual Italian and Provençal—thus, Mediterranean Rim. The recipes are uncomplicated, full of flavor, and well worth the journey.

■ CHAPTERS

Appetizers, Soups, and Mezze ▪ Salads ▪ Risotto, Grains, and Pasta ▪ Seafood ▪ Poultry and Game Birds ▪ Meats and Large Game ▪ Vegetables and Side Dishes ▪ Desserts ▪ Condiments

■ SPECIFICS

168 pages, approximately 90 recipes, approximately 50 color photographs, $24.95. Published by Chronicle Books.

fennel salad with clementines and moroccan olives

serves 4

This dish is traditionally made with oranges, but I prefer the sweeter clementines we see in winter, imported from Spain and Morocco in those cute little wooden crates. Shiny, jet black oil-cured Moroccan olives offer a nice color contrast as well as a salty counterpoint to the clementines. This is a good finish to a heavy meal or it can be used as part of a mezze table.

5 teaspoons anise seeds
Juice of 4 clementines or 2 juice oranges
1 tablespoon minced onion or shallot
¼ cup extra virgin olive oil
2 small bulbs fennel
10 clementines or 5 navel oranges, peeled with membranes or white pith removed, and sectioned
24 black Moroccan or other black oil-cured olives, pitted
1 tablespoon chopped chives
½ cup (loosely packed) arugula leaves, washed and dried
Salt and freshly ground black pepper

Put the anise seeds in a heavy skillet over medium heat. Toast for 4 minutes, stirring a few times. Grind 2½ teaspoons of the seeds with a mortar and pestle. Set ground and whole toasted seeds aside separately.

Combine the clementine juice, onion, and ground anise seeds in a small bowl. Slowly whisk in the olive oil. Set aside.

Remove green tops from fennel and discard. Cut the bulbs lengthwise in half and cut out the firm center core. Cut lengthwise into strips, about ⅛ inch wide.

Place the fennel, clementines, olives, chives, and arugula in a large bowl and toss with the dressing. Season with salt and pepper to taste. Divide the salad among 4 plates. Sprinkle with the reserved whole anise seeds.

pan-roasted cod with
provençal fava bean ragout

serves 4

⅓ cup coarse bread crumbs

2 tablespoons coarsely cracked coriander
    seeds

4 cod steaks or fillets (6 ounces each)

Salt

8 ounces fava beans, shelled (about
    ½ cup)

5 tablespoons olive oil

2 cloves garlic, minced

1 small tomato, diced

⅓ cup kalamata olives, pitted

4 teaspoons small capers, drained

¼ cup dry white wine

½ cup Shellfish or Chicken Stock
    (page 78)

12 basil leaves, stacked, rolled like a
    cigar, and cut crosswise into thin strips

Freshly ground black pepper

Mix the bread crumbs with the coriander seeds and spread on a large plate. Press one side of the steaks firmly into the bread crumb mixture to coat well. Refrigerate up to 1 hour, if desired.

Cook the shelled fava beans in 1 quart of boiling salted water for 3 minutes. Drain and run under cool water. When cooled, peel skins by tearing off a small piece of peel from the rounded end with your fingernail. Squirt out the beans by pinching the opposite end. Set aside.

Preheat the oven to 200 degrees. Heat 4 tablespoons of the olive oil in a large nonstick skillet over medium-high heat. Add the fish, crust side down, and cook for about 3 minutes, or until the coating turns golden brown. Turn the fish over and cook for 5 to 6 minutes, or until the fish is springy to the touch and cooked through. Remove the fish to an ovenproof platter, cover loosely with foil, and put into the oven.

Wipe out the skillet with a paper towel and heat the remaining tablespoon of olive oil over high heat. Add the garlic and tomato and cook for 2 minutes. Reduce the heat to medium, add the fava beans, olives, and capers and cook for 1 minute. Add the wine and stock and turn the heat to high. Reduce the liquid by half, about 5 minutes. Remove from the heat, stir in the basil, and season with salt and pepper to taste.

Divide the fish among 4 plates and spoon the sauce evenly over and around the fish. Serve immediately.

The old definition of a ragout was a French meat stew, with the flavors melding together after long, slow cooking. But to me, a ragout is a combination of ingredients in which each one retains its flavor while at the same time producing a superior finished product. Such is the result achieved with fava beans, ripe summer tomatoes, garlic, and olives in this dish, which comes together much more quickly than a traditional ragout. Liberal substitutions can be made, such as green olives or caperberries for the kalamata olives, other fresh shell beans for the favas, and halibut, grouper, or other firm-flesh white fish for cod.

shellfish stock

makes 2 quarts

2 pounds shrimp or lobster shells
¼ cup olive oil
2 cups dry white wine
1 cup fresh tomatoes or tomato scraps
2 medium onions, coarsely chopped
2 ribs celery, coarsely chopped

5 sprigs of parsley
3 sprigs of thyme
2 bay leaves
10 black peppercorns
Pinch of saffron (optional)

Rinse the shells under cold running water. Put the oil in a large stockpot over high heat. Add the shells and sauté for 12 to 14 minutes, stirring regularly. Add 4 quarts water and the remaining ingredients. Bring to a boil. Skim the top of the stock to remove any foam.

Reduce the heat and simmer for 1 hour and 20 minutes, skimming foam every 20 minutes. Remove the shells with a wire mesh strainer or skimmer and strain the liquid through a cheesecloth-lined strainer into a large (at least 4½ quarts) saucepan.

Bring to a boil and reduce the heat to a simmer. Reduce to 2 quarts, about 1 hour and 40 minutes. Cool in an ice bath in the sink or large bowl until warm. Refrigerate. When completely cool, skim the fat that congeals on top. Bring to a boil before using. Refrigerate for up to 3 days. Freeze in small containers.

chicken stock

makes 4 quarts

6 pounds chicken necks, backs, wings,
    and giblets (no livers)
2 medium onions, coarsely chopped
2 carrots, coarsely chopped
2 ribs celery, coarsely chopped

Green tops of 2 leeks, coarsely chopped
12 sprigs of parsley
2 sprigs of thyme
3 bay leaves
½ teaspoon black peppercorns

Thoroughly rinse the chicken parts under cold running water. Put in a large stockpot, cover with 6 quarts cold water, and bring to a boil over high heat. Skim the top of the stock to remove any foam as it forms.

Add the remaining ingredients, reduce to a simmer, and cook, uncovered, for 5 hours, skimming foam every 40 to 60 minutes.

Remove the chicken and vegetables with a wire mesh strainer or skimmer and strain the liquid through a cheesecloth-lined strainer into a 4-quart pot or heatproof plastic container. Put the container in ice in the sink or a large bowl until cooled to warm. Refrigerate. When completely cool, skim the fat that congeals on top. Bring to a boil before using. Refrigerate for up to 3 days. Freeze in small containers.

loin of venison in black pepper—pomegranate marinade

serves 6

2 large onions, coarsely chopped

1 piece of fresh ginger (about 1 inch),
    coarsely chopped

½ orange (unpeeled), seeded and cut into
    ½-inch chunks

2 tablespoons coarsely ground black pepper

1 ½ cups pomegranate juice or 1 cup
    pinot noir with 2 tablespoons
    pomegranate molasses (available in
    Middle Eastern markets and specialty
    stores)

1 clove garlic, coarsely chopped

Pinch of ground allspice

1 boneless loin of venison (about 3
    pounds)

2 tablespoons olive oil

Salt

2 tablespoons chopped chives

In a blender, puree the onions, ginger, orange, black pepper, pomegranate juice, garlic, and allspice. Cut the venison crosswise into 12 medallions. Lay the medallions flat in 1 layer in a nonreactive (glass, enamel, or ceramic) dish and pour the marinade over. Turn to coat well, cover, and refrigerate 24 to 36 hours.

Remove the venison from the marinade and wipe off excess marinade with a paper towel. Put the olive oil in a large skillet over medium-high heat. Or use 2 skillets, each with 2 tablespoons of oil. Season the venison with salt and cook the medallions for 2½ minutes per side. Meat should be medium-rare, with plenty of red in the center.

To serve, place 2 medallions on each plate and sprinkle with chives.

Pomegranates are used frequently in the eastern Mediterranean (as well as Morocco) in everything from breakfast drinks to salads. The lively sweet-tart quality of the fruit's juice is also good as a marinade with strong meats like lamb and game like venison. Venison and other lean cuts of meat benefit from marinating because the marinade is in direct contact with the meat, unencumbered by fat or skin. Thus the marinade penetrates easily and provides flavor that the fat normally would.

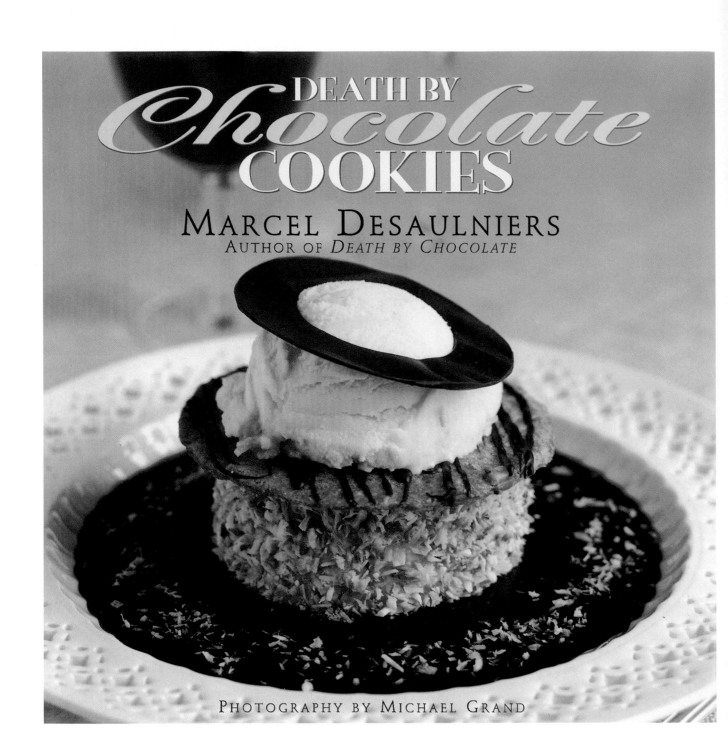

DEATH BY *Chocolate* COOKIES

MARCEL DESAULNIERS

AUTHOR OF *DEATH BY CHOCOLATE*

PHOTOGRAPHY BY MICHAEL GRAND

Marcel Desaulniers, much-lauded chef of The Trellis Restaurant in Colonial Williamsburg, Virginia

■ WHY HE WROTE IT

" . . . chocolate is not just the most deliciously intoxicating substance in the cosmos, it might be the key to universal peace."

■ WHY IT MADE OUR LIST

Desaulniers is clearly mad about chocolate, and leafing through this collection of chocolate cookies, bars, brownies, praline, ice-cream sandwiches, candies, and shortcakes, we're feeling a little crazed, too. Most of these are "pop in your mouth" treats, not the towering confections of his earlier books, and all the easier to make and gorge on for that. A chocoholic's dream.

■ CHAPTERS

Easy Street ▪ Family Secrets ▪ For Kids at Heart ▪ Celebrate! ▪ Keep It on Ice ▪ More Than a Mouthful

FROM THE BOOK

■ CHEF'S CHOICE

"I love peanuts. Peanuts are one of my vices. The only thing better than peanuts is peanuts with chocolate. Add peanut butter to that, and the only thing missing from this picture of Nirvana is my soulmate and a South Pacific setting. But I digress . . . ."

■ PREVIOUS CREDITS

The dastardly Desaulniers previously tempted our sweet tooths with *Death by Chocolate* and *Desserts to Die For.*

■ SPECIFICS

144 pages, 80 recipes, 80 color photographs, $30. Published by Simon & Schuster.

CHOCOLATE CRACKUPS
Yields 3 dozen 2½-inch cookies

MAKE THE CHOCOLATE CRACKUPS

Heat 1 inch of water in the bottom half of a double boiler over medium heat. With the heat on, place the unsweetened chocolate in the top half of the double boiler. Use a rubber spatula to stir the chocolate until completely melted and smooth, about 3 minutes. Transfer the melted chocolate to a 1-quart bowl and set aside until needed.

Combine the granulated sugar and vegetable oil in a 7-quart bowl, using a stiff whisk to stir until the sugar resembles wet (white) sand. Add the eggs and vanilla extract and whisk vigorously until incorporated. Add the melted chocolate and stir until silky. Add the flour, baking powder, and salt, and blend with a rubber spatula until smooth. Tightly cover the bowl with plastic wrap and refrigerate for 1 hour.

Preheat the oven to 350 degrees Fahrenheit.

Remove the dough from the refrigerator and discard the plastic wrap. Divide the cookie dough into 36 slightly heaping tablespoon-size pieces (approximately 1 ounce per piece) onto a large piece of wax paper. Place the confectioners' sugar in a 1-quart bowl. Gently roll each portion in the palms of your hands to form a smooth ball (keep a towel close by since it gets a little sticky between the first and the thirty-sixth ball). Then roll each ball in the confectioners' sugar to coat evenly and generously.

Divide the balls onto 3 nonstick baking sheets, 12 evenly spaced balls per sheet (they expand so don't crowd). Place the baking sheets on the top and center racks of the preheated oven and bake for 12 to 14 minutes, rotating the sheets from top to center halfway through the baking time (at that time also turn each sheet 180 degrees). Remove the cookies from the oven and cool to room temperature on the baking sheets, about 30 minutes. Store the cooled cookies in a tightly sealed plastic container until ready to serve.

INGREDIENTS

4 ounces unsweetened chocolate, chopped into ¼-inch pieces
2 cups granulated sugar
½ cup vegetable oil
4 large eggs
2 teaspoons pure vanilla extract
2 cups all-purpose flour
1½ teaspoons baking powder
½ teaspoon salt
1 cup confectioners' sugar

EQUIPMENT

Cook's knife, cutting board, measuring cups, measuring spoons, double boiler, rubber spatula, 1-quart bowl, 7-quart bowl, stiff whisk, plastic wrap, wax paper, 3 nonstick baking sheets, plastic cookie storage container with lid

THE CHEF'S TOUCH

Chocolate Crackups will keep for several days at room temperature if stored in a tightly sealed plastic container. For long-term storage, up to several weeks, the cookie may be frozen. Freeze the Crackups in a tightly sealed plastic container to prevent dehydration and to protect them from freezer odors.

CHOCOLATE BOULDERS

Yields 3 dozen 2½-inch cookies

INGREDIENTS

1½ cups pecan pieces

1 pound semisweet chocolate, 8 ounces chopped into ¼-inch pieces and 8 ounces chopped into ⅛-inch pieces

½ pound unsalted butter, cut into 1-ounce pieces

1 cup tightly packed light brown sugar

3 large eggs

1 teaspoon pure vanilla extract

3 cups all-purpose flour

1 teaspoon baking powder

1 teaspoon salt

EQUIPMENT

Measuring cups, cook's knife, cutting board, measuring spoons, 3 nonstick baking sheets, double boiler, rubber spatula, 1-quart bowl, table-model electric mixer with paddle, plastic cookie storage container with lid

THE CHEF'S TOUCH

If you love sweets but haven't put in many hours in the kitchen (and prefer to keep it that way), these cookies are for you. Chocolate Boulders are best eaten within a day or two of baking. In fact, they are at their best when served within a few hours of being removed from the oven.

MAKE THE BOULDERS

Preheat the oven to 350 degrees Fahrenheit.

Toast the pecans on a baking sheet in the preheated oven for 10 minutes. Remove the nuts from the oven and set aside to cool to room temperature before using.

Heat 1 inch of water in the bottom half of a double boiler over medium heat. With the heat on, place the ¼-inch pieces of chocolate in the top half of the double boiler. Use a rubber spatula to stir the chocolate until completely melted and smooth, about 4 to 6 minutes. Transfer the melted chocolate to a 1-quart bowl and set aside until needed.

Place the butter and brown sugar in the bowl of an electric mixer fitted with a paddle. Beat on medium speed for 3 minutes until soft. Use a rubber spatula to scrape down the sides of the bowl, then beat on high for 2 minutes until fairly smooth. Scrape down the bowl. Add the eggs and the vanilla extract and beat on medium for 3 minutes until smooth. Scape down the bowl. Beat on high for 2 minutes until very smooth. Add the melted chocolate and beat on medium for 1 minute until incorporated. Operate the mixer on low speed while gradually adding the flour, baking soda, and salt and mix until incorporated, about 30 seconds. Stop the mixer and add the chocolate chopped into ⅛-inch pieces and the toasted pecans, and mix on low for 30 seconds. Remove the bowl from the mixer and use a rubber spatula to finish mixing the dough until thoroughly combined.

Using a heaping tablespoon of dough for each cookie (approximately 1¾ ounces), portion 12 cookies, evenly spaced, onto each of 3 nonstick baking sheets. Place the baking sheets on the top and center racks of the preheated oven and bake for 12 to 14 minutes, rotating the sheets from top to center halfway through the baking time (at that time also turn each sheet 180 degrees). Remove the cookies from the oven and cool to room temperature on the baking sheets, about 30 minutes. Store the cooled cookies in a tightly sealed plastic container.

CHOCOLATE DROP SHORTCAKES

Yields 2 dozen 2½-inch biscuits

INGREDIENTS

1 cup whole milk

¼ cup granulated sugar

1¾ cups all-purpose flour

½ cup unsweetened cocoa powder

2 tablespoons baking powder

1 teaspoon salt

8 tablespoons unsalted butter, chilled

8 ounces semisweet chocolate mini-morsels

EQUIPMENT

Measuring cups, measuring spoons, 1½-quart saucepan, 4-quart bowl, instant-read test thermometer, plastic wrap, sifter, 7-quart bowl, fork, rubber spatula, 2 nonstick baking sheets, plastic cookie storage container with lid

MAKE THE CHOCOLATE DROP SHORTCAKES

Preheat the oven to 400 degrees Fahrenheit.

Heat the milk and the granulated sugar in a 1½-quart saucepan over medium-high heat. When hot, stir to dissolve the sugar. Bring to a boil. Immediately remove from the heat and transfer to a 4-quart bowl. Cool in an ice-water bath to a temperature of 40 to 45 degrees Fahrenheit. Cover with plastic wrap and refrigerate until needed.

In a sifter combine the flour, cocoa powder, baking powder, and salt. Sift into a 7-quart bowl. Add the butter. Use a fork to "cut" the butter into the sifted flour mixture until the mixture develops a mealy texture. Add the chocolate mini-morsels and use a rubber spatula to mix until combined. Add the chilled milk mixture and mix with the spatula until the dough comes together.

Using a heaping tablespoon of dough (approximately 1½ ounces) per shortcake, portion 12 shortcakes, evenly spaced, onto each of 2 nonstick baking sheets. Place the baking sheets on the center rack of the preheated oven and bake for 12 minutes. Remove the shortcakes from the oven and cool at room temperature for 10 minutes. Serve the warm shortcakes immediately, or cool completely and store in a tightly sealed plastic container.

THE CHEF'S TOUCH

My mother loved serving our family strawberry shortcake after dinner on Sundays in the summer. Although hers wasn't chocolate, we loved it anyway (my siblings share my passion for chocolate). It is probably a good thing she didn't have this chocolate shortcake recipe—she may never have gotten rid of us.

Chocolate Drop Shortcakes will keep for 3 to 4 days at room temperature in a tightly sealed plastic container. The shortcakes come to life when served warm; just pop them in a 275-degree-Fahrenheit oven for 3 to 4 minutes. Before serving, use a serrated knife to cut the shortcakes in half horizontally.

Strawberries are delicious with this recipe. But if you really want to indulge, use raspberries instead and serve with lots of whipped cream. The shortcakes are also great with ice cream.

ALMIGHTY CHOCOLATE DIVINITY

Yields 2 dozen 2-inch bites

THE CHEF'S TOUCH

For the ultimate texture and flavor for the Almighty Chocolate Divinity, be sure to toast the walnuts in a 350-degree-Fahrenheit oven for 5 to 6 minutes. Don't chop the nuts until they have cooled to room temperature. A food processor fitted with a metal blade will finely chop the nuts in just a few seconds, or you can use a cook's knife to chop the nuts.

Practice makes perfect with this lovely, cloudlike candy. If your Divinity looks less like a cumulus and more like a downpour, don't despair; it will still be quite tasty.

Almighty Chocolate Divinity will keep for 2 to 3 days at room temperature if stored in a tightly sealed plastic container. The Divinity will keep for a few more days under refrigeration (I actually prefer this candy chilled). For long-term storage, up to several weeks, the candy may be frozen in a tightly sealed plastic container to prevent dehydration and to protect it from freezer odors.

INGREDIENTS

- **3** cups granulated sugar
- **½** cup water
- **⅓** cup light corn syrup
- **2** large egg whites
- **1** cup finely chopped toasted walnuts
- **8** ounces semisweet chocolate mini-morsels

EQUIPMENT

Measuring cups, baking sheet, food processor with metal blade, 3-quart saucepan, whisk, instant-read test thermometer, table-model electric mixer with balloon whip, rubber spatula, measuring spoons, wax paper, plastic cookie storage container with lid

CREATE THE DIVINITY

Heat the granulated sugar, water, and corn syrup in a 3-quart saucepan over medium-high heat, stirring to dissolve the sugar. Bring to a boil. Continue to boil, stirring often, until the temperature of the syrup reaches 250 degrees Fahrenheit, about 5 minutes.

As soon as the syrup begins boiling, place the egg whites in the bowl of an electric mixer fitted with a balloon whip. Whisk on high until soft peaks form, about 4 minutes. Change the mixer speed to medium. Carefully and slowly pour the 250-degree-Fahrenheit syrup into the whisked egg whites, and continue to whisk on medium until the meringue is very thick, about 4 minutes. Remove the bowl from the mixer. Working quickly, use a rubber spatula to fold the walnuts and then the chocolate morsels into the meringue, creating a variegated mixture. Divide the mixture into 24 heaping tablespoons onto two large pieces of wax paper, using your finger to push the mixture off the spoon and onto the wax paper. Allow to cool to room temperature for about an hour before storing in a tightly sealed plastic container.

Chapter 2
Italian and Mediterranean Cooking

No matter how hard chefs and food writers try to tempt us with more exotic cuisines, Mediterranean fare holds its position as the current American favorite. Since the category continues to be hot, cookbook authors have cast their nets both broader and deeper. In this country, the designation *Mediterranean* used to mean just Italian, Southern French, and maybe Spanish, but our horizons have expanded to include the cooking of every country around the Mediterranean Sea, and recipes sometimes include elements from more than one of the countries. Writers are also delving into every last corner of the area. (This year you can take a cookbook visit to never-before-covered Puglia, for instance.) Each book here treats a popular subject in a uniquely personal way.

■ **MARCELLA CUCINA** BY MARCELLA HAZAN

Onion Risotto Beaten with Butter and Sage **94**

Pan-Roasted Veal with Radicchio **96**

Sautéed Cauliflower with Green Olives and Tomato **98**

Orange Cake, Ancona-Style **100**

■ **FLAVORS OF PUGLIA: Traditional Recipes from the Heel of Italy's Boot**
BY NANCY HARMON JENKINS

Spaghetti with Oven-Roasted Tomatoes **105**

Salt-Baked Snapper **106**

Roast Stuffed Chicken **108**

Easter Lamb with Fresh Green Peas and Parmesan Sauce **110**

■ **KITCHEN CONVERSATIONS: Robust Recipes and Lessons in Flavor from One of America's Most Innovative Chefs** BY JOYCE GOLDSTEIN

Yesil Domates Batisi/Turkish Green Tomato Salad with Feta Cheese **114**

Risotto with Mussels, Ouzo, Green Onions, and Hot Pepper **116**

Roast Fish with Sicilian Sweet-and-Sour Onions **118**

Spiced Figs with Lemon, Fennel, and Cloves **120**

■ **A FRESH TASTE OF ITALY: 250 Authentic Recipes, Undiscovered Dishes, and New Flavors for Every Day** BY MICHELE SCICOLONE

Salmon Carpaccio **124**

Grilled Jumbo Shrimp with Sage and Pancetta **125**

Gardener's Risotto **126**

Apple Lattice Tart **132**

■ **INVITATION TO MEDITERRANEAN COOKING: 150 Vegetarian and Seafood Recipes** BY CLAUDIA RODEN

Bulghur Salad with Walnuts **136**

Spaghetti with Herbs and Roasted Cherry Tomatoes **139**

Fish Soup with Saffron and Cream **140**

Roasted Peaches **143**

■ **THE FOODS AND FLAVORS OF HAUTE PROVENCE** BY GEORGEANNE BRENNAN

Chicken Ragout with Black Olives **146**

Figs Grilled with *Roulade* and Chicken Livers **148**

Lamb with Rosemary Sauce **149**

■ **IN NONNA'S KITCHEN: Recipes and Traditions from Italy's Grandmothers** BY CAROL FIELD

Polenta Concia/Polenta Layered with Cheeses and Black Pepper **153**

Pollo con le Olive/Roast Chicken Stuffed with Black Olives **155**

MARCELLA CUCINA

Marcella cooks by your side
with an inspirational collection
of new recipes that brings
to your table the flavors,
the textures,
the essence of Italy

Marcella Hazan

PHOTOGRAPHY BY ALISON HARRIS

■ **AUTHOR**

Marcella Hazan, the "godmother of Italian cooking in America"

■ **WHY SHE WROTE IT**

". . . I am prompted to say that this book has written itself . . . . It was not mapped out like a military campaign, so many objectives to reach, so much territory to cover, so many positions to hold. It advanced, unforced, day by day, and the features of the cooking it describes have been shaped by the life that my husband and I live. There can be no doubt about its being a cookbook, but when here and there it decided to step over the line into autobiography I allowed it to have its way."

■ **WHY IT MADE OUR LIST**

It's hard to tell what's more delicious here: Hazan's always-wonderful recipes or the anecdotes she's sprinkled throughout—of discovering new recipes in restaurants, finding a perfect ingredient at a street market, bridling at the notion that broccoli *must* be cooked in olive oil. Hazan has said that this will be her last cookbook; let's hope she doesn't mean it.

■ **CHAPTERS**

Appetizers ▪ Soups ▪ Pasta ▪ Risotto and Polenta ▪ Fish ▪ Poultry and Rabbit ▪ Meat ▪ Vegetables ▪ Salads ▪ Desserts

■ **PREVIOUS CREDITS**

Hazan has fed our love of Italian food with *The Classic Italian Cookbook, More Classic Italian Cooking, Marcella's Italian Kitchen,* and *Essentials of Italian Cooking.*

FROM THE BOOK

■ **WORDS OF WISDOM**

"It happens too often when I eat the food of highly trained chefs, food that is ingeniously contrived, elaborately described in the menu, and eye-catchingly presented, that virtually nothing registers on my palate. Such occasions remind me of a plea that the composer Richard Strauss once made to an orchestra he was rehearsing: 'Gentlemen, you are playing all the notes perfectly, but please, now let me hear some music.' "

■ **SPECIFICS**

472 pages, 184 recipes, 110 color photographs, $35. Published by HarperCollins.

Onion Risotto Beaten with Butter and Sage

RISOTTO CON LE CIPOLLE MANTECATO ALLA SALVIA

1½ cups very thinly sliced onion

1 tablespoon vegetable oil

1 tablespoon butter

Salt

5 cups homemade meat broth OR a bouillon cube dissolved in 5 cups simmering water OR ½ cup canned beef broth diluted with 4½ cups water

1½ cups *carnaroli, arborio,* or other imported Italian rice for risotto

FOR *MANTECARE*

2 tablespoons butter

16 to 20 fresh sage leaves cut into thin lengthwise strips

¾ cup freshly grated Parmigiano-Reggiano cheese

Black pepper ground fresh

For 4 to 6 persons

I have put *mantecato* into the Italian title because here that process carries 50 percent of the responsibility for the risotto's taste. The base is rigorously simple and pure, endowing the risotto with a lovely, sweet foundation of flavor. All of the sage is added off the heat, its fragrance coaxed free by the warmth of the steaming risotto.

1. Put the sliced onions, 1 tablespoon vegetable oil, 1 tablespoon butter, and a sprinkling of salt into the pot where you will be making the risotto, and turn on the heat to medium. Cook the onion, stirring it from time to time, until it is very soft, first letting it wilt completely, then continuing to cook it until it becomes colored a tawny gold.

2. When the onion is just about done, pour the broth into a saucepan, bring it to and keep it at a slow, sputtering simmer on a burner close to the risotto pot.

3. Turn up the heat under the onion to medium high, and add the rice. Turn it over thoroughly and continuously for at least 1 minute to coat it well, so that its white color takes on some of the onions' warmer hue. Add 1 cup of simmering broth, and cook the rice, stirring it and periodically adding liquid. Finish cooking the rice, stirring always and adding broth when needed, until it is tender but firm to the bite, about 25 minutes.

4. Off heat, do the *mantecare* step, whisking in 2 tablespoons of butter, the shredded sage leaves, the grated Parmesan, and liberal grindings of black pepper. Turn the risotto over four or five times with your wooden spoon. Taste and correct for salt, transfer to a warm platter, and serve at once.

AHEAD-OF-TIME NOTE: You can cook the onions a couple of hours in advance. Reheat them thoroughly and have the heat going strong when you put in the rice.

THE PRINCIPAL RISOTTO RICE VARIETIES

Rice for risotto must satisfy two complementary but separate requirements: On the kernel's surface it must have a soft starch, part of which will dissolve in the cooking to produce a clinging, creamy texture; and within the kernel it must have a different starch that will stay firm and give the cooked rice an *al dente* consistency. If you look at a single grain of rice against the light, you will see both starches—the firm one, chalky white in the center of the kernel, the soft one translucently surrounding it.

Even among the rice varieties grown specifically for risotto, the proportions of the two starches differ, and thus each kind of rice will cook somewhat differently and lead to the making of risottos that vary in style.

Arborio. A large, plump, beautiful grain that abounds in amylopectin, the starch that dissolves in cooking, while it is less rich in amylose, the firm, inner starch. It is the rice of preference to achieve the denser consistency that is popular with cooks in the regions of Lombardy, Piedmont, and Emilia-Romagna where they make risotto with saffron, or with Parmesan and white truffles, with meat sauce, or with game. This can be a fine all-purpose variety yielding a luscious risotto, but because of all the soft starch that envelops it, it must be followed with great care in the cooking. When inattentive cooks use arborio they are rewarded with gummy risottos.

Vialone Nano. A small, stubby, homely grain well endowed with amylose, the starch that does not soften easily in cooking, although it has enough of the softer starch to qualify it as a suitable variety for risotto. It is the nearly unanimous choice in the Veneto, where the preferred consistency is loose—rippling or *all'onda*, to use the Venetian expression—and where people are partial to a kernel that offers considerable resistance to the bite. It is an excellent variety to use for the delicately conceived Venetian-style risottos with seafood or spring vegetables.

Carnaroli. A premium variety developed in 1945 by a Milanese rice grower who crossed *vialone* with a Japanese strain. It has become more easily available than it was when I first wrote about it several years ago, but it is still less abundant and costs more than either *arborio* or *vialone nano*. The *carnaroli* kernel is sheathed in enough soft starch to dissolve deliciously in cooking, but it also contains more of the tough starch than any other risotto variety so that it cooks to an exceptionally satisfying firm, beautifully balanced consistency.

Pan-Roasted Veal with Radicchio

VITELLO IN TEGAME COL RADICCHIO

½ pound long-leaf
   Treviso radicchio OR
   Belgian endive

2 tablespoons extra virgin
   olive oil

1½ pounds veal
   tenderloin OR boned
   shoulder; see headnote

2 garlic cloves, peeled and
   lightly mashed with the
   handle of a knife

1½ tablespoons very
   finely chopped
   pancetta

Salt

⅓ cup dry white wine

Black pepper ground
   fresh

---

*For 4 persons, or for 6 if
preceded by a substantial first
course*

The succulence and tastiness of this roast derive in part from the cooking method and in part from the specific combination of meat and vegetable. The method is the characteristically Italian one of cooking meat on top of the stove rather than in the oven, a procedure that, as I have mentioned elsewhere in these pages, produces very satisfying depth of flavor.

You should also note that once the veal is cooked and sliced, you return it to the pot and turn the slices over at low heat in the combined cooking juices and vegetables. This is a brief step, taking less than a minute, which does wonders for the finished dish because every surface of the meat becomes impregnated by the flavors of the roast, and at the same time the meat recovers some of the heat lost during the slicing. I follow this step any time that I am roasting a whole piece of meat, whether it is veal, beef, or pork.

The radicchio helps the naturally mild-flavored veal achieve a greater intensity and richness of taste than it would otherwise be capable of. If the long-leafed Treviso radicchio is available to you, it should be your first choice, but failing that you can obtain equally satisfactory results with that closely related member of the chicory family, Belgian endive.

Tenderloin yields the most tender and juicy results with this recipe, but a nice boned shoulder will certainly not disappoint. If you are using shoulder, do not have the butcher roll it up and truss it, because you would then not be able to brown all its parts.

1. If you are using Treviso radicchio with its long root still attached, pare the root down to a short nub. If the root has been cut off, as it is in endive, trim away a thin slice from the butt end and detach the leaves from the radicchio or endive, discarding any blemished ones. Shred the leaves lengthwise into narrow strips about ¼ inch wide, soak briefly in cold water, and drain.

2. Choose a sauté pan or skillet into which the meat can fit cozily, put in the olive oil, and turn the heat on to medium high. When the oil

is hot enough that it sizzles instantly on contact with the meat, put in the veal. Brown it thoroughly on one side, then turn it, adding the mashed garlic cloves.

3. When the meat has been browned on all sides, transfer it to a plate and add the pancetta to the pan. Turn the pancetta over three or four times during 1 minute of cooking, then put in the shredded radicchio or endive, sprinkling it lightly with salt. Turn the vegetable over a few times to coat it well, and cook it until it becomes limp and colored a light brown.

4. Return the meat to the pan, and add the wine. While you let the wine bubble completely away, use a wooden spoon to scrape loose any browning residues stuck to the bottom of the pan. Sprinkle the meat with salt and several grindings of pepper, turn it a few times, then lower the heat and put a lid on the pan. Cook at a slowly sputtering simmer, turning the meat over occasionally. Whenever you find that the juices in the pan are insufficient to keep the meat from sticking, add 2 to 3 tablespoons of water. Cook until the meat feels very tender when poked with a sharp fork, about 1 hour or more.

5. When done, transfer the piece of veal to a cutting board, slice it thin, and return the slices to the pan. Over low heat, for about half a minute, turn the slices over to coat them well. Serve from a warm platter, pouring the full contents of the pan over the meat.

AHEAD-OF-TIME NOTE: You can prepare the dish, including the slicing of the meat, several hours in advance, but preferably not overnight. Reheat gently but thoroughly, adding 2 tablespoons of water.

Sautéed Cauliflower with Green Olives and Tomato

CAVOLFIORE CON OLIVE VERDI E POMODORO

A head of cauliflower, about 1½ pounds

¼ cup extra virgin olive oil

⅓ cup very thinly chopped onion

16 green olives in brine, pitted and quartered

Salt

Black pepper ground fresh

1 cup really ripe fresh tomatoes, peeled raw, seeds scooped away, and cut into fine dice

For 4 persons

I don't think of myself as a fancy cook. Presentation is not one of my first thoughts, but I am not insensible to an attractive-looking dish as long as its appearance signals the flavors I am about to experience. The tomato dice and the green olive sections look very pretty in this Apulian-style cauliflower, but they are there for reasons of taste. Cauliflower, if it hasn't been around too long, can be quite mild, sometimes tediously so. Here, however, the residual bitterness of the olives and the acidulousness of the tomato help the cauliflower's potential sweetness make taste impressions that, by contrast, are both more intense and more lively. Bear in mind that cauliflower is one vegetable that wants to be cooked thoroughly—not until it is mushy, of course, but it has to be decidedly tender; otherwise, it will always retain a disagreeable trace of sourness.

1. Trim away the cauliflower's green leaves and wash it in cold water.

2. Choose a saucepan that can amply contain the whole cauliflower head, fill it three-quarters full with water, and bring the water to a boil. Drop in the cauliflower and cook until it feels very tender when tested with a fork, about 20 to 25 minutes. Drain and, as soon as the cauliflower is cool enough to handle, cut it into pieces about 1½ inches big.

3. Put the olive oil and the chopped onion in a 10- or 12-inch skillet, and turn the heat on to medium high. Cook the onion, stirring once or twice, until it becomes colored a pale gold, then add the cut-up cauliflower, the olives, salt, and a liberal grinding of black pepper.

4. Cook over lively heat for 2 to 3 minutes, occasionally turning over the contents of the pan with a wooden spoon. Add the diced tomato, turn all the ingredients over, and continue cooking for another 5 minutes or so. Serve at once when done.

AHEAD-OF-TIME NOTE: You can boil the cauliflower a few hours in advance, keeping it at cool room temperature, but preferably out of the refrigerator.

Orange Cake, Ancona-Style

TORTA DI ARANCE ALL'ANCONETANA

2 cups plus 2 tablespoons
all-purpose flour, plus
flour for dusting the
pan

3 eggs

The grated peel, avoiding
the spongy white pith,
of 3 oranges

4 tablespoons (½ stick)
butter, softened to
room temperature, plus
butter for greasing the
pan

1 cup plus 3 tablespoons
sugar

2 tablespoons ouzo
liqueur; see headnote

1 tablespoon whole milk

2½ teaspoons baking
powder

2 cups freshly squeezed
orange juice with
3 tablespoons sugar
dissolved in it

---

8 to 10 servings

A tube pan with loose bottom

Of all the cakes that I have worked on for this and for my previous books, none has been more gratifying than this tribute to the orange. It is so soft, so juicy, so tenderly aromatic, so easy to make.

I call it *all'Anconetana* because I had it and obtained the recipe for it in Ancona, the large port town in the Marches. But I understand it is made elsewhere in this happy central Italian region between the mountains and the sea. One ingredient of the original recipe is apparently native to the Marches. It is *mistrà*, the driest of the anise-based liqueurs. I have tried such Italian and French alternatives as Sambuca and Pernod, but they are too cloying, too stickily anise-tasting. I was about to abandon trying to duplicate this wonderful cake until I was prompted to try ouzo, which works very nicely.

Another ingredient you may want to replace is the Sicilian blood oranges that one would use in Italy. The Italian blood orange is full of juice and exceptionally fragrant. The ones from California I have tried are stingy with juice, short on fragrance, and, considering the amount of liquid that is required here, extravagantly expensive. You'd be better off forgoing the drama of the red juice and employing an orange such as the tangelo or the temple or any other comparably fragrant variety.

1. Turn on the oven to 350°.

2. Put flour, eggs, grated orange peel, 4 tablespoons softened butter, sugar, and liqueur in a food processor and run until all ingredients are evenly amalgamated.

3. Add the milk and baking powder, and process again to incorporate into the mixture.

4. Thickly smear the tube pan with butter and dust with flour. Put the cake mixture in the pan and place the pan in the upper level of the preheated oven. Bake for 45 minutes or slightly longer, until the top of the cake becomes colored a rich gold.

5. When the cake is done, place the bottom of the pan over a tumbler or tall mug, using pot holders, and push down to raise the loose

bottom. Take the tube with the cake out of the hoop, work the cake loose from the bottom with a knife, and lift it away from the tube. Place it on a plate with a slightly raised rim.

6. While the cake is still warm, poke many holes in it using a chopstick or any similar narrow cylindrical tool. Into each of the holes slowly pour some of the orange juice. At first the hole fills to the brim with juice, but this is subsequently—in about 1 hour—absorbed by the cake. Always serve at room temperature.

NOTE: You can keep the cake for up to 1 week in the refrigerator, fully covered by plastic wrap.

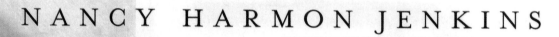

NANCY HARMON JENKINS

Author of *The Mediterranean Diet Cookbook*

Flavors of Puglia

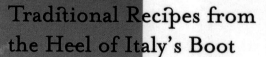

Traditional Recipes from
the Heel of Italy's Boot

AUTHOR

Food writer Nancy Harmon Jenkins, who spends half of her time in Italy

■ **WHY SHE WROTE IT**

To lead the reader on a culinary tour through the kitchens and countryside of this charming and largely overlooked Italian region.

■ **WHY IT MADE OUR LIST**

It's refreshing to find an Italian cuisine that hasn't been written about again and again, and this first-ever book on Puglia's cucina povera is an adept introduction. Light on meat, rich in fruits and vegetables, olive oil, and pasta, these healthful recipes show off the region's home cooking at its best. And with numerous descriptions of the landscape and a section on visiting Puglia, it doubles as a guidebook.

FROM THE BOOK

■ **CULINARY CONUNDRUM**

"Not just in Puglia, but all around the Mediterranean, each tiny fishing port, each major coastal city, claims a version of fish soup—and not just a version, but the version—unique, close to perfect, the best, putting all others to shame, indeed, truth to tell, the original from which all others are derived and of which they are but pale imitations."

■ **CHAPTERS**

Ingredients and Basic Recipes ▪ The Small Dishes of Puglia: Antipasti, Snacks, and Little Meals ▪ Soups: For All Seasons ▪ Pasta: Homemade and Store-bought with Sauces ▪ From Field and Garden: Puglia's Vegetable Traditions ▪ Between Two Seas: Puglia's Bountiful Seafood ▪ Farmyard Bounty: Meat and Poultry ▪ From the Ovens of Puglia: Breads, Focaccie, and Pizze ▪ From the Pantry: Preserving Flavors Year-round ▪ Sweet Celebrations: Desserts ▪ When You Go to Puglia

■ **PREVIOUS CREDITS**

Jenkins has already contributed to the olive-oil craze with *The Mediterranean Diet Cookbook*.

■ **SPECIFICS**

262 pages, more than 100 recipes, 26 black-and-white photographs, $25. Published by Broadway Books.

spaghetti with oven-roasted tomatoes

PASTA CON POMODORI AL FORNO

6 servings

This recipe comes from my landlord and friend Pino Marchese. He makes this in the summertime when Puglia's pride, big plump Sammarzano plum tomatoes, weighing nearly a pound each, are at their peak. Whatever tomatoes you use, make sure they are absolutely ripe, juicy, and full of flavor—this is one recipe where canned tomatoes simply won't work. Pino uses spaghetti, but linguine, vermicelli, or bucatini will do as well.

---

8 large very ripe tomatoes

Coarse sea salt to taste

4 garlic cloves, coarsely chopped

$^1/_2$ cup minced flat-leaf parsley

$^1/_2$ cup freshly grated bread crumbs

$^1/_2$ cup extra virgin olive oil

1 pound thin spaghetti or linguine

Freshly ground black pepper

$^1/_2$ cup shredded basil leaves

Freshly grated Parmigiano-Reggiano
  or pecorino, optional

PREHEAT the oven to 425°F.

SLICE each tomato in half and set, cut side up, in a lightly oiled oven dish that will hold all the tomatoes in one layer. Sprinkle the halves with salt, garlic, and parsley.

TOAST the bread crumbs in a frying pan over medium heat until they are light golden-brown. Sprinkle the bread crumbs over the tomato halves and drizzle all the olive oil over them. Place the dish in the preheated oven and roast for 30 to 45 minutes, or until they are very soft and juicy.

MEANWHILE, bring a large pot of salted water to a rolling boil, timing it so the pasta will finish when the tomatoes are ready. Add the pasta and cook, partially covered, until the pasta is done, about 10 minutes depending on its size and shape. Drain the pasta well and turn it into a heated bowl. Scrape in the cooked tomatoes fresh from the oven, together with any juices. Mix furiously, taste, and add more salt if necessary, an abundance of ground black pepper, the basil, and, for those who wish, a handful of grated Parmigiano-Reggiano or pecorino.

salt-baked snapper

PESCE ARROSTO IN SALE

6 to 8 servings

I was taken aback when a vendor in the Monópoli market told me that his favorite way to cook fish at home was to roast it in salt, a method I knew only from fancy restaurants in other parts of the world. "Completely cover it with salt and then put in a very hot oven *(al massimo)* for fifteen to twenty minutes. That's all," he said. Later, Gianna Greco, a gifted cook with a fine country restaurant at Torre Casciani on the coast south of Gallípoli, confirmed this. And naturally you must use sea salt to cover it, she said.

Wherever it originated, salt-baked fish has become widely, wildly, and deservedly popular in recent years for its simplicity of execution and its fresh, direct, and uncomplicated flavor. That flavor, of course, depends entirely on the quality of the fish itself. You will need a whole fish for this, head, tail, bones, everything but the innards, which the fishmonger will clean out for you. And don't stint on quality—only the best will do. A whole snapper would be my choice here, though the preparation is also fine with a whole salmon, or any other whole fish, although flat fish like sole and halibut will not be successful. This is one technique that will not work with fish steaks or fillets.

---

1 whole fresh snapper or salmon (head and tail included), weighing at least 4 pounds, cleaned

4 pounds coarse sea salt

2 egg whites

Lemon wedges

Very fine extra virgin olive oil

PREHEAT the oven to 425°F.

RINSE the fish carefully, inside and out, in running water. Pat dry with paper towels. Measure the thickness of the fish at its thickest part.

POUR the sea salt into a large bowl, add the egg whites, and mix vigorously until all the grains of sea salt are coated with egg white. Spread about a third of the salt mixture over the bottom of a large rectangular or oval oven dish big enough to hold the whole fish. The bottom layer should be at least 1 inch thick. Place the fish on top, then cover it completely with the rest of the salt. It is important to encase the fish completely in salt, so that no part of it is visible. The topmost part of the fish should be covered at least 1 inch thick.

PLACE the oven dish in the preheated oven, turn the heat down to 400°F., and bake for 20 to 30 minutes, depending on the thickness of the fish—the so-called Canadian rule says fish should cook for 10 minutes per inch, measured at the thickest part.

REMOVE the fish from the oven. The salt will have formed a hard crust over the fish. It's nice to present the fish like this at the table, then dramatically crack the crust with the handle of a knife. Some people even add to the drama by using a small hammer to crack the crust. As you remove the crust, you will be pulling away the fish skin and, of course, any scales. The flesh will be pleasantly salty and very moist.

SERVE with wedges of lemon and a cruet of the finest extra virgin olive oil you can obtain for dressing the fish.

roast stuffed chicken

POLLO ARROSTO

6 to 8 servings

The chicken roasted for a Pugliese Sunday lunch will be a plump, young farmyard bird, a *pollo ruspante,* her brief life spent in relative freedom, pecking away at the greens and grains, the bugs and worms, that give her juicy flesh so much savor. The stuffing speaks decisively of the Italian South and could be adapted for use with capons or even a small, fresh, free-range turkey. Slip a few slivers of garlic and some parsley leaves beneath the skin of the breast to make a handsome presentation. If the chicken you buy comes without giblets, buy a few chicken livers to add to the stuffing.

One 4½- to 5-pound free-range roasting chicken with giblets

1 medium onion, finely chopped

1 garlic clove, finely minced

3 tablespoons extra virgin olive oil

1 cup plain unflavored bread crumbs, preferably freshly grated

1 tablespoon coarsely chopped capers

¼ cup finely minced flat-leaf parsley

2 tablespoons freshly grated pecorino or Parmigiano-Reggiano

2 ounces Genoa salami, finely chopped

1 large egg

1 garlic clove, thinly sliced

8 whole leaves flat-leaf parsley

Sea salt and freshly ground black pepper to taste

1 cup dry white wine, at room temperature, plus 2 tablespoons for deglazing

PREHEAT the oven to 400°F.

REMOVE the giblets from the chicken and set the bird on a rack in a roasting pan. Tuck the gizzard in a corner of the pan; it will add to the flavor of the pan juices.

CHOP the liver and heart as finely as possible (or use about ¼ pound of chicken livers purchased separately) and place in a small frying pan along with the chopped onion, minced garlic, and 2 tablespoons of the olive oil. Over medium-low heat, sauté gently until the chicken parts are thoroughly brown and the vegetables are starting to soften. Scrape into a bowl and mix with the bread crumbs, capers, minced parsley, cheese, and salami. Break the egg in a bowl, beat lightly with a fork, then stir into the stuffing mixture, using your hands to blend rapidly. The mixture should be moist but not runny. If necessary, add a little water or a few more bread crumbs to attain the right consistency. Stuff the chicken loosely with the stuffing mixture.

WITH your fingers, loosen the skin over both sides of the breast meat and gently slide a few slivers of sliced garlic and a few whole parsley leaves into place between the skin and the flesh. Tie the legs loosely over the opening with kitchen twine.

RUB the chicken all over with the remaining tablespoon of olive oil, then sprinkle with salt and pepper to taste. Place in the preheated oven and roast for 45 minutes, by which time the skin should be nicely brown. Turn down the heat to 350°F. and baste the chicken with 1 cup of the wine. Return to the oven to roast for an additional 30 to 45 minutes, basting with the pan juices every 10 minutes. The chicken is done when the juices around the thigh bone run clear yellow when the leg is pierced with a fork.

REMOVE from the oven and let rest for 15 minutes before serving. While the chicken is resting, pour the pan juices into a measuring cup. Deglaze the pan with the remaining 2 tablespoons wine and add to the juices in the cup. Skim off the fat that rises to the top of the cup (save this flavorful fat, if you wish, for sautéing potatoes). Put the juices in a small saucepan and boil a few minutes to reduce and concentrate the flavors. Serve as a sauce with the chicken.

easter lamb with fresh green peas and parmesan sauce

VERDETTO

6 servings

As it is in most of the Mediterranean, lamb is the great celebratory ritual food of Puglia, the very symbol of feasting and sacrifice. In the old, pre-Christian Mediterranean described in the verses of *The Iliad,* no feast began without a sacrifice, an offer of the best part of the meal to the gods. The Paschal lamb served at Easter and Passover, like the lamb for the great Id at the end of Ramadan, is a symbol meant, even if unconsciously, to recall this ancient pagan rite.

In the region around Bari, if the Easter lamb isn't roasted, then it will most likely be turned into *verdetto,* lamb cooked with peas—or sometimes with fresh green asparagus, or young, tender cardoons, the choice of vegetable depending in part on where in the spring season Easter happens to fall. At the end of cooking, this savory stew is made richer by the addition of eggs and grated cheese to coat the meat and vegetables with an unctuous cream.

This is a traditional dish for Easter (Pasqua) but more especially for the Monday following, called Pasquetta or Pasqualino, a national holiday.

2 ounces pancetta or blanched bacon, diced

2 tablespoons extra virgin olive oil

1 onion, halved and very finely sliced

2 pounds very young boneless lamb shoulder, or 2½ to 3 pounds lamb shoulder with bones, cut in pieces (see Note)

Salt to taste

1 cup dry white wine

1½ pounds (shelled weight) fresh green peas—about 2½ pounds peas in their pods (see Note)

½ cup finely minced flat-leaf parsley

Freshly ground black pepper to taste

3 large eggs

⅓ cup freshly grated pecorino or Parmigiano-Reggiano

PREHEAT the oven to 325°F.

IN a heavy ovenproof saucepan over medium-low heat, sauté the pancetta or blanched bacon in 1 tablespoon oil until the pieces are crisp and brown. Add the onion slices and continue cooking, stirring frequently until the onion is soft but not turning brown.

PUSH the onion and pancetta out to the sides of the pan, raise the heat to medium-high, and add the remaining tablespoon of oil and lamb pieces to the center. Sprinkle with salt to taste and brown the lamb on all sides—about 10 minutes. When the lamb pieces are thoroughly brown, stir in the wine. Let the wine boil rapidly to throw off the alcohol, then cover the pan and place in the preheated oven to bake for 1 hour, or until the lamb is very tender. Check from time to time and if the lamb juices are drying up add a very little boiling water.

AFTER 1 hour of cooking, remove the pot from the oven and stir in the peas and half the parsley. Add black pepper to taste, stir to combine well, then cover and continue cooking, on medium-low heat on top of the stove for about 20 minutes, or until the peas are tender, again adding boiling water from time to time if necessary.

FIVE minutes before you are ready to serve the dish, mix the eggs with the cheese and remaining parsley, beating with a fork. Quickly beat a few tablespoons of hot juices from the pan into the egg mixture to warm it up, then, off the heat, stir the egg mixture into the lamb and peas, using a wooden spoon to reach all the meat and vegetables and coat them well with the eggs. There should be sufficient heat to set the eggs into a creamy sauce, but not so much heat that they will scramble. If necessary, the dish may be returned to the heat, but be very careful. If the eggs scramble, there's not much you can do about it except pretend that's what you intended all along.

SERVE immediately. The dish should *not* be reheated.

NOTE: *In Puglia the lamb for verdetto is usually shoulder, cut into chunks with the bones, the wise observation being that bones add considerable flavor. In my experience, most Americans will be happier with boneless meat, in which case the quantity served should be no more than 2 pounds.*

If you wish to serve cardoons or asparagus instead of peas, clean the vegetable in the usual manner; the quantity used should be the trimmed *weight. Cook the vegetable, like the peas above, until it is tender.*

KITCHEN CONVERSATIONS

Robust Recipes
and Lessons
in Flavor from One
of America's Most
Innovative Chefs

JOYCE GOLDSTEIN

Author of *Back to Square One* and
The Mediterranean Kitchen

Cooking teacher and Mediterranean maven Joyce Goldstein

■ WHY SHE WROTE IT

"I want you to learn how to bring flavors to their peak, or how possibly to rescue a dish if it has gone astray, to recognize when it is approaching success and when the dish is in balance, to stop and savor it when it is 'right,' and to learn to remember its taste so you can make it again."

■ WHY IT MADE OUR LIST

It's like having your own personal cooking teacher standing beside you, talking you through the recipes, telling you why different flavors work together, suggesting other combinations to try, urging you to taste as you cook, to learn how to rely on your own instincts until a dish tastes right. The interactive format and boldly flavored but uncomplicated recipes make this a conversation worth having.

FROM THE BOOK

■ ADVICE ON VEGETABLES

"Be sure to cook the vegetables for as long as it takes to maximize their flavor. Not every vegetable is meant to be al dente. Some need longer cooking to shine and reveal their flavor. Green beans, cauliflower, and broccoli profit from a few extra minutes in the pan. Undercooked eggplant is bitter and tough. Fennel is either best served raw or braised to a melting tenderness. Carrots are fine to munch on when raw, but as a cooked vegetable they don't develop sweetness until they've simmered for a while. On the other hand, Brussels sprouts taste less cabbagy with briefer cooking."

■ CHAPTERS

Evan Goldstein's Wine Guide ▪ Salads ▪ Appetizers ▪ Savory Pastries ▪ Soups ▪ Pasta, Rice & Grains ▪ Fish & Shellfish ▪ Poultry & Meat ▪ Vegetables ▪ Sauces ▪ Desserts: Compotes, Custards & Cakes

■ PREVIOUS CREDITS

Formerly the chef/owner of San Francisco's Square One Restaurant, Goldstein previously penned *The Mediterranean Kitchen* and *Back to Square One*.

■ SPECIFICS

378 pages, 60 recipes, 46 black-and-white photographs, $25. Published by William Morrow and Company, Inc.

Yesil Domates Batisi Turkish Green Tomato Salad with Feta Cheese

I ate this tart and tangy salad at a buffet dinner where there were at least fifty dishes to sample from various regions of Turkey. This recipe, reportedly from Izmir, along the Aegean coast of Turkey, really caught my attention. We rarely utilize green tomatoes, except for pickles, and I thought this was a novel and tasty way to serve this underappreciated food. Serve slightly warm or at room temperature.

Serves 6

4 tablespoons olive oil

3 onions, chopped

1 tablespoon finely minced garlic

6 large green tomatoes, very coarsely chopped, about 6 cups

1 cup vegetable or **chicken stock**

3 to 4 tablespoons extra virgin olive oil

Lots of salt

Freshly ground black pepper

1 cup crumbled feta cheese

2 tablespoons chopped fresh dill

Warm the olive oil in a large sauté pan. Add the onions and cook over moderate heat until translucent, about 8 to 10 minutes. Add the garlic, tomatoes, and stock and cook, covered, for 15 minutes until the tomatoes are softened.

Do not overcook. Stir in the olive oil. Season to taste with salt and pepper. Place on a serving platter and top with crumbled feta cheese and dill. Serve slightly warm or at room temperature.

Kitchen Conversation

I love the tanginess of the tomatoes and how it is tempered by the salty, creamy feta. Freshly ground black pepper is an essential element of this salad, as it brings a very subtle heat. The dill adds its own grassy perfume, which complements the tomatoes. As a change of pace, try oregano for a deeper taste.

Wine Notes

Pairing Pointers: *With these tomatoes we seek a wine to be a vivid "highlighter" to bring out the tart, clean flavors of the salad. The simpler and sharper the wine, the better.*

Categories:

Light, dry white, sparkling, or rosé wines. Lower alcohol. No or very light use of oak. Clean and refreshing.

Medium, dry white, sparkling, or rosé wines. Moderate alcohol. No, light, or moderate use of oak. Reasonably rich.

Specific Recommendations:

Muscadet—current vintage, as fresh as possible ■ *Chardonnay—light, crisp, floral—Italy and France*

Sauvignon Blanc—green, leafy styles ■ *Viura, Verdejo— refreshing, fragrant, exuberant*

Cheese in Salads

Adding cheese to a salad does two things. It provides another kind of salt and it adds interesting texture. Crumbly mild goat cheese or salty feta cheese, slightly pungent Gorgonzola or Roquefort, waxy Gruyère or fontina, each changes the balance of the equation. Cheeses pair especially well with bitter elements like toasted walnuts.

Risotto with Mussels, Ouzo, Green Onions, and Hot Pepper

Risotto uses a short-grain rice as opposed to the long-grain basmati preferred for pilaf. Unlike a pilaf, in risotto the liquids are added 1 cup at a time until the short-grain rice becomes creamy. Although the addition of feta cheese breaks the Italian rule of no cheese with seafood, this is not a classic risotto but one that combines Italian technique and Greek flavors. The feta adds a wonderful note of salt, which contrasts with the sweetness of the mussels and ouzo and softens the impact of the wine and green onions.

Serves 4

4 dozen mussels, well scrubbed and debearded

1 cup white wine

4 cups fish stock or **a combination of chicken stock and water**

4 tablespoons olive oil

1¹/₂ cups green onions, chopped

1 teaspoon hot pepper flakes

1¹/₂ cups arborio rice (or carnaroli or vialone)

¹/₂ cup ouzo

1 cup chopped Italian parsley

1 cup crumbled feta cheese (optional)

Steam the mussels open in the wine. Remove the mussels from the shells and pull off any remaining beards. Discard the shells (unless you want a few mussels in the shell as a garnish). Strain the mussel liquor and add to the fish or chicken stock. Bring the stock up to a boil. Reduce the heat and keep at a simmer.

Warm the olive oil in a large sauté pan or wide, shallow saucepan. Add the green onions and cook for 5 minutes. Add the hot pepper flakes and rice, and toss in the oil for 3 minutes. Add the ouzo to the pan and cook until absorbed. Add 1 cup hot stock and cook, stirring occasionally, until the stock is absorbed. Add the remaining stock, 1 cup at a time, stirring occasionally, until the stock is absorbed. Add mussels and heat through. Sprinkle with lots of chopped parsley and top with crumbled feta if desired.

Kitchen Conversation

Taste this with and without the cheese. What do you think? If you choose not to use cheese, remember to increase the salt and pepper. Another time try making this with regular onions instead of green. You will find they are sweeter, less high and grassy in flavor, and less of a contrast to the mussels. This is neither good nor bad, just different. If you use regular onions, you may want to add diced chopped tomatoes for balance. Or do you find the ouzo makes up for the sweetness?

Wine Notes

Pairing Pointers: *A pungent and bold white wine is necessary with this risotto. The feta is critical, because if it's too salty it will wreak havoc on your wine choice. The mussels and ouzo demand a more generous and alcoholic wine. Keep the hot pepper in balance so as not to gut the wine.*

Categories:

Medium, dry white, sparkling, or rosé wines. Moderate alcohol. No, light, or moderate use of oak. Reasonably rich.

Full, dry white or rosé wines. Moderate to ample alcohol. Little to significant use of oak. Quite rich.

Dry, fortified white wines.

Specific Recommendations:

Chardonnay —less oaked, moderately complex, steely ■
Riesling—rich, light or no oak, powerful style—Australia

Gewürztraminer—spicy, floral, ample—France, USA ■
Marsanne—packed with fruit, textured, earthy—France

If served as an appetizer ■ *Sherry—fresh, exuberant fino or manzanilla*

Roast Fish with Sicilian Sweet-and-Sour Onions

Many years ago, I stood on a terraced hillside in the ancient Sicilian town of Ragusa Ibla, looking at the spectacular view. All along the rock walls were trays of tomatoes and tomato paste, spread out to dry in the hot sun. Although sun-dried tomatoes appear to be trendy in America, they are part of a strong Italian tradition of keeping tomatoes in the repertoire of the cuisine when fresh, ripe tomatoes are out of season. ☛ *Sun-dried tomatoes are available dry or packed in oil. The dry ones need to be reconstituted in a little water or they will be too chewy. However, soaking them can leach out a lot of the flavor. (If you use oil-packed sun-dried tomatoes, you do not have to soak them.) With the dry tomatoes, soak a third in hot water to get a full-flavored tomato liquid to add to the onion mixture, then add the rest of the tomatoes without soaking. They will soften enough if you prepare the onion mixture a few hours ahead of time. Combining the tomatoes with currants is an Arabic touch, also part of the Sicilian tradition.*

Serves 4

¹/₄ cup olive oil

3 yellow onions, sliced ¹/₄ inch thick (4 to 5 cups)

2 tablespoons red wine vinegar or **to taste**

1 tablespoon honey or **to taste**

¹/₃ cup sun-dried tomatoes, preferably oil packed, cut in thin slivers

3 tablespoons currants, plumped in hot water, drained and liquids saved

6 tablespoons chopped fresh mint

4 5- to 6-ounce fillets of cod, snapper, flounder, halibut, or **sea bass**

Salt and freshly ground black pepper to taste

Preheat the oven to 450 degrees.

Heat the olive oil in a large sauté pan. Add the onions, sprinkle lightly with salt, and cook over moderate heat until very tender, 15 to 20 minutes, stirring occasionally. Do not let them brown. Add the vinegar and honey, and cook for 5 minutes. Add the sun-dried tomatoes, currants, and 4 tablespoons of the mint. Cook for a few minutes longer. Taste for seasoning. You may not need any additional salt if the tomatoes have been salted, but you will need pepper. Adjust the sweet-and-sour ratio. If you'd like it sweeter, add some of the currant soaking liquids. Check again for salt.

Sprinkle the fish fillets with salt and pepper, and place in a lightly oiled baking dish. Cover with the onions. Bake for 8 to 10 minutes, or until the fish tests done (poke with a knife and take a peek). You may need to cook this a little longer if the onions were cool when you put them on top of the fish. Remove the fish to serving plates and top with the remaining chopped mint.

Kitchen Conversation

Our palates seem to like counterpoint and contrast, so sweet and sour is an appealing taste combination. By cooking onions until they are sweet, and adding elements that play up the sweetness, you'll find that the key to balance is a tart component such as vinegar. Sweet fragrant mint, salty-sweet sun-dried tomatoes and sweet currants lend complexity to the onions. It's all a question of balance, balance, balance. Can you taste the tomatoes under the sweetness of the onions and currants?

Wine Notes

Pairing Pointers: *The balance of sweet and tart is what wine is all about. Don't let the vinegar in this scare you. Just make certain that the wine is sharper than the dish. The sweetness of the onions can be mirrored through ripe fruit.*

Categories:

Medium, dry white, sparkling, or rosé wines. Moderate alcohol. No, light, or moderate use of oak. Reasonably rich.

Full, dry white or rosé wines. Moderate to ample alcohol. Little to significant use of oak. Quite rich.

Light, dry red wines. Lower alcohol. No or very light use of oak. Fresh, effusive fruit. Little, if any, tannins.

Specific Recommendations:

Garganega—lean, minty, and ripe—Italy

Riesling—rich, medium full, and opulent—France, Washington State

Pinot Noir—dense, attractive, and seemingly sweet—USA

Spiced Figs with Lemon, Fennel, and Cloves

Figs are quite fragile when ripe. But ripe is the only way to eat them. You can make a light syrup and poach whole figs very gently, then cool them in the syrup. However, there's always the danger of overcooking, having them rupture and lose their sexy shape. One alternative is to make a syrup and pour it over fresh figs that have been cut in quarters, as if you were serving a macedonia or fruit salad. Or leave the figs whole (really the prettiest way to serve them) and bake them. If you can find lemon verbena, the leaves will perfume the figs in a most exotic way. If not, use lemon zest (or if you are feeling in an experimental mood, try lemongrass). Instead of water you may use port for a more intense syrup.

Serves 4

1 pound figs, 2 large or 3 small per person

¼ cup sugar or **honey**

⅔ cup water (or part or **all port)**

2 strips lemon zest, or **4 lemon verbena leaves,** or **1½ inches lemongrass,** sliced paper thin and chopped coarsely

½ teaspoon fennel or **aniseed** (optional)

2 to 3 whole cloves

Toasted pine nuts or **walnuts** (optional)

Cut the stems off the figs and prick lightly with a fork in a few places so that the figs will absorb the syrup.

Combine the sugar or honey and water or water and port in a medium saucepan. Put the lemon zest, lemon verbena leaves, or lemongrass and spices in a spice ball or tie in cheesecloth and add to the saucepan. Bring up to a boil, reduce the heat, and simmer for 5 to 6 minutes.

Pour over the figs and bake in a 350 degree oven for 15 to 20 minutes. Or poach the figs gently in this syrup for 5 to 8 minutes. Cool in the syrup. Discard the spice ball. Serve garnished with toasted pine nuts, walnuts, or lemon verbena leaves, if desired.

Kitchen Conversation

If you used port in your syrup, the dessert is considerably richer and more intense than if you used water. With port all of the spices will be muted. However, with a water-based syrup the dessert will seem lighter and the spices and lemony herbs more prominent. The fennel, anise, and cloves add a complex undertone to the syrup. If you used port, garnish with walnuts if crunch is desired. Pine nuts will be overpowered by the port-based syrup. If you used water, the pine nuts will add sweetness to play off the lemon.

Wine Notes

Pairing Pointers: *Despite the use of fresh figs (as opposed to dried) I find this dessert works better with fortified wines, especially Madeira, fortified Muscats, and Muscat ports (Australia). The nature of the spices mandates a wine with some oomph!*

Category:

Dessert style and sweet wines. Varied levels of alcohol and oak.

Specific Recommendations:

Muscat—luscious and fragrant—Australian port, Southern France ■ Madeira—Malmsey style ■ Vin Santo—rich, syrup version

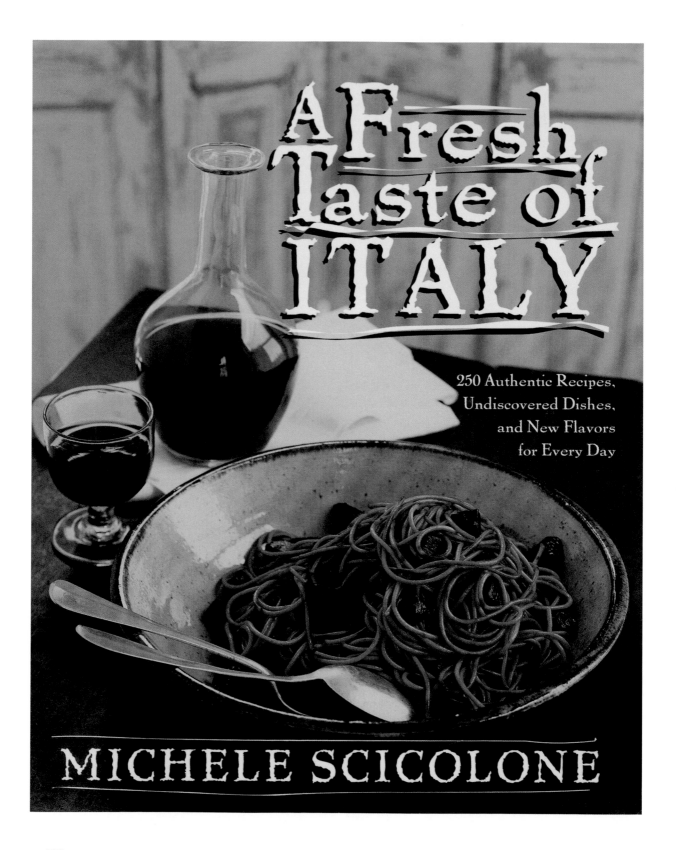

250 Authentic Recipes,
Undiscovered Dishes,
and New Flavors
for Every Day

A Fresh Taste of ITALY

MICHELE SCICOLONE

Italophile Michele Scicolone

"With this book I have reproduced as closely as possible the fresh tastes and simple flavors of contemporary Italian food from all over Italy."

Scicolone has been traveling to Italy twice a year for twenty-five years, seeking out new restaurants, revisiting old favorites, collecting recipes from chefs and other good cooks. This latest collection is a delicious overview of what's happening in Italian cooking today; and, thanks to the detailed headnotes, a nice restaurant guide for your next visit.

Regional Tastes of Italy ▪ Ingredients and Equipment ▪ Antipasto ▪ Soup ▪ Sauces ▪ Pasta ▪ Rice, Barley, and Polenta ▪ Seafood ▪ Chicken and Other Birds ▪ Meat and Game ▪ Vegetables ▪ Bread ▪ Fruit Desserts ▪ Biscotti, Tarts, Cakes, and Other Desserts ▪ Wine

FROM THE BOOK

■ **TRAVEL GUIDANCE**
"A famous author was asked where she likes to go when she travels. She replied, 'Italy. I often think, "While there is Italy, why go anywhere else?" ' "

Scicolone also wrote about Italian cooking in *The Antipasto Table* and *La Dolce Vita*.

392 pages, 250 recipes, 24 color photographs, $30. Published by Broadway Books.

Carpaccio is said to have been invented at Harry's Bar in Venice. Owner Giuseppe Cipriani came up with the recipe to please an important and fussy client who was on a special diet. He had his chef thinly slice the finest raw beef and dress the slices with a caper and mayonnaise sauce. He named it carpaccio after the famous artist because the colors resembled those he had seen in his paintings.

Today there are many variations made with meat, fish, or vegetables. The only thing they seem to have in common is that the ingredients are thinly sliced and sometimes raw or only partly cooked. In this version, thin slices of browned salmon fillet are topped with a lemony arugula salad.

Salmon Carpaccio

CARPACCIO DI SALMONE

SALAD

4 cups arugula or watercress

2 tablespoons olive oil

1 tablespoon fresh lemon juice

Salt and freshly ground pepper, to taste

1 tablespoon olive oil

1 pound salmon fillet, cut into thin slices

Salt and freshly ground pepper, to taste

1　Rinse the arugula in several changes of cool water. Pinch off the tough stems and dry the leaves thoroughly. Cut into 1-inch pieces and place them in a bowl. Just before cooking the fish, whisk together the olive oil, lemon juice, salt, and pepper. Set aside.

2　Heat the olive oil in a large nonstick skillet over high heat. Add enough fish to make a single layer. Cook until lightly browned on the bottom yet still undercooked on top, about 1 minute. With a large spatula, remove the salmon from the skillet and turn it, browned side up, onto a large serving platter. Sprinkle with salt and pepper. Cook the remaining salmon in the same way and add it to the platter.

3　Toss the arugula with the dressing. Pile the salad on top of the salmon. Serve immediately.

Grilled Jumbo Shrimp with Sage and Pancetta

GAMBERONI ALLA GRIGLIA

12 thin slices pancetta

12 jumbo shrimps, peeled and deveined

12 fresh sage leaves

1   Preheat the broiler or grill.

2   Unroll the pancetta slices and wind each slice around a shrimp. Tuck a sage leaf between the shrimp and pancetta. Thread 2 or 3 shrimps on each skewer.

3   Place the skewers on the grill rack or broiler pan about 4 inches from the source of the heat. Cook for 2 to 3 minutes on each side, or until the shrimps are cooked through and the pancetta is crisp.

4   Serve immediately.

SERVES 6

The Antica Osteria del Bai is located in a little stone building that was once a lookout post for the nearby port of Genoa. From the beach below, Garibaldi and his thousand, as his troops were called, embarked on their heroic journey south that eventually led to the unification of Italy. The age-old look of the building has been carefully preserved even to the maritime pines sprouting among its crumbling roof tiles. Inside, though, the restaurant is quite modern. We feasted on fat, juicy shrimps wrapped in a jacket of pancetta and cooked on the grill. Terre Alte, a dry complex white wine from Livio Felluga, is perfect with the shrimp.

Antica Osteria del Bai
Via Quarto, 12
Quarto dei Mille (Genoa)

Gardener's Risotto

RISOTTO AL ORTOLANO

3 tablespoons unsalted butter

1 tablespoon olive oil

1 medium onion, finely chopped

1/2 cup diced carrot

1/2 cup diced celery

2 cups medium-grain rice, such as Arborio, Carnaroli, or
*   Vialone Nano*

6 cups hot homemade chicken broth or a combination of half
*   canned broth and half water*

1/2 cup fresh or frozen baby lima beans or peeled fresh
*   fava beans*

1 cup finely diced zucchini

1/2 cup sliced mushrooms

4 plum tomatoes, seeded and diced

Salt and freshly ground pepper, to taste

1/4 cup finely chopped fresh basil

1/2 cup freshly grated Parmigiano-Reggiano

1 In a large heavy saucepan over medium heat, melt 2 tablespoons of the butter with the olive oil. Add the onion, carrot, and celery. Cook until the vegetables soften, about 5 minutes. Add the rice and cook, stirring, for 2 minutes. Turn the heat up to medium-high. Add 1/2 cup of the broth and cook, stirring constantly with a wooden spoon, until most of the liquid is absorbed. The spoon should leave a wide track on the bottom of the pan, yet there should be a small amount of liquid surrounding each grain. Continue adding broth 1/2 cup at a time and stirring constantly.

2 After 10 minutes, stir in the lima beans, zucchini, mushrooms, tomatoes, salt, and pepper. Continue adding broth 1/2 cup at a time and stirring until the rice is tender yet firm to the bite and a creamy

sauce forms around the rice. If there is not enough broth, switch to hot water. Remove from the heat.

3 Vigorously stir in the basil, cheese, and remaining 1 tablespoon butter. Serve immediately.

The Rice Aria

Giocchino Rossini, who was born in Pesaro in Emilia-Romagna, was famous for his musical compositions, his great wit, and his devotion to good eating. He could write beautiful melodies seemingly without effort even while sitting with friends in a café or restaurant. His famous aria, *"Di tanti palpiti"* from the opera *Tancredi,* was written as the author waited for a plate of risotto with truffles. When word of the circumstances under which it was written got out, the romantic aria, which tells of the pangs of love, became known as the *aria dei risi,* or rice aria.

Salmon Carpaccio (page 124)

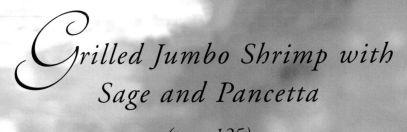

Grilled Jumbo Shrimp with Sage and Pancetta

(page 125)

Gardener's Risotto
(page 126)

Apple Lattice Tart

(page 132)

January in Milan can be cold and bleak, but it's a great time for shopping. All the expensive shops on the Via Montenapoleone are open, and their splendid goods are on sale. Exhausted by the effort of shopping, we fell into the elegant Caffè Sant'Ambroeus and restored ourselves with a wedge of this tart. The tender apple and raisin filling in a buttery pastry shell was crowned with a golden almond paste lattice. With a cup of cappuccino to warm us, we were soon out again.

Making this tart at home is not difficult, but piping the lattice topping can be a bit tricky if you've never worked with a pastry bag before. Practice by piping a series of parallel lines on a flat plate. Then give the plate a 180° turn and pipe out another series of parallel lines perpendicular to the first set. When you feel comfortable with the procedure, scrape the practice lattice lines back into the bag and repeat it on top of the filled tart.

Caffè Sant'Ambroeus
Corso Matteotti 7
Milan (Lombardy)

Apple Lattice Tart

CROSTATA DI MELE AL MARZAPANE

CRUST

1¹/₃ cups all-purpose flour

3 tablespoons sugar

¹/₂ teaspoon salt

8 tablespoons (1 stick) cold unsalted butter, cut into bits

1 large egg, lightly beaten

1 teaspoon pure vanilla extract

FILLING

1¹/₂ pounds Golden Delicious apples, peeled and cut into thin slices (3 large apples)

1 cup sugar

¹/₂ cup golden raisins

3 tablespoons fine dry bread crumbs

1 teaspoon ground cinnamon

2 tablespoons fresh lemon juice

TOPPING

1 package (7 to 8 ounces) almond paste

1 tablespoon unsalted butter, softened

1 large egg

1 teaspoon pure vanilla extract

1 teaspoon grated lemon zest

¹/₄ cup all-purpose flour

1 large egg yolk plus 2 teaspoons water

Confectioners' sugar, in a shaker

1 To make the crust, in a large bowl, combine the flour, sugar, and salt. With a pastry blender or 2 knives, cut in the butter until the mixture resembles a coarse meal. In a small bowl, beat the egg and

vanilla until blended. Stir the liquid into the flour mixture just until a dough forms. Add a few drops of cold water if it seems dry. On a piece of plastic wrap, shape the dough into a flat disk. Wrap the plastic around the dough and refrigerate for at least 1 hour or overnight.

2   On a lightly floured surface, roll out the dough to an 11-inch circle. Transfer the dough to a 9-inch tart pan with a removable bottom. Trim off all but a $1/2$-inch border of dough. Fold the border against the inside of the pan and press it into place, building it up slightly above the rim. Refrigerate the shell while you prepare the filling, about 30 minutes.

3   Preheat the oven to 350°F. Place the oven rack in the center of the oven.

4   To make the filling, combine all of the filling ingredients in a large bowl. Pile the apple mixture into the prepared tart shell, pressing it lightly to fit.

5   To make the topping, crumble the almond paste into a food processor fitted with a steel blade or an electric mixer bowl. Add the butter, egg, vanilla, and lemon zest and blend or beat until smooth. Add the flour and stir just until blended. Spoon the mixture into a pastry bag fitted with a $1/2$-inch tip. Pipe the mixture around the border of the dough being careful not to let it touch the pan or it will stick when it bakes. Pipe the remainder in a lattice pattern over the filling. Beat the egg yolk and water. Brush the glaze over the lattice topping. Place the tart in the oven. Place a baking sheet on the rack beneath it to catch any drips. Bake for 1 hour and 15 minutes, or until the topping is browned and the apple juices are bubbling. If the topping browns too rapidly, fold a sheet of aluminum foil into a tent and loosely cover the tart.

6   Cool the tart on a rack for 10 minutes. The apple juices will settle and thicken as the tart cools. Place the pan on a coffee can or similar tall object and slide the rim down. Let the tart cool completely.

7   Sprinkle with confectioners' sugar before serving. Use a serrated knife to cut the tart. Cover with foil or plastic wrap and store in the refrigerator for up to 3 days.

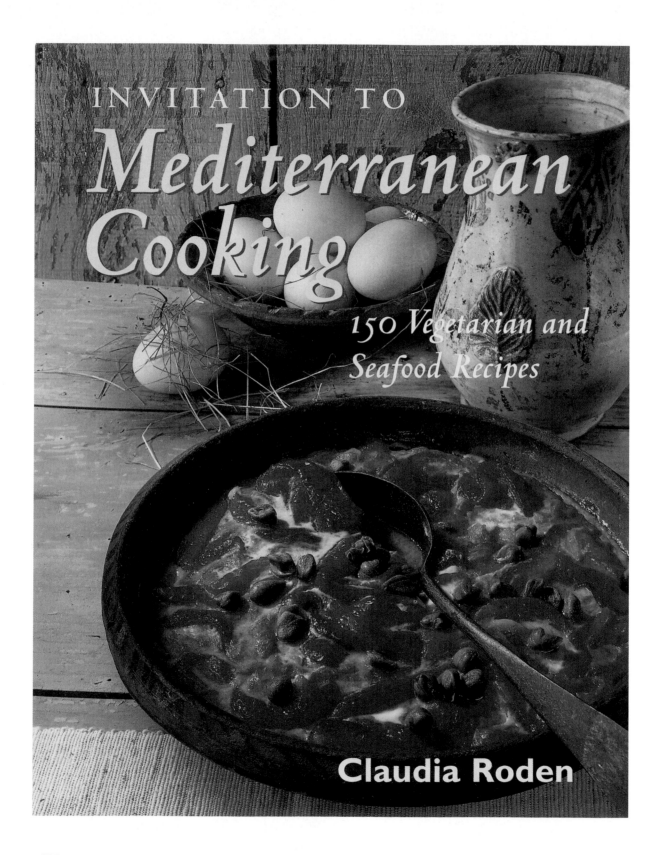

INVITATION TO

Mediterranean Cooking

150 Vegetarian and Seafood Recipes

Claudia Roden

Mediterranean-and-Middle-Eastern-cooking expert Claudia Roden

"My goal was not to cover all of the countries, to feature famous dishes, or to include an example of every type of food. It was to offer fresh, light, delicious, casual food for every day, and quick and easy to cook, as well as some more elaborate dishes that are ideal for entertaining and special occasions and are fun to serve. The dishes are naturally in line with the ideals of healthy eating, but the pleasures of cooking and eating are the main focus of this book."

Roden writes with enthusiasm and knowledge about a part of the world that our part of the world never seems to tire of reading about, and her light and easy recipes are utterly enticing. Since fish and vegetables have always been at the heart of Mediterranean cooking, the narrow focus here makes sense and gives these ingredients room to shine.

Salads and Appetizers ▪ Soups ▪ Savory Pies and Tarts ▪ Pasta ▪ Grains: Bulghur, Rice, and Couscous ▪ Mixed Vegetable Dishes ▪ Omelets and Egg Dishes ▪ Flans, Gratins, and Cheese Bakes ▪ Vegetable Side Dishes ▪ Fish and Seafood ▪ Desserts

Roden's last book of many was the impressive and geographically wide-ranging *A Book of Jewish Food*.

224 pages, 150 recipes, approximately 85 color photographs, $30. Published by Rizzoli International Publications, Inc.

FROM THE BOOK

"Although Mediterranean dishes are extraordinarily varied and there are many cooking styles in the sixteen or so countries around the little inland sea, there is a certain unity throughout the Mediterranean basin, which means that if you know one cuisine, you will be able to understand the others, and many of the dishes can be seen as variations on a theme. The unity has to do with the sharing of climate and produce, with the intense traffic and trading activity between the port cities, and with an incestuous history."

3/4 CUP FINE OR MEDIUM
GROUND BULGHUR

ABOUT 6 MEDIUM TOMATOES,
PEELED AND PURÉED IN A FOOD
PROCESSOR

JUICE OF 1/2 LEMON

1 TEASPOON TOMATO PASTE

3 TO 4 TABLESPOONS EXTRA
VIRGIN OLIVE OIL

SALT

CHILI FLAKES OR CHILI POWDER
TO TASTE

1 SMALL MILD ONION OR 5
SCALLIONS, FINELY CHOPPED

2/3 CUP WALNUTS OR PISTACHIOS,
OR A MIXTURE OF THE TWO

BULGHUR SALAD
WITH WALNUTS

In this scrumptious and nutritious Turkish
salad, called *batrik*, bulghur is soaked in
the juice of fresh puréed tomatoes and is enriched
with walnuts, pistachios, and onions.
It can be made with mild or hot chili pepper.

Serves 4 to 6

Mix the bulghur with the tomatoes, lemon juice, and
tomato paste and set aside for 1 hour, or until the grain
has absorbed the juice and become tender. Add oil, salt,
and chili flakes to taste. Just before serving, add the
onion and walnuts.

1 1/2 POUNDS CHERRY TOMATOES, CUT IN HALF

SALT

3 TO 4 CLOVES GARLIC, CHOPPED

1 TO 1 1/2 SMALL HOT RED CHILI PEPPERS, SEEDED AND CHOPPED (OPTIONAL)

1/2 CUP EXTRA VIRGIN OLIVE OIL

4 SUN-DRIED TOMATOES, FINELY SLICED (OPTIONAL)

1 LARGE BUNCH (3/4 TO 1 CUP) MIXED FRESH HERBS SUCH AS BASIL, MARJORAM, OREGANO, MINT, CHERVIL, CHIVES, AND TARRAGON, CHOPPED

14 OUNCES SPAGHETTI OR OTHER LONG PASTA

FRESHLY GRATED PECORINO ROMANO OR PARMIGIANO-REGGIANO

SPAGHETTI WITH HERBS AND ROASTED CHERRY TOMATOES

Serves 4

Cook the tomatoes, cut side up, under the broiler, until they soften slightly, and sprinkle very lightly with salt.

For the sauce, fry the garlic and chili peppers in 2 tablespoons of the oil until the aroma rises, then remove from the heat. Add the remaining olive oil, the sun-dried tomatoes, and herbs.

Cook the pasta in boiling salted water until *al dente* and drain. Mix with the sauce and serve topped with the broiled cherry tomatoes. Accompany with grated cheese.

2 TABLESPOONS BUTTER

1 TABLESPOON SUNFLOWER OR LIGHT VEGETABLE OIL

1 MEDIUM ONION, CHOPPED

3 CLOVES GARLIC, FINELY CHOPPED

1 MEDIUM LEEK, SLICED

1 CELERY RIB, SLICED

1 CUP DRY WHITE WINE

SALT AND FRESHLY GROUND WHITE PEPPER

3-INCH STRIP ORANGE PEEL

1 LARGE POTATO, CUT INTO CUBES

1/2 TEASPOON SAFFRON THREADS

1 1/4 POUNDS SKINNED FISH FILLET

2/3 CUP HEAVY CREAM

VARIATION

Replace about 7 ounces of the fish with cooked shrimp and add them to the pan just before you add the cream.

FISH SOUP WITH SAFFRON AND CREAM

This delicate, creamy soup with the flavors of the South of France is one of our family favorites. It is extremely easy to make with boneless fish fillets such as cod, haddock, whiting, or other white (not oily) fish, or with a mixture of fish and cooked shrimp. Serve it with warmed or slightly toasted bread.

Serves 4

Heat the butter and oil in a large saucepan over medium heat. Add the onion, garlic, leek, and celery and sauté until they are soft and beginning to color slightly.

Pour in the wine and 2 1/4 cups water. Season with a little salt and white pepper to taste and add the orange peel. Simmer for 5 minutes.

Add the potato and cook for 20 minutes, adding water if necessary as the liquid evaporates. Add the saffron and fish and cook for 8 to 10 minutes or until the fish turns opaque. Break the fish into pieces, remove the orange peel, stir in the cream, and cook for 1 to 2 more minutes. Serve hot.

8 PEACHES, CUT IN HALF,
UNPEELED, STONES REMOVED

$1/2$ CUP AMARETTO OR MARSALA

2 TO 3 DROPS VANILLA EXTRACT

4 TABLESPOONS SUGAR, OR TO
TASTE

ROASTED PEACHES

**This very simple and delicious way of
preparing peaches is from southern Italy**

Serves 4

Preheat the oven to 375°F.

Arrange the peaches in a shallow baking dish, cut side up. Mix the Amaretto with the vanilla and 2 tablespoons of the sugar, and pour over the peaches, so that a little settles in the hollows.

Bake for 10 to 20 minutes or until soft (the time varies, depending on the size and ripeness of the fruit).

Sprinkle the tops with the remaining sugar and put under the broiler until caramelized. The baking can be done in advance, but the last step must be carried out just before serving. Serve hot.

The Food
and
Flavors
of Haute Provence

G E O R G E A N N E
B R E N N A N
foreword by
Patricia Wells

Cooking and gardening aficionado Georgeanne Brennan

"Above all, I want the recipes in this book to convey the sense and the ease of cooking seasonally with local and regional ingredients that is the essence of life in Haute Provence."

Rustic Haute Provence has been a second home to Californian Brennan since 1970, and she makes a convincing case for the pleasures of planting your own vegetables, growing your own herbs, making your own cheese, raising your own pigs. Lovely, evocative descriptions of the way food is harvested and handled in Haute Provence fill the book, and though you may not actually be seized by the desire to make your own blood sausage, Brennan's world is sure a nice place to visit.

FROM THE BOOK

■ ON HAUTE PROVENCE HOSPITALITY

"When my children were little, each morning I would find on my doorstep a wooden crate with several melons in it, and we were expected to eat them all because the next morning there would be more. We ate valiantly."

Wild Herbs & Lavender ▪ Olives & Olive Oil ▪ Wild Mushrooms & Truffles ▪ Cheese ▪ The Potager ▪ Sheep, Goats & Pigs ▪ Game & Fish ▪ Nuts ▪ Honey & Fruits

Among Brennan's earlier food-and-garden books are *Potager* and *The Glass Pantry*.

320 pages, 109 recipes, line drawings throughout, $24.95. Published by Chronicle Books.

Chicken Ragout with Black Olives

SERVES 6

This is comfort food in Haute Provence. I have been served it many times over the years and often make it myself, and it is always satisfying. The chicken parts are first browned in a little olive oil in a heavy pan or skillet, then topped with herbed tomatoes and a handful of oil-cured black olives to finish cooking. The olives bring the salt and a mellowness to the dish and add texture and spots of intensity. Brined black or green olives can be used in place of oil-cured olives, and will impart a sharper flavor to the dish. Rabbit, pork, or beef can be prepared this way as well. In Haute Provence, any leftovers appear the following day as a sauce for pasta, polenta, or rice, with perhaps a few mushrooms and some fresh herbs added.

1 fryer chicken, about 3 pounds, cut into serving pieces,
   or a selection of breasts and thighs
1 teaspoon freshly ground black pepper
3 tablespoons fresh thyme leaves
1 teaspoon chopped fresh rosemary
1 tablespoon extra-virgin olive oil
1½ teaspoons unsalted butter
½ cup minced yellow onion
2 cloves garlic, minced
4 to 6 large, very ripe fresh tomatoes, chopped, or 3 cups chopped
   canned Roma tomatoes and their juice
2 fresh bay leaves, or 1 dried
16 oil-cured black olives

◆ Rub the chicken pieces all over with the pepper, half of the thyme, and half of the rosemary. In a skillet large enough to hold all the chicken pieces in a single layer, heat the olive oil and butter over medium-high heat. When it is nearly smoking, add the chicken pieces. Reduce the heat to medium, and sauté for 2 or 3 minutes until lightly browned. Turn the pieces over and cook for another minute or two to brown on the other side. Add the onion and garlic and continue to cook for another minute or two. Pour the tomatoes over the chicken. Add the bay leaves, and stir in the olives. Cover tightly. Reduce the heat to medium-low and cook until the juices run clear when the thickest part of a thigh is pierced with a knife, about 15 minutes.

◆ Remove the cover, increase the heat to medium, and cook for another 5 minutes to reduce and thicken the sauce. Stir in the remaining thyme and rosemary and serve hot.

NOTE: *If skinned chicken pieces are used, add 1 to 2 additional tablespoons olive oil to the pan.*

Figs Grilled with *Roulade* and Chicken Livers

SERVES 6 TO 8 AS AN HORS D'OEUVRE, OR 4 AS A FIRST COURSE

Sweet figs, chicken livers, and the roulade *of Haute Provence make an excellent hors d'oeuvre or first course, or can be served as a main dish accompanied with polenta or rice and a green salad. Dried figs may be used in place of fresh, as long as they are supple.*

> 16 soft, large, ripe figs, any kind
> 8 chicken livers
> 16 thin slices *roulade* (pancetta), each 6 inches long, or
>   thick bacon slices

◆ Prepare a charcoal or wood fire.

✳ Make a slit in each fig from the stem to the blossom end, but do not cut all the way through. Pat the chicken livers dry with paper towels and cut them in half, discarding any veins. Slip a piece of chicken liver into a slit fig and wrap a piece of *roulade* around the fig. Slip it onto a skewer. Repeat, preparing 4 skewers, each with 4 wrapped figs.

◆ Place the prepared skewers in a long-handled grill basket, close tightly, and place over hot coals. (Alternatively place the skewers directly on the grill rack or in a preheated broiler.) Grill for 4 or 5 minutes, then turn and cook until the *roulade* is lightly browned and the chicken livers are done, 3 or 4 minutes longer. The chicken livers should be a pinkish brown when they are ready.

◆ To serve, slide the figs from the skewers onto individual plates.

Lamb with Rosemary Sauce

SERVES 4

Lamb and mutton chops are common fare in Haute Provence households today, and in local restaurants as well, and they are often dressed up with the addition of a sauce based on regional flavors. Here, rosemary and goat cheese add their unique Southern French accents.

½ teaspoon salt
4 lean lamb chops cut from the leg, sliced about ½ inch thick, or
    lamb shoulder chops of the same thickness, ⅓ to ½ pound each
1 teaspoon freshly ground black pepper
1 teaspoon minced fresh rosemary, plus 5 sprigs
¾ cup dry white wine
½ cup chicken broth
2 ounces fresh goat cheese

◆ Preheat a broiler. In a flameproof skillet large enough to hold the chops in a single layer, heat the salt over high heat. The pan is ready when a drop of water flicked into it sizzles. Add the lamb chops and sear on the first side until browned, 2 or 3 minutes. Turn over the chops, add the pepper, and sear on the other side, about 2 minutes. Add the minced rosemary to the pan and turn the chops, then turn them again. Remove from the heat and slip under a broiler to finish cooking to the desired degree of doneness, about 5 minutes more for rare, 7 minutes for medium, turning as necessary. Remove from the pan and keep warm.

◆ Return the skillet to the stove top over medium-high heat. Add the white wine and deglaze the pan by scraping up any bits clinging to the bottom. Add the chicken broth and 1 sprig of the rosemary. Cook until reduced by one-third, then remove and discard the rosemary. Swirl in the goat cheese to form a thick sauce.

◆ Place the hot chops on a warmed serving platter or individual dishes and spread each with a spoonful of the sauce. Garnish with the remaining rosemary sprigs.

In
Nonna's
Kitchen

RECIPES AND TRADITIONS
FROM
ITALY'S GRANDMOTHERS

CAROL FIELD

Author of *Celebrating Italy*
AND *The Italian Baker*

Carol Field, chronicler of Italian food and culture

". . . *la cucina della nonna*, the comfort food of home, is staging a comeback . . . . Even though Italy has become a land of change and accelerated options, where almost half of the men no longer return home for lunch, where Nutella, a chocolate and hazelnut spread in a jar, has become the afternoon snack of children, where television is erasing regional differences and fax machines are speeding up life, even so, people are looking backward as they look ahead."

Not just a loving backward glance but an attempt to preserve a way of life before it disappears from view, this collection of interviews with and recipes from Italy's nonnas, women who "built an entire cuisine on leftover bread," is full of reminiscences both heartwarming and hardscrabble. Many of the women found the idea of recording their recipes using specific ingredients and quantities almost ludicrous; we're glad Field went to the trouble to do so.

Le Nonne ▪ Basic Ingredients ▪ Before the Meal ▪ Soups ▪ Bread and Pizza ▪ First Courses ▪ Second Courses ▪ One-Dish Meals ▪ Eggs ▪ Vegetables ▪ Desserts ▪ Pantry

FROM THE BOOK

■ WHY WASTE NOT
"Wasting bread is considered such a sin that when someone dies, that person is immediately sent to Purgatory where an inventory is taken of how much bread he or she might have wasted during a lifetime. For every crumb wasted, the punishment is always the same: collect an equivalent number using only the eyelashes to pick them up."

Field has written about Italian cuisine in *The Italian Baker*, *Celebrating Italy*, *Italy in Small Bites*, and *Focaccia*.

452 pages, approximately 200 recipes, approximately 80 black-and-white photographs, $30. Published by HarperCollins Publishers, Inc.

Polenta

Polenta today is both rustic and chic, a dish appearing in restaurants all over northern and central Italy topped with everything from a wreath of quail to wild mushroom ragù. It is only recently that many women would think of making polenta voluntarily. So many years of scarcity had cast it as the food of deprivation and every bite was overlaid with memories of sadness and hard times. Earlier in this century, people ate polenta because they had no choice. They ate it two or three times a day, perhaps cooked in a little milk or broth, perhaps with a bit of salami, cabbage, cicoria, or green beans. In many families the big dome of polenta was poured onto a board in the center of the table and everyone sat around—no plates required—scooping out a space for sauce or flavoring and spooning up the polenta right in front of them. For holidays and very special days in the lives of the poor, the glowing golden circle of polenta was turned out onto a wooden board and a single herring was slapped against each person's piece, the rare moment in the countryside when the taste of meat or fish came to the table.

The implements of cooking polenta are almost sacred. When the fascist government decreed that metal and iron be collected to serve the country during the war, people didn't want to give up their pots and pans for patriotic use. Women's first small resistance to the war came when they held onto their copper pots. How, they asked themselves, could they possibly give away the *paiolo* in which polenta had always been cooked? They represented the connection of one generation to the next—"this one was Mother's, this one Grandmother's." Confronted with an almost universal refusal, the prefects from the National Institute relented and announced that *paioli* didn't need to be given up. At which point so many countrywomen decided that if *paioli* didn't need to be handed over, surely they could also hold on to their *testi*, the terra-cotta or cast-iron disks that were heated in the embers and used for cooking.

Polenta can be creamy, as it is in Lucca, where Renata Marsili makes matuffi, soft scoops of polenta topped with a layer of tomato sauce; or it can be as firm as it is in Friuli, where it is cut with a taut piece of wire or string. Some families in Piedmont serve polenta with a garlic and anchovy sauce—not the famous, more elaborate bagna cauda—and others with a mixture of anchovies and greens. Tuscans and Ligurians beat polenta right into their minestrones and vegetable soups, making a thick rib-sticking meal in a bowl called *intruglia* or *polenta incatenata*. Many people eat polenta with whatever greens they can gather—wild asparagus, rucola, cicoria—with crayfish from the stream, with snails from the fields, or with the bounty of hunters—small birds such as thrush (in Bergamo they are placed in a hollow on top of the polenta and the dish is known as *polenta e osei*) or quail, partridge, pheasant, and guinea hen. Families eat *polenta concia* sprinkled with cheese and black pepper, *polenta pasticciata* layered with a wash of tomato sauce and blizzards of grated grana, *polenta incatenata* with greens cooked in the pot right along with the cornmeal, or *polenta in furla*, cooked in cream and served with grated cheese.

POLENTA CONCIA

Polenta Layered with Cheeses and Black Pepper

Serves 8 to 10 as a first course, 4 to 6 as a main course

*P*olenta is to the arc of land that runs from Friuli through Lombardy and the Veneto what pasta is to Emilia Romagna and what bread is to Tuscany: a delicious base for flavorings that are limited only by the imagination of the cook and the ingredients on hand. Polenta can be seasoned with beans, favas, fish, sausages, cheeses, or meat; it can be compact, high, soft, or dense. Entire cookbooks have been devoted to polenta. Lina Vitali makes polenta concia, a simple dish from the mountainous Valtellina, where impressive quantities of cow's milk cheeses are produced. This version of polenta is cooked and then layered with the local cheese called bitto—Italian fontina with its nutty flavor most approximates its taste—handfuls of grated Parmesan cheese, and lots of freshly grated black pepper.

> 6 cups water
>
> 2½ teaspoons coarse sea salt
>
> 1⅔ cups (8 ounces) medium-grind cornmeal
>
> ½ pound bitto or fontina cheese
>
> 4 to 6 tablespoons freshly grated Parmigiano-Reggiano cheese
>
> Substantial gratings of black pepper
>
> 4 tablespoons unsalted butter
>
> 2 garlic cloves, lightly smashed with the side of a large knife
>
> Leaves of fresh sage (optional)

Bring 6 cups water and 2½ teaspoons coarse salt to a vigorous boil in a very large pot. If you have a *paiolo*, an unlined copper pot with a slightly concave bottom, by all means use it, but a heavy-bottomed copper or stainless steel saucepan will be fine. Reduce the heat to medium-low. Let the cornmeal fall into the pot from your left hand in a slow steady stream while using a whisk in your right hand to keep lumps from forming. Continue stirring sporadically with a long-handled wooden spoon, being very careful to eliminate any lumps by crushing them against the sides of the pot. Keep the water at a steady simmer and stir from the bottom of the pot toward the top, almost as if you were folding egg whites into a batter. The polenta will thicken, bubble, and hiss as it cooks. When it comes away from the sides of the pot, after 30 to 45 minutes, the polenta is ready. Be sure to taste for salt.

Pour the polenta out onto a marble slab or onto a wooden board covered with a kitchen towel and let cool.

Preheat the oven to 350°F. Butter a shallow 3-quart baking dish.

Cut the polenta into ½-inch-thick slices. Italian grandmothers cut slices of polenta using a wire or thick cotton string; if you use a knife, dip it in hot water so it won't stick to the polenta. Place one layer of polenta slices in the dish, cover with a layer of finely sliced fontina or bitto cheese and a large dusting of grated Parmigiano-Reggiano cheese and black pepper, and keep layering the polenta, cheeses, and pepper, finishing with a layer of cheese. Brown the butter with the garlic and (if you are using it) the sage, discard the garlic, and pour over the top. Bake in the oven for 30 minutes, or until the layers of polenta are very hot.

VARIATION:

POLENTA TARAGNA CONCIA (Buckwheat Polenta Layered with Cheese and Black Pepper): Use buckwheat polenta. Sauté 2 minced onions in the butter and layer them in the pan with the polenta, bitto or fontina, and Parmigiano-Reggiano cheese.

POLLO CON LE OLIVE

Roast Chicken Stuffed with Black Olives

Serves 4 to 6

*T*his is a roast chicken for real lovers of olives and olive oil. It is as delicious as it is simple, although I am hard-pressed to explain why a mere handful of olives inside the cavity of a chicken can make such a difference. Call it a miracle from Adele Rondini in Le Marche. Serve the chicken with boiled or roasted potatoes.

> 1 (5-pound) roasting chicken, preferably free-range and organically raised, room temperature
> ¹/₂ teaspoon sea salt
> Freshly ground black pepper
> 4 medium garlic cloves, unpeeled
> 2 cups (12 ounces) black olives in brine, preferably Niçoise type, pitted
> 1 lemon
> 2 tablespoons extra-virgin olive oil
> 3 sprigs flat-leaf parsley

Preheat the oven to 425°F.

Remove the giblets and excess fat from the cavity of the chicken. Rinse the chicken inside and out under cold running water. Dry it thoroughly. Sprinkle salt and pepper inside the cavity, then fill it with the garlic and black olives. Squeeze the juice of half a lemon over the skin, then rub it with the extra-virgin olive oil. Put both halves of the lemon and the three parsley sprigs inside the cavity. Truss it closed.

Place the chicken, breast side down, on a roasting rack in a heavy roasting pan or heavy ovenproof skillet. Roast for 30 minutes, then turn the chicken over to brown the breast for 20 to 30 minutes longer. To test for doneness, insert an instant thermometer under the leg or at the thickest part of the thigh to see if the internal temperature is 170°F. (be careful not to pierce the cavity), or insert a knife in the same place and see if the juices run slightly rosy. They should not be red, which indicates that the chicken is not ready; nor should they be clear, which indicates that it is overcooked. Remove the chicken from the oven and allow it to rest at room temperature for 15 minutes before carving and serving with the olives. You may mash the roasted garlic with juices from the roast, warm them together, taste for salt and pepper, and pass at table.

Chapter 3
Best-Sellers

Every year there are cookbooks that virtually sell themselves, and sell extremely well, at that. The latest entry in a well-known series, the latest revision of a much-loved classic, the latest collection from a celebrity—these are all cookbooks likely to make the best-seller list, and though in some cases their success may be due as much to the name on the cover as to the recipes within, they certainly merit our attention. We promise you won't be disappointed with any of the dishes here.

■ **THE JOY OF COOKING** BY IRMA S. ROMBAUER, MARION ROMBAUER BECKER, AND ETHAN BECKER

Creamed Mushrooms with Dried Porcini 161

Grilled Ratatouille Salad 161

Pulled Pork Sandwiches 162

Sour Cream Pumpkin Pie 163

■ **THE GOOD HOUSEKEEPING STEP-BY-STEP COOKBOOK** EDITED BY SUSAN WESTMORELAND

Olive Sticks 166

Braised Fennel with Two Cheeses 167

Savory Tomato Tart 168

Chocolate Truffle Cake 171

■ **NAOMI'S HOME COMPANION: A Treasury of Favorite Recipes, Food for Thought, and Kitchen Wit and Wisdom** BY NAOMI JUDD

Polly's Fried Chicken with Tan Gravy 174

Macaroni and Cheese Casserole 178

Cornmeal Mush 181

■ **SHEILA LUKINS U.S.A. COOKBOOK** BY SHEILA LUKINS

Boarding House Potato Salad 185

Larry Smith's Mother's Pork Chops 186

Sour Cherry Lamb Shanks 186

■ **SWEETIE PIE: The Richard Simmons Private Collection of Dazzling Desserts**
BY RICHARD SIMMONS

"I'm Late, I'm Late" Carrot Cake 190

Pink Ice Granita 192

■ **MR. FOOD® COOL CRAVINGS: Easy Chilled and Frozen Desserts** BY ART GINSBURG

Frozen Fruit Salad 196

Chocolate Malted Pops 197

Healthier recipes, healthier eating • Desserts for you, desserts for entertaining • New measure for meat • Reduced-fat recipes for today's lifestyles • Ethnic foods • All new grain section • Main course salads • Vegetarian Dinners Italian pasta, Asian noodles • Better nutrition, better food • New preparations for poultry • Exciting new recipes • Turkey on the grill New temperatures for meat • Bake your own bread • New pie, tarts, pastries, and American fruit desserts • Grilled salmon, roast monkfish with garlic and herbs, and other quick, tasty seafood recipes • Heavenly muffins, coffeecakes, scones, biscuits, and cornbread • Tapas, Dim Sum, and Antipastos • Homemade pizzas • Learn about fresh herbs, vinegars, oil, spices, and chili peppers • Bean and soy recipes for the vegans and meat eaters in your family • Homemade breads and pizzas

The ● All New All Purpose Joy of Cooking

Irma S. Rombauer, Marion Rombauer Becker and Ethan Becker

■ AUTHORS
Founding-family members Irma S. Rombauer, Marion Rombauer Becker, and Ethan Becker, plus a host of editors, food writers, and assorted experts

■ WHY THEY REVISED IT

"... we have held fast to *Joy*'s revision focuses: provision of new recipes and the latest food and nutrition knowledge; collaboration with the best cooks; and, ultimately, a cookbook that is useful to the novice and experienced cook alike."

■ WHY IT MADE OUR LIST

It's not your mother's *Joy of Cooking*, but that's not all bad; though we miss the idiosyncratic style and personal touch of Irma Rombauer's original, the fact is, hardly anyone cooks porcupine anymore, and it was time to bring the old book into the new age. What this revision-by-committee, really more a new book than a new *Joy of Cooking*, lacks in charm, it makes up for in the quality of the recipes and the sheer breadth of knowledge and experience it offers. Still a must-own title, after all these years.

FROM THE BOOK

■ ON CHANGING TASTES

"They say love comes when you least expect it, and that's what's been happening with grains. People pampered their whole lives with thick steaks, flashy salads, and rich desserts are suddenly finding that what they really crave are homely little wheat berries, bowls of cornmeal mush, even tiny amaranth."

■ CHAPTERS

Diet, Lifestyle & Health ▪ Entertaining ▪ Menus ▪ Coffee, Tea & Hot Chocolate ▪ Stocks & Sauces ▪ Condiments, Marinades & Dry Rubs ▪ Soups ▪ Eggs ▪ Hors d'Oeuvre ▪ Little Dishes ▪ Sandwiches, Burritos & Pizzas ▪ Salads ▪ Salad Dressings ▪ Grains ▪ Beans & Tofu ▪ Pasta, Dumplings & Noodles ▪ Vegetables ▪ Fruits ▪ Stuffing ▪ Shellfish ▪ Fish ▪ Poultry ▪ Game ▪ Meat ▪ Yeast Breads ▪ Quick Breads ▪ Pancakes, Waffles, French Toast & Doughnuts ▪ Cookies ▪ Candy ▪ Pies & Tarts ▪ American Fruit Desserts ▪ Puff Pastry, Strudel & Danish Pastries ▪ Cakes, Tortes & Cupcakes ▪ Frostings, Fillings & Glazes ▪ Custards, Puddings, Mousses & Dessert Soufflés ▪ Dessert Sauces

■ PREVIOUS CREDITS

Originally published in 1931, *Joy* was last updated in 1975.

■ SPECIFICS

1,136 pages, approximately 2,600 recipes, 1,000 line drawings, $30. Published by Scribner.

MUSHROOMS

Mushrooms lend both elegance and earthiness to a dish. While we are grateful for the abundance of cultivated small button mushrooms, wild mushrooms have considerably more character, and an assortment of them is available in specialty groceries and supermarkets. Choose mushrooms that are heavy for their size, with dry, firm caps and stems—nothing damp or shriveled, no dark or soft spots, and all close to the same size. If the gills are open, the mushrooms are more mature and their flavor will be stronger, and with a wild mushroom, this may be a plus. Open-gilled mushrooms should be used as soon as possible. A trick: When a costly mushroom is needed to flavor a dish, buy one or two, depending on the intensity of its flavor, then fill in with neutral-tasting button mushrooms.

White button or commercial mushrooms are rounded, plump, creamy, and mild. Select only those with closed caps. If they are very small, use them whole.

Porcini, also called cèpes or boletes, look like very large button mushrooms with thick stalks and reddish caps. They are among the tastiest of wild mushrooms, something to enjoy simply in a risotto or sauté of mixed mushrooms. Brush large ones with olive oil and lemon juice and broil or grill as you would meat. Look for fresh porcini in late spring and fall.

Chanterelles, or girolles, resemble a curving trumpet. Their golden or orange-brown caps and slender stems can hint of apricots or be delicately earthy. They have an affinity with cream, whether over toast, pasta, chicken, or polenta. The similarly shaped black mushrooms variously called black trumpets, horns of plenty, or trumpets of death are closely related and similar in taste but have thinner flesh. Both are gathered from summer into winter.

Creminis, or Italian browns, are the same as button mushrooms, only grown outdoors and bigger. They have light brown caps and a naturally more developed flavor.

Enoki are as slender as bean sprouts and, with their tiny dots of caps, look like an ivory sea creature. They are a pretty salad ingredient, adding a faintly sweet taste. They are also lovely barely heated and served in broth. To use, trim off the spongy base and separate the strands.

Morels are small, with dark brown, conical, spongelike caps. The honeycombed surface that allows them to soak up sauces can also harbor sand. Swish morels around in a bowl of water, being sure to pat them dry thoroughly before using. Morels have a special affinity with tender young vegetables.

Oyster mushrooms can be cultivated or wild. They grow in clusters of small fan-shaped caps with short stems, cream colored to grayish brown. Their texture is smooth, and their flavor can have a touch of the sea.

Portobellos are cultivated mushrooms, full-blown creminis (above). They are generous in size (up to 6 inches wide), meaty, and robustly flavored (although they have no wild taste). Their open gills and large, flat caps make them naturals for grilling and broiling. They are also useful in sautés.

Shiitakes are umbrella shaped, brown or brown-black. They are cultivated on logs and have a distinctive earthy taste. Save the tough stems to simmer in stock.

Wood or cloud ear mushrooms are the dark, very thin, almost crunchy mushrooms that give so many Chinese dishes a subtly woodsy taste. Unlike other fresh mushrooms, these should look damp. They are available in Asian markets.

Mushrooms go well with cream, lemon, garlic, shallots, onions, cheese, fennel, fish, chicken, veal, peas, dill, chervil, parsley, tarragon, basil, oregano, and capers. Allow 4 to 5 ounces per serving.

Caution! A number of poisonous forms of wild mushrooms, during various stages of their development, resemble edible forms. Take the time to become familiar with the mushrooms you wish to pick—accompany someone you are absolutely sure is an experienced forager until you know your mushrooms as well as he or she does.

Common button mushrooms

Porcino, also called cèpe or bolete

Chanterelles, also called girolles

To Store: Wrap unwashed mushrooms in a loosely closed paper bag or wrap loosely in damp paper towels. Leave packaged mushrooms in their unopened package. Store on a refrigerator shelf, not in the crisper (too much moisture hastens spoilage).

To Prepare: Clean mushrooms with a soft brush or wipe with a damp cloth. Or if the mushrooms are truly grimy, rinse them quickly under cold running water and pat dry. Never soak mushrooms—their delicate tissues will absorb water. If desired, slice $^1\!/_8$ inch off the bottom of the stems to refresh them but do not discard the flavorful stems. If only caps are called for in a recipe, cut the stem flush with the cap. Either chop the stems fairly fine, toss them until lightly browned in a little butter, and add them to the dish or use within a day to flavor something else. As a general rule, use intense heat when cooking mushrooms, and cook just enough to lightly brown them and heat them through. The best methods are sautéing, stir-frying (for 3 to 4 minutes), grilling, and broiling.

To Brown: When mushrooms are to be added to a soup or stew, never add them raw. Mushrooms simmered from the raw state always seem to have a raw flavor. Bring out their flavor by browning them first in a little butter or oil, tossing them in a skillet over high heat just until you can smell them. To brown without fat, heat a cast-iron skillet very hot. Add whole small mushrooms, quarters, or large slices and stir over high heat without stopping until the pieces have lightly browned. Remove at once. Be sure to scrape all pan juices into the dish.

To Use Dried Mushrooms: Dried mushrooms provide intensified mushroom flavor in a sauce, soup, or stew. Soak dried mushrooms in lukewarm water to cover until softened, at least 15 minutes, then rinse well and remove the hard stems. To make a stock base for a sauce or stew, simmer dried mushrooms for an hour in stock or water to cover by several inches with a pinch each of salt and sugar. Strain the soaking liquid or cooking liquid through a damp coffee filter, paper towel, or cheesecloth to remove sand.

CREAMED MUSHROOMS WITH DRIED PORCINI

4 servings

A very rich side dish or sauce, or an opulent first course when spooned over toast.

Soak in warm water just to cover until softened, about 15 minutes:

> 1 ounce dried porcini mushrooms

Drain, reserving ¼ cup liquid. Finely chop the mushrooms. Heat in a large skillet:

> 2 tablespoons butter
> 2 tablespoons olive oil

Add and cook over medium heat until translucent, about 5 minutes:

> ½ cup finely diced onions

Add the chopped porcini along with:

> 1 pound assorted fresh mushrooms, wiped clean and thinly sliced

Increase the heat to medium-high and cook, stirring often, until the mushrooms release and then reabsorb their juices, about 5 minutes. Add the reserved mushroom liquid along with:

> ½ cup heavy cream or crème fraîche
> 2 cloves garlic, minced
> 1½ teaspoons fresh thyme leaves
> Salt and ground black pepper to taste

Reduce the heat to medium and simmer until the sauce is slightly thickened. Taste and adjust the seasonings, then add:

> 2 tablespoons chopped fresh parsley

GRILLED RATATOUILLE SALAD

6 servings

Prepare a medium-hot charcoal fire.
Combine in a bowl:

> 2 to 4 tablespoons olive oil
> 2 to 3 tablespoons red wine vinegar, to taste

When the coals are covered with gray ash, coat with the oil mixture:

> Twelve ½-inch-thick eggplant slices

Black trumpets, also called horns of plenty or trumpets of death

Cremini

Enoki

Morel

2 fennel bulbs, quartered lengthwise

2 medium zucchini, cut lengthwise into thick slices

4 plum tomatoes

3 slender leeks (white part only), split up to the root ends
and washed thoroughly

3 red, orange, or yellow bell peppers, or a combination

½ head garlic, unpeeled

Fennel bulb

Grill the vegetables, turning as needed, until the tomatoes and peppers are charred on the outside and the other vegetables are tender, about 5 minutes for the zucchini, up to 20 minutes for the garlic. Remove from the grill and let cool slightly. Peel, seed, and dice the tomatoes and bell peppers. Dice the fennel and zucchini into ½-inch pieces. Trim the root ends from the leeks and slice. Squeeze the garlic cloves from their skins and mash. Combine the vegetables, except the eggplant slices, in a bowl. Just before serving, stir in:

3 tablespoons minced fresh basil

1 tablespoon extra-virgin olive oil

Pinch of grated orange zest

Salt and ground black pepper to taste

Arrange the eggplant slices on a platter, top with the ratatouille, and serve at room temperature.

PULLED PORK SANDWICHES   *About 12 sandwiches*

In many parts of the country, this is what is meant by barbecue. Pulled pork is pork shoulder cooked until it is tender enough to be shredded with a fork. After being pulled apart, it is mixed with a sauce and served on a bun. Trim the excess fat from:

1 boneless Boston butt or pork shoulder blade roast
(about 4 pounds)

Rub the meat with:

Southern Dry Rub for Barbecue, NEXT COLUMN

The meat can be cooked at once or wrapped in 2 layers of aluminum foil and refrigerated for up to 24 hours.

Position a rack in the center of the oven. Preheat the oven to 325°F.

Heat a heavy ovenproof pot large enough to hold the meat over medium heat. Add and heat:

2 tablespoons lard or vegetable oil

Add the meat and brown well on all sides. Cover the pot tightly with foil or a lid, place in the oven, and bake until the meat is tender enough to be shredded easily with a fork, 3 to 3½ hours. Skim off the fat from the pan juices. Shred the meat into strings with a fork and mix with the pan juices. Stir in:

1½ to 2 cups barbecue sauce

Have ready:

Cole Slaw, BELOW

12 hamburger buns

If necessary, gently reheat the pork over medium-low heat. To make each sandwich, spoon the pork on the bottom half of the buns, top with some slaw, and cover with the top half of the buns.

SOUTHERN DRY RUB FOR BARBECUE

About 2 cups

Southern barbecue chefs rub spice mixtures like this one into pork or beef before it starts the long, slow cooking that will transform it into barbecue.

Spread in a small dry skillet over medium heat and toast, shaking the pan often to prevent burning, until fragrant, 2 to 3 minutes:

¼ cup cumin seeds

Remove from the heat, let cool to room temperature, and grind to a fine powder in a spice grinder, coffee grinder, or blender, or with a mortar and pestle. Transfer to a small bowl and add:

¼ cup packed light or dark brown sugar

½ cup sweet or hot paprika

¼ cup chili powder

2 tablespoons ground red pepper

1 teaspoon ground mace

¼ cup salt

¼ cup cracked black peppercorns

Stir together well. This rub will stay potent, covered and kept in a cool, dark, dry place, for up to 6 weeks.

COLE SLAW   *6 servings*

A basic recipe for an American favorite; improvisations on the theme are encouraged.

Stir together until well blended:

¾ cup mayonnaise

¼ cup white vinegar

1 tablespoon sugar

Finely shred or chop:

1 small head chilled green or red cabbage, cored and
outer leaves removed

Stir in just enough dressing to moisten the cabbage.

Season with:

Salt and ground black pepper to taste

If desired, add any of the following:

    Dill, caraway, or celery seeds, or a combination

    Chopped fresh parsley, chives, or other herb

    Crumbled crisp bacon

    Pineapple chunks

    Grated peeled carrots

    Coarsely chopped onions, bell peppers, or pickles

Stir again and serve immediately.

PULLED PORK, NORTH CAROLINA-STYLE

In North Carolina, cooks season pulled pork with a tangy vinegar-based sauce in place of barbecue sauce.

Prepare Pulled Pork Sandwiches, above, replacing the barbecue sauce with a combination of ¾ cup white vinegar, ¾ cup cider vinegar, 1 tablespoon hot red pepper sauce or more to taste, 1 tablespoon sugar, 2 teaspoons crushed red pepper flakes, and salt and cracked black peppercorns to taste.

SOUR CREAM PUMPKIN PIE

One 9-inch pie; 8 servings

A tangy pie with a light, soufflélike texture.

Position a rack in the center of the oven. Preheat the oven to 350°F.

Building up a high fluted rim, prepare in a 9-inch pan, preferably glass, glazing with the egg yolk:

    Pat-in-the-Pan Butter Crust, NEXT COLUMN

In a large, heavy saucepan, whisk together thoroughly:

    1½ cups freshly cooked or canned pumpkin puree

    8 ounces (scant 1 cup) sour cream

    ¾ cup sugar

    3 large egg yolks

    1 teaspoon ground cinnamon

    ½ teaspoon ground ginger

    ½ teaspoon freshly grated or ground nutmeg

    ¼ teaspoon ground cloves or allspice

    ¼ teaspoon salt

Whisking constantly, heat over medium heat until just warm to the touch. Beat on medium speed until foamy:

    3 large egg whites, at room temperature

Add:

    ¼ teaspoon cream of tartar

Continue to beat until soft peaks form, then gradually beat in:

    ¼ cup sugar

Increase the speed to high and beat until the peaks are stiff and glossy. Using a large rubber spatula, gently fold the egg whites into the pumpkin mixture. Pour the filling into the prepared crust. Bake until the top has browned lightly and feels softly set when touched, 40 to 50 minutes. Let cool completely on a rack. At this point the pie can be refrigerated for up to 1 day. Let warm at room temperature for 30 minutes before serving. Serve with:

    Whipped cream

PAT-IN-THE-PAN BUTTER CRUST

One 9-inch pie or 9½- or 10-inch tart crust

Those who are daunted by flaky pastry will find this simple alternative more than satisfactory.

This dough will also make about eight 3½-inch tartlet crusts. Press the dough into the tartlet molds and bake until firm and golden, about 15 minutes, pricking several times during baking with a fork.

Position a rack in the center of the oven. Preheat the oven to 400°F.

Whisk together in a bowl or process for 10 seconds in a food processor:

    1½ cups all-purpose flour

    ½ teaspoon salt

Add:

    8 tablespoons (1 stick) unsalted butter, softened, cut

      into 8 pieces

Mash with the back of a fork or process until the mixture resembles coarse crumbs. Drizzle over the top:

    2 to 3 tablespoons heavy cream

Stir or process until the crumbs look damp and hold together when pinched. Transfer the mixture to a 9-inch pie pan or 9½- or 10-inch two-piece tart pan. Pat evenly over the bottom and sides with your fingertips. If making a pie, form a crust edge and crimp or flute. Prick the bottom and sides with a fork. Bake until the crust is golden brown, 18 to 22 minutes, pricking the bottom once or twice if it bubbles. If you are filling the crust with an uncooked mixture that requires further baking, whisk together, then brush the inside with:

    1 large egg yolk

    Pinch of salt

Return to the oven until the egg glaze sets, 1 to 2 minutes.

The Good Housekeeping

Step -by- Step Cookbook

ALL NEW!

More than 1,000 Recipes
1,800 Photographs

■ **EDITOR**

Susan Westmoreland, *Good Housekeeping*'s food director

■ **WHY THEY WROTE IT**

"It's the next best thing to having a wise and patient grandmother who's a great cook and teacher. We start with a basic technique: Want to panfry chicken-breast cutlets? Our step-by-step photos will show you the way and—voilà!—the finished dish. With the turn of a page you'll have eight more recipes—all using the same technique."

■ **WHY IT MADE OUR LIST**

The perfect primer for beginning cooks and general reference for old hands, this wide-ranging guide, chock-full of information, makes preparing everything from burgers to biscotti as simple and clear as possible. If you thought that all women's-magazine recipes start with canned soup, the sophisticated dishes and ingredients here will be downright startling. Squid ink, anyone?

■ **CHAPTERS**

Appetizers ▪ Soups ▪ Eggs and Cheese ▪ Shellfish ▪ Fish ▪ Poultry ▪ Meat ▪ Vegetables ▪ Salads ▪ Pasta ▪ Grains and Beans ▪ Quick and Yeast Breads ▪ Sandwiches ▪ Desserts ▪ Pies and Tarts ▪ Cookies and Cakes

■ **PREVIOUS CREDITS**

Good Housekeeping has been publishing cookbooks since 1903; the most recent was *The New Good Housekeeping Cookbook*.

■ **SPECIFICS**

576 pages, more than 1,000 recipes, 1,800 color photographs, $30. Published by Hearst Books.

FROM THE BOOK

■ **ETYMOLOGICAL CREDITS**

▪ *"(The Dutch) called their creation of shredded cabbage, seasonings, and a boiled dressing* koolsla, *from the Dutch* kool, *for cabbage, and* sla, *for salad."*

▪ *"The word 'streusel' is German for 'sprinkle' or 'strew.'"*

OLIVE STICKS

◆◆◆◆◆◆◆◆◆◆◆◆

Prep: 30 minutes

Bake: 12 to 15 minutes per batch

Makes about 56

1 package (8 ounces) feta cheese, well drained and crumbled

⅓ cup minced fresh parsley

⅓ cup olive paste or ½ cup Kalamata olives, pitted and pureed with

1 tablespoon olive oil

2 large egg whites

1 package (17¼ ounces) frozen puff-pastry sheets, thawed

OLIVE PASTE

◆◆◆◆◆◆◆◆◆◆◆◆

This pungent puree is known as tapenade in the South of France and olivada in Italy; it is traditionally made from black or green olives, garlic, capers, anchovies, herbs, and olive oil. Olive paste is delicious slathered on toasted bread, added to sandwiches of grilled vegetables or creamy cheeses, or stirred into mayonnaise to make a dip for crudités.

1 Preheat oven to 400°F. In small bowl, with fork, mix feta cheese, minced parsley, olive paste, and egg whites until thoroughly blended. On lightly floured surface, unfold 1 pastry sheet (keep other sheet refrigerated). With floured rolling pin, roll pastry sheet into 16" by 14" rectangle.

2 Cut pastry crosswise in half. Spread half of olive mixture evenly over 1 pastry half; top with remaining pastry half.

3 With rolling pin, gently roll over pastry layers to seal them together.

4 Grease large cookie sheet. With large chef's knife, cut pastry rectangle crosswise into ½-inch-wide strips, taking care not to tear pastry.

5 Place pastry strips, about 1 inch apart, on cookie sheet, twisting each strip 3 or 4 times. Bake strips 12 to 15 minutes, until pastry is puffed and lightly browned. With pancake turner, transfer sticks to wire rack to cool. Repeat with remaining pastry sheet and olive mixture. Serve at room temperature. Store in tightly covered container.

EACH PIECE: ABOUT 55 CALORIES, 1g PROTEIN, 5g CARBOHYDRATE, 4g TOTAL FAT (1g SATURATED), 4mg CHOLESTEROL, 80mg SODIUM

BRAISED FENNEL WITH TWO CHEESES

◆◆◆◆◆◆◆◆◆◆◆◆◆◆◆◆◆◆◆◆◆◆◆◆◆◆◆◆◆

Prep: 15 minutes   *Cook:* 45 minutes plus broiling

Makes 6 accompaniment servings

**3 small fennel bulbs
(8 ounces each)**
**1 can (13¾ to 14½ ounces)
chicken broth**
**6 ounces mozzarella cheese,
shredded (1½ cups)**

**2 tablespoons freshly grated
Parmesan cheese**
**1 tablespoon chopped fresh
parsley**

1 Rinse fennel bulbs with cold running water; cut off root end and stalks from bulbs. Slice each bulb lengthwise in half. In deep 12-inch skillet, heat chicken broth and *1½ cups water* to boiling over high heat. Add fennel; heat to boiling.

2 Reduce heat to low; cover and simmer 35 minutes, turning bulbs once, or until fennel is fork-tender; drain. Preheat broiler. Place fennel, cut-side up, in shallow broiler-safe 1½-quart casserole. In small bowl, mix mozzarella and Parmesan cheeses and parsley.

3 Sprinkle cheese mixture evenly over fennel in casserole. Place casserole in broiler at closest position to heat source. Broil 1 to 2 minutes, until cheese topping is golden and bubbly and fennel is heated through.

BRAISED CELERY WITH GRUYÈRE

Substitute 2 bunches celery for fennel; trim stalks from bases of celery. Cut each stalk in half to give 5- to 6-inch lengths. Proceed as directed, but simmer only 20 minutes in Step 2 and use 4 ounces Gruyère or Swiss cheese, shredded (about 1 cup), instead of mozzarella.

Each serving: About 125 calories, 8g protein, 7g carbohydrate, 8g total fat (4g saturated), 28mg cholesterol, 530mg sodium

EACH SERVING: ABOUT 135 CALORIES, 8g PROTEIN, 10g CARBOHYDRATE, 8g TOTAL FAT (4g SATURATED), 29mg CHOLESTEROL, 490mg SODIUM

SAVORY TOMATO TART

◆◆◆◆◆◆◆◆◆◆◆◆

Prep: 30 minutes
Bake: 35 minutes
Makes 6 main-dish servings

Pastry for 11-inch Tart (see
 opposite page)
1 tablespoon olive or
 vegetable oil
3 medium onions (about
 1 pound), thinly sliced
Salt
1 package (3½ ounces) goat
 cheese, crumbled
3 large tomatoes (about
 1½ pounds), cut into ¼-inch-
 thick slices
½ teaspoon coarsely ground
 black pepper
¼ cup Kalamata olives, pitted
 and chopped
Sliced fresh basil leaves for
 garnish

1 Prepare Pastry for 11-inch Tart and use to line tart pan as directed. Preheat oven to 425°F. Line tart shell with foil; fill with pie weights, dry beans, or uncooked rice. Bake 20 minutes; remove foil with weights. Bake tart shell 10 minutes longer, or until golden. (If crust puffs up during baking, gently press it down with back of spoon.)

2 Meanwhile, in nonstick 12-inch skillet, heat oil over medium heat; add onions and ¼ teaspoon salt and cook, stirring frequently, about 15 minutes, until onions are tender and browned.

3 Turn oven control to broil. Spoon cooked onions in even layer over bottom of tart shell; sprinkle with half of goat cheese.

4 Arrange tomato slices in concentric circles over onion layer. Sprinkle black pepper and ¼ teaspoon salt over tomatoes. Sprinkle remaining goat cheese over top of tart. Place pan in broiler about 5 to 7 inches from heat source. Broil tart about 5 minutes, until cheese just melts. Sprinkle with chopped Kalamata olives and sliced basil leaves. To serve, cut tart into wedges.

EACH SERVING: ABOUT 415 CALORIES, 8g PROTEIN, 33g CARBOHYDRATE, 28g TOTAL FAT (7g SATURATED), 15mg CHOLESTEROL, 650mg SODIUM

PASTRY FOR 2-CRUST PIE

◆◆◆◆◆◆◆◆◆◆◆◆◆

2¼ cups all-purpose flour
½ teaspoon salt
¼ cup shortening
½ cup cold margarine or

butter, cut up

1 In large bowl, mix flour and salt. With pastry blender or two knives used scissor-fashion, cut in shortening and margarine until mixture resembles coarse crumbs.

2 Sprinkle in *4 to 6 tablespoons ice water*, a tablespoon at a time. Mix lightly with fork after each addition, until dough is just moist enough to hold together.

3 Shape dough into 2 balls, one slightly larger. Wrap and refrigerate 30 minutes, or overnight (if chilled overnight, let stand at room temperature 30 minutes before rolling). On lightly floured surface, with floured rolling pin, roll larger ball 2 inches larger all around than inverted 9-inch pie plate.

4 Roll dough round gently onto rolling pin; gently ease into pie plate. Trim edge, leaving 1-inch overhang. Reserve trimmings for decorating pie, if you like. Fill pie crust.

5 Roll small ball of dough into 10-inch round. Cut several slashes; center over filling. Trim edge, leaving 1-inch overhang; fold overhang under. Make decorative edge.

PASTRY FOR 1-CRUST PIE

1¼ cups all-purpose flour
¼ teaspoon salt
2 tablespoons shortening

4 tablespoons cold margarine
or butter, cut up

Prepare pastry as directed for 2-Crust Pie, but in Step 2 sprinkle in *3 to 5 tablespoons ice water*, and in Step 3 make only 1 ball of dough.

PASTRY FOR 11-INCH TART

1½ cups all-purpose flour
½ teaspoon salt
2 tablespoons shortening

½ cup cold margarine or
butter, cut up

Prepare pastry as directed for 2-Crust Pie, but in Step 2 sprinkle in *3 to 4 tablespoons ice water*, and in Step 3 make only 1 ball of dough and, after chilling, roll dough to a 14-inch round. Ease dough into 11" by 1" round tart pan with removable bottom. Fold overhang in and press against side of tart pan to form rim ⅛ inch above pan edge.

PASTRY FOR 9-INCH TART

1 cup all-purpose flour
¼ teaspoon salt
1 tablespoon shortening

6 tablespoons cold margarine
or butter, cut up

Prepare pastry as directed for 2-Crust Pie, but in Step 2 sprinkle in only *2 to 3 tablespoons ice water*, and in Step 3 make only 1 ball of dough and, after chilling, roll dough to an 11-inch round. Use to line 9" by 1" round tart pan with removable bottom as directed for 11-inch tart.

FOOD PROCESSOR METHOD

◆◆◆◆◆◆◆◆◆◆◆◆

In food processor with knife blade attached, combine flour, salt, shortening, and margarine. Process for 1 to 2 seconds, until mixture forms fine crumbs. Add smaller amount of *ice water* all at once; process for 1 to 2 seconds, until dough leaves sides of bowl. Remove dough from bowl; with hands, shape into ball.

Whether they're whipped into a cloud-like meringue or simply boiled, fried, poached, baked or scrambled, eggs are one of our most versatile foods. As a cooking ingredient, their uses are virtually endless — from thickening and enriching custards to aerating cakes and puffy soufflés. Nutritionally speaking, eggs are a good (and inexpensive) source of protein, iron, and vitamins. And, while the yolks are relatively high in fat and cholesterol, egg whites are completely fat- and cholesterol-free.

Treat eggs with care — their delicate structure is sensitive to handling and heat. To ensure that your egg dishes have a fluffy, light texture, use low to medium heat and do not overcook, or the yolks may toughen and the whites become rubbery.

BUYING, STORING, AND USING

• When buying eggs, pass on any that are dirty, cracked, or leaking. Move each egg in the carton to make sure it isn't stuck to the bottom.
• The color of an egg – white or brown – is determined by the breed and diet of the hen and has no bearing on taste, nutritional value, or cooking performance.
• The "pack date" on the carton is the day the eggs were packed. It runs from 001 (for January 1) through 365 (for December 31). Eggs can be used up to 5 weeks beyond the pack date. In some states and localities, the carton also indicates an expiration date after which the eggs should not be sold.
• A blood spot does not signal a fertilized or bad egg. It can, in fact, be an indication of freshness. It means that while the egg was forming, a blood vessel ruptured on the egg's surface. The spot can be removed with the tip of a knife.
• Store eggs in the coldest part of the refrigerator — not in the refrigerator door. Keep them in their carton to prevent the porous shells from absorbing other refrigerator odors.
• Store eggs pointed end down to keep the yolk centered.
• For baked goods, bring eggs out of the refrigerator about 30 minutes before you'll use them, or place them in a bowl of warm (not hot) tap water for 5 minutes (room-temperature eggs will beat to a greater volume, yielding lighter cakes). However, cold eggs are easier to separate; so do this right when you take them out of the refrigerator. For all other recipes, use refrigerator-cold eggs.
• Cover leftover egg yolks (unbroken) with cold water and refrigerate to use within 2 days. Drain before using.

• Refrigerate leftover egg whites in a tightly covered container; use within 4 days.
• You can safely refrigerate hard-cooked eggs in their shells for up to 7 days (mark to identify them as cooked).
• All recipes in this book use large eggs.
   1 large egg white = about 2 tablespoons
   1 large egg yolk = about 1 tablespoon
   5 large eggs = about 1 cup
   8 large egg whites = about 1 cup

FREEZING FACTS

To freeze extra raw eggs, beat to blend the whites and yolks, transfer to a freezer container, and seal. Egg whites can be frozen on their own. So can egg yolks, but you must add salt or sugar or corn syrup (depending on whether they'll be used in a sweet or savory dish) to prevent the yolks from thickening on freezing. For every 4 yolks, stir in ⅛ teaspoon salt or 1½ teaspoons sugar or corn syrup, then freeze as usual. Thaw frozen eggs in the refrigerator.

TESTING FOR FRESHNESS

Crack the egg onto a saucer. A fresh egg has a round yolk and a thick, translucent white. An older egg's yolk is flat, the white thin and runny. For poaching or frying, use a fresh egg so it holds its shape. Use older eggs for scrambling or baking.

To test without breaking the egg, place in a glass of cold water: If fresh, it will stay on the bottom or stand upright (if less fresh). If older, it will float. For hard-cooking, a less-fresh egg is easier to peel.

EGGS TO ORDER

Scrambled For each serving, beat together 2 eggs, 2 tablespoons milk, and salt and pepper to taste just until blended. In 8-inch skillet, heat 2 teaspoons margarine or butter over medium heat until hot. Add eggs and, as they begin to set, draw an inverted pancake turner across the bottom of the pan, forming large soft curds; stir occasionally. Continue cooking until eggs are thickened and set.

Poached In skillet, heat 1 to 1½ inches of water to boiling. Reduce heat so water gently simmers. Break cold eggs, 1 at a time, into a cup; holding cup close to water, slip in eggs. Cook 3 to 5 minutes, until whites are set and yolks begin to thicken. With a slotted spoon, lift out each egg; drain in the spoon over paper towels.

Fried In 8-inch skillet, melt 1 tablespoon margarine or butter over medium-high heat. Break 2 eggs into pan; reduce heat to low. For "sunny-side up," cover and cook slowly until whites are set and yolks have thickened. For "over easy," carefully turn eggs to cook second side.

Cooked in shell Place eggs in saucepan with cold water to cover by at least 1 inch. Cover and quickly heat just to boiling. Remove from heat. Let eggs stand, covered, 4 to 5 minutes for soft-cooked eggs, or 15 minutes for hard-cooked eggs. To cool hard-cooked eggs, immediately run cold water over them to keep them from overcooking.

SMART SEPARATING

Many recipes call for separated eggs. An egg separator can be used, but the half-shell method (top right) works just as well.
• It is easiest to separate refrigerator-cold eggs.
• Remove any trace of egg yolk in the whites using a half-shell as a scoop.

• When separating several eggs, transfer the whites to a different bowl as you go in case a yolk breaks.
Sharply tap the egg on the side of the bowl to crack the shell. With your thumbs, carefully pull open shell along the crack, letting some of the white run into the bowl. Transfer the yolk carefully back and forth from one half-shell to the other until all the white has run into the bowl.

EGG WHITE MAGIC

• For maximum volume, use room-temperature whites.
• Fat inhibits whites from foaming; for fullest volume, avoid all traces of yolk. Don't use plastic bowls; they absorb fat.
• If whites are underbeaten, the result will not be as light. If overbeaten, they won't blend easily with other ingredients.
• Soft peaks: When beaters are lifted, peaks form and curl over slightly.
• Stiff peaks: Whites do not slip when bowl is tilted.

CHOCOLATE TRUFFLE CAKE

Prep: 1 hour plus chilling overnight and standing   *Bake:* 35 minutes
Makes 24 servings

1 cup butter (do not use margarine)	9 large eggs, separated
14 squares (14 ounces) semisweet chocolate	½ cup granulated sugar
	¼ teaspoon cream of tartar
2 squares (2 ounces) unsweetened chocolate	Confectioners' sugar for garnish

◆ Preheat oven to 300°F. Remove bottom from 9" by 3" springform pan and cover bottom with foil, wrapping foil around to the underside (this will make it easier to remove cake from pan). Replace bottom. Grease and flour foil bottom and side of pan.

◆ In heavy 2-quart saucepan, melt butter with all chocolate over low heat, stirring frequently. Pour chocolate mixture into large bowl.

◆ In small bowl, with mixer at high speed, beat egg yolks and granulated sugar about 5 minutes, until very thick and lemon-colored. With rubber spatula, stir egg-yolk mixture into chocolate mixture until blended.

◆ In another large bowl, with clean beaters, with mixer at high speed, beat egg whites and cream of tartar to soft peaks. With rubber spatula or wire whisk, gently fold beaten egg whites into chocolate mixture, one-third at a time.

◆ Spread batter evenly in pan. Bake 35 minutes. (Do not overbake; cake will firm on chilling.) Cool cake completely in pan on wire rack. Refrigerate overnight in pan.

◆ To remove cake from pan, run a hot knife around edge of cake; remove side of pan. Invert cake onto cake plate; unwrap foil on bottom and lift off bottom of pan. Carefully peel foil from cake.

◆ Let cake stand 1 hour at room temperature before serving. Just before serving, sprinkle confectioners' sugar through fine sieve over star stencil or doily for a pretty design, or dust top of cake with confectioners' sugar. Store any leftover cake in refrigerator.

Each serving: About 200 calories, 4g protein, 15g carbohydrate, 16g total fat (9g saturated), 100mg cholesterol, 100mg sodium

Naomi's
HOME COMPANION

A Treasury of
Favorite Recipes,
Food for Thought,
and Kitchen
Wit and Wisdom

by Naomi Judd

Naomi Judd, the mother half of the popular country-music duo The Judds

■ WHY SHE WROTE IT

"I've seen that America's hungry for moral nutrition and spiritual sustenance, so I'm offering some food for thought . . . . We all live in a family-unfriendly culture. With the increasing power and influence of the mass media, our society really has become Hollywood versus America. Don't want to spoil your appetite, but the collapse of a nation begins in every home. Chew on that a while!"

FROM THE BOOK

■ CULINARY OBSERVATION

"Broth is like a Southern debutante—it should be from good stock."

■ WHY IT MADE OUR LIST

It's not often you find a cookbook that's as concerned with what goes on around the dinner table as what's on top of it. Though this colorful, chatty book full of personal photos and homespun homilies will probably be of most interest to fans of Judd and her celebrity daughters, Wynonna (the singer) and Ashley (the actress), many of the recipes are appealing in their own right—the kind of good ol' down-home comfort-food favorites that always bring the family to the table.

■ CHAPTERS

The Family Powwow ▪ Food For Our Family ▪ It Can Only Get Better: Comfort Food ▪ Mind, Body, and Spirit Connection ▪ On the Road ▪ Welcome Home ▪ Slow Down and Simplify: "My Cup of Solitude" ▪ Times of Sickness and Health ▪ Dinner on the Ground ▪ A Mother's Love ▪ Single-Mom Food ▪ From One Generation to Another ▪ Eat, Relax, and Unite ▪ Thanksgiving ▪ Fourth of July ▪ Halloween ▪ Christmas ▪ Milestones

■ PREVIOUS CREDITS

Judd's autobiography, *Love Can Build a Bridge*, was a *New York Times* bestseller.

■ SPECIFICS

214 pages, approximately 90 recipes, approximately 160 color photographs, 10 black-and-white photographs, $25. Published by GT Publishing Corporation.

Polly's Fried Chicken with Tan Gravy

Mom in her kitchen teaching Ashley how to make fried chicken

"Let the mealtimes be far more than the fulfillment of a necessity. In this home, food shall be prepared with grace, and eaten with gratitude."

—FROM *A HOUSE BLESSING,* BY WELLERAN POLTARNESS

Practically every Sunday when I was a kid, this was the after-church dinner—Mom's delicious fried chicken with mashed potatoes and gravy. Mom believes we're spiritual beings in an earthly body. Our souls were fed in Sunday school and church, and then she fed our bodies.

My Mom Polly has always been around food. As a teenager, she was the cashier at the family-run Hamburger Inn in Ashland, the most popular gathering place in our town. Each booth and table usually had its own little powwow going on. It was there Mom learned how to cut up a whole chicken by watching her grandmother, Cora Lee Burton. Saturday night Grandma would do the chickens, soaking them overnight in salt water to keep them moist. In this recipe, my mother uses her special toasted flour to make the gravy. If you've bought already-packaged chicken parts, figure two pieces per person, more if you love leftovers. Hot or cold, this dish is always good.

MAKES 4 SERVINGS

1 **whole chicken (about 3½ pounds), giblets and liver removed for other uses, cut into 8 serving pieces**
Cold salted water (about 1 tablespoon of salt)
1 **cup all-purpose flour**
1½ **teaspoons black pepper**
1½ **teaspoons salt**
Vegetable oil, for frying (enough to come up halfway on chicken pieces—about 1½ inch depth in skillet)
Tan Gravy (recipe, page 176)

1. In a large bowl, soak the chicken in enough salted water to cover in the refrigerator overnight.

2. Drain the chicken and shake off the excess water.

3. In a pie plate, mix together the flour, pepper, and salt. (Mom lists the pepper before the salt because people often slack off on the pepper—don't!) Roll the chicken in the flour to coat.

4. Into two 12-inch cast-iron skillets, pour enough vegetable oil to come to a depth of 1½ inches in each skillet or about halfway up on the chicken pieces. Heat over medium-high

heat until very hot (350° on a deep-fat frying thermometer)—the chicken should sizzle when it hits the oil. Using tongs, carefully add the chicken pieces to the hot oil, making sure there is a lot of space between the pieces. (Fry all the chicken at the same time, but be careful not to crowd the skillets—you don't want to lower the temperature of the cooking oil.)

5. Cover the skillets and lower the heat to medium. Learn to listen to the chicken; if you don't hear it sizzling or cooking, carefully uncover the skillets to see if the oil is bubbling. If not bubbling, turn up the heat and cover the skillet immediately. After 15 minutes, the bottom sides should be brown. Turn the pieces over with the tongs, and continue to cook, covered, browning on all sides, and adjusting the heat as necessary. Remove the breast pieces after another 12 minutes—the white meat cooks faster than the dark meat. All the chicken should be cooked in about 30 minutes.

6. Transfer the chicken to paper towels to drain. Serve immediately.

Tan Gravy

MAKES 1¼ CUPS,
ENOUGH TO SERVE 3 OR
4 PEOPLE

**2 tablespoons cooking oil from
the fried chicken**
**3 tablespoons Polly's Toasted
Flour (below)**
About 1 cup milk
¼ teaspoon black pepper

1. Carefully pour the hot cooking
   oil from the chicken-frying skillets into a heatproof container
   to reuse for future frying.
   Return 2 tablespoons of the oil
   to one of the skillets and heat
   over medium-high heat.

2. Add the 3 tablespoons flour and
   cook, whisking up the browned
   frying bits from the bottom of
   the skillet. Let the mixture
   cook, whisking constantly, until
   a deep brown, about 3 minutes.

3. Gradually add the milk, whisking constantly, until the mixture
   is well blended and smooth.
   Reduce the heat and simmer
   until thickened, 3 to 5 minutes.
   Add the pepper. Serve in a
   sauceboat with the fried
   chicken.

*The food chain: My great grandmother Cora Lee Burton with
her son Carl in her general store at the turn of the century*

POLLY'S TOASTED
FLOUR
In a dry 9-inch cast-iron skillet,
spread all-purpose flour to a
depth of ¼ inch, about 1 cup.
Place the skillet over low to
medium heat and cook the
flour, stirring, and watching
closely, until it turns a light
brown color, 12 to 15 minutes.
Remove to a bowl, let cool, and
store in a a tightly covered container in a cool, dry place. This
will keep for months.

*If you could have
been present at any
event in your family's
history, which would
it have been?*

Let's All Play Family Feud: Powwow Rules

It's important to have a pleasant atmosphere when digesting food, so we have our meetings to deal with problems, separately from our meals. It's taken many years of hurt feelings, tantrums, and unresolved conflicts to get to where we are now! The room for improvement will always be the biggest room at our house.

A family is like a tossed salad—each ingredient is distinct and identifiable.

These are the guidelines we've all agreed on:

1. No interrupting.

2. No shouting.

3. Everyone must realize we each have our own realities.

4. Everyone gets as much time as they need to express themselves completely.

5. Everyone should be prepared with their thoughts and solutions so time isn't wasted.

6. Stop and think before you speak so you talk to the person as if they were a friend instead of a relative.

The Judd women at a family reunion: (left to right, back row) Wy, Grace, Ashley, niece Erin, and sister-in-law Middy; (front row) Mom, me with Boogaloo, and Margaret

7. Everyone needs to remember that these are just issues! Our commitment to communicating is the bottom line to making sure the family endures.

Chew on this a while: Conflict can't survive without your participation. Confrontation gets easier when you give up your need to be right, and no matter how you slice it, there's always two sides.

The Girls Next Door

When Wynonna and I got to stay in one place for a whole week in Omaha, Nebraska in 1989, we'd gotten so tired of room service we chose to stay at the Residence Inn so we could have a kitchen to cook in. We pretended we were secretaries living in apartments. I called her Betty and she called me Norma Normal (the name I used to wrestle under). The first night, after our show, still in our outrageous stage outfits, we headed for the local supermarket with our grocery list at about one in the morning. The place was empty, except for a couple of cab drivers and the stock people sitting on the floor loading up the shelves. Here come Wy and I done up in our sparkly outfits, spike heels, and serious big hair, skipping as we pushed the carts through the aisles, merrily singing Judd songs. Such looks we got! One night I would make fried chicken and mashed potatoes with gravy, and invite "the neighbors" over. Then Wy—I mean Betty—would cook lasagne, and even our fanatically devoted road manager Mike McGrath (code name Aqua Boy) would dazzle us with macaroni and cheese and a fresh fruit salad sprinkled with shredded coconut. Happy days!

Macaroni and Cheese Casserole

If I were alone on a desert island, this is the one dish I would want to have.

MAKES 4 SERVINGS AS A MAIN DISH, OR 6 SERVINGS AS A SIDE DISH

- **8 ounces uncooked elbow macaroni or medium shells**
- **½ stick or ¼ cup butter**
- **¼ cup all-purpose flour**
- **2 cups milk**
- **6 ounces Velveeta or sharp Cheddar cheese, cut into small chunks, plus a little extra shredded for topping**
- **Salt and pepper, to taste**

1. Preheat the oven to 350°.

2. Cook the macaroni according to the package directions. Drain well.

3. Meanwhile, in a large, heavy saucepan, melt the butter. Whisk in the flour to make a paste. Gradually whisk in the milk. Bring to a simmer over medium heat, whisking, until thickened, about 1 minute. Add the cheese, salt, and pepper and whisk until smooth.

4. Stir the cooked macaroni into the cheese sauce. Scrape into a shallow 2-quart baking dish.

5. Bake in the 350° oven, uncovered, until bubbly and lightly golden on top, 20 to 25 minutes. Add the extra shredded cheese for the last 5 minutes of baking. Let stand 10 minutes before serving.

Blessed are they who can laugh at themselves, for they shall never cease to be amused.

Cornmeal Mush

Multiple-choice question for definition of mush:
(1) what you say to sled dogs
(2) something soggy and boggy
(3) when lovebirds are overly romantic
(4) a warm, alternative carbohydrate side dish.

MAKES 6 SERVINGS

3½ **cups water**
1 **cup white cornmeal**
1 **cup cold water**
1 **teaspoon salt**
About 8 teaspoons vegetable oil or bacon fat, for frying
Butter and maple syrup, for serving

1. In a 3-quart heavy saucepan, bring the 3½ cups of water to a boil. Meanwhile, grease an 8 × 8 × 2-inch square baking dish.

2. In a medium bowl, stir together the cornmeal, cold water, and salt. Very gradually whisk the cornmeal mixture into the boiling water, whisking constantly to avoid any lumping. When the mixture returns to the boil, reduce the heat to a simmer. Cover the saucepan and simmer, whisking every 5 minutes, until thickened, about 25 minutes.

3. Pour the mixture into the prepared baking dish. Refrigerate until firm enough to slice, about 4 hours.

4. Onto a cutting board, unmold the cornmeal mixture. Cut into slices about ⅓ inch wide. (You should have 24 slices, 4 slices per serving.)★

5. In a large nonstick skillet, heat 2 teaspoons of the oil or bacon fat over medium-high heat. Working in batches and adding more oil or bacon fat as needed, add the slices of mush and cook until crisp and brown, about 10 minutes on the first side, and then 6 to 8 minutes on the second side. Transfer to paper towels to drain and then serve hot with butter and maple syrup.

★ TIP
When you unmold the mush from the baking dish, you can, for variety, cut it up in the following way: Cut the square into quarters, and then cut each quarter into 9 slices, for a total of 36 slices. Each serving is then 6 slices.

Home is the anchor of our existence, our little corner of peace, a resting place for the heart.

Former *Silver Palate* collaborator Sheila Lukins

■ WHY SHE WROTE IT

"This book is a celebration that I'd like you to join—a celebration of American pride, ingenuity, and individuality. It's a paean to our fearless style of cooking, free to be anything it wants in a brave new culinary world."

■ WHY IT MADE OUR LIST

Fans of the *Silver Palate* series, who are legion, are always interested in what Lukins is up to now. This time, she's spent three years traveling around the country, sampling chowder in New England, salsa in the Southwest, and the specialties of the house at high-toned restaurants and roadside eateries all over. The result is as sprawling as America itself, with Creamy Potato Salad keeping company with Autumn Duck Salad, and drinks from New York's Rainbow Room served with good old Deviled Eggs.

> FROM THE BOOK
>
> ■ ON THE TWILIGHT TIPPLE
> *"The cocktail hour . . . is when people from every walk of life lay down the accumulated baggage of their trip through the day and pick up their spirits."*

■ CHAPTERS

Breakfast Fruits & Cereals ▪ Eggs & Hash ▪ Pancakes, Waffles & Sides ▪ Muffins & Sweet Breads ▪ The Salad Plate ▪ Sandwiches ▪ Mixed Drinks ▪ Complements ▪ The Relish Tray ▪ Breads ▪ Soups ▪ Dinner Side Salads ▪ The Farmers' Market ▪ Noodles, Grains & Beans ▪ Beef ▪ Pork & Ham ▪ Lamb ▪ Poultry & Game ▪ Fish ▪ Shellfish ▪ Fruit Desserts, Puddings & Pies ▪ Cakes & Cookies ▪ The Big Scoop

■ PREVIOUS CREDITS

Lukins, the food editor of *Parade* magazine, went even further afield with her last book, *Cooking Around the World*.

■ SPECIFICS

606 pages, more than 600 recipes, black-and-white illustrations, $29.95 (hardcover) and $19.95 (paperback). Published by Workman Publishing Company, Inc.

THE POTATO BIN

— ❦ —

This book is full of potatoes, prepared every which way. I use them constantly—most cooks do, and for good reasons. I can't think of another food that is altogether so versatile, filling, delicious, inexpensive, and chock full of vitamins, minerals, and complex carbohydrates as the potato. This humblest of vegetables comes with more history than most, too.

The first potatoes to travel from the Americas to Europe ended their journey at the Vatican in 1588—a gift to the Pope from the Spanish sovereign, via the conqueror Pizarro. The Pope's botanist planted them and drew beautiful pictures of the results, which he called "little truffles" (*taraturfli*). Little did anyone know what effect this curious tuber (which the botanist did not eat) would have on the entire Western world. Within two centuries, it was sustaining millions, from southern Spain to the British Isles. Without it, many would doubtless have starved. After the French Revolution, the Paris Commune declared it Republican and made eating it compulsory. More than a million Irish fled to the United States because of potatoes—the lack of them, in this case. And without those refugees, of course, our story would be a very different one.

Generation after generation, we never tire of potatoes. These days, we can buy many more kinds than our mothers and grandmothers could—dozens of different spuds in a marvelous array of shapes, sizes, and textures. I often spot heirloom varieties at farmers' markets. Though there are far too many kinds to detail here (or for anyone to remember!), some guidelines will help you when you're shopping.

• Starchy potatoes (Idahos or russets) are best for baking or mashing.

• Waxy, low-starch varieties that hold their shape well make the best gratins and non-creamy potato salads. Round Whites and Round Reds work well, as do new (immature) potatoes of any kind. True new potatoes are thin-skinned and highly perishable, available only in spring and early summer.

• Specialty potatoes, such as Bintje, Carole/Carola, Yellow Finn, and Yukon Gold (among others), are golden-hued, low-starch varieties and retain their shape better when cooked. You can roast or steam and slice these; you can also prepare them as you would a baking potato.

• Blue potatoes are showing up in markets more frequently now and are temptingly colorful. I find them bland and mealy, however, with the exception of Peruvian Blues. Try these as homemade potato chips, or toss them together with red-skinned new potatoes to make an eye-catching potato salad.

Store potatoes in a paper bag in a cool, dark spot. Keep them out of the refrigerator; the cold will convert their sugars to starch. If for some reason they have been refrigerated, bring them to room temperature before cooking.

BOARDING HOUSE POTATO SALAD

★ ★ ★

I wish I could say that I just stumbled upon Mrs. Wilkes's Boarding House, but when I was in Savannah, Georgia, I made a beeline for the renowned family-style restaurant, located, as it has been since the 1940s, at 107 West Jones Street at Whitaker. An address is scarcely necessary—just keep an eye out for lines around the block and the seductive aromas emanating from

within—home-fried chicken, greens, baked ham, barbecued pork, and on and on. After all of us sat down at tables and the food was served family-style, for the first time I truly understood the term "boarding house reach."

Mrs. Wilkes's potato salad served as an inspiration for this variation. While at first glance the ingredients may seem a little "old hat," I think of them as tried and true. I know that when I serve this salad, everyone around my table has at least one big helping (usually more), and I happily share the kudos with Mrs. Wilkes. I urge you to get this one cooking for your next family get-together or summertime picnic. The recipe easily doubles to feed a crowd.

4 to 5 russet potatoes (2½ pounds total), peeled and cut into ½-inch dice
Salt
½ cup diced (¼ inch) celery
½ cup diced (¼ inch) red bell pepper
⅓ cup chopped gherkin pickles
2 tablespoons minced red onion
4 hard-cooked eggs, chopped
1 cup mayonnaise
1 teaspoon Dijon mustard
1 tablespoon red wine vinegar
Freshly ground black pepper, to taste

1. Place the potatoes in a saucepan and cover with cold water. Add 1 teaspoon salt. Bring to a boil, reduce the heat slightly, and simmer until tender, about 10 minutes. Drain and transfer to a bowl.

2. Add the celery, bell pepper, gherkins, red onion, and eggs. Toss thoroughly.

3. Combine the mayonnaise, mustard, vinegar, pepper, and salt, to taste, in a small bowl. Blend well, and fold into the potatoes with a large rubber spatula. Cover and refrigerate for 3 to 4 hours, bringing to room temperature to serve.

Serves 6 to 8

★★★★★★★★★★★★★★★★★★★★★★★

DRESSING OR VINAIGRETTE

— ❧ —

Salad dressings can be made with vinegar, but they don't have to be. Sometimes a mayonnaise or lemon juice and olive oil base makes for a nice change of pace. On the other hand, a true vinaigrette, a word we've borrowed from the French, must contain some kind of vinegar. If it doesn't, it isn't a vinaigrette—it's a dressing.

★★★★★★★★★★★★★★★★★★★★★★★

LARRY SMITH'S MOTHER'S PORK CHOPS

★ ★ ★

My good friend and colleague Larry Smith, born and bred in northern Michigan farm country, has long regaled me with tales of his mom's bean soup and her skillet pork chops, which were a once-a-week staple in the Smith family kitchen during his formative years. I think it's the sage and onions that make the chops so memorable. Thanks, Mom, and thanks, Larry, for passing along some really good home cooking! Serve the chops with buttered egg noodles and applesauce.

Wine: Washington State Merlot
Beer: Midwestern pale ale

4 pork loin chops, 1 inch thick
    (about ½ pound each)
Salt and freshly ground black pepper, to taste
1 tablespoon dried sage leaves, crumbled
2 tablespoons olive oil
4 large onions, halved lengthwise and slivered
¼ cup dry white wine
2 tablespoons chopped fresh sage

1. Sprinkle the pork chops on both sides with salt and pepper. Rub well with the dried sage.

2. Heat the olive oil in a large cast-iron skillet over medium-high heat, and brown the pork chops on both sides, 3 to 4 minutes per side. Reduce the heat to low and cook the chops uncovered, turning once, until cooked through, 20 minutes. Transfer the chops to a plate and set aside.

3. Add the onions to the skillet, raise the heat to medium-high, and cook, stirring, until wilted, 10 minutes. Add the wine and cook 5 minutes more, scraping up the browned bits on the bottom of the skillet. Season with salt and

pepper, and stir in the chopped fresh sage. Return the chops to the skillet and bury them in the onions. Cook until warmed through, about 5 minutes. Serve immediately.
Serves 4

SOUR CHERRY LAMB SHANKS

★ ★ ★

The slightly tart flavor of northern Michigan's wonderful dried sour cherries is just the right foil for lamb's richest flavor. The added carrots and tomatoes round out the stew, which I scoop over couscous and serve with plenty of crusty bread to mop up all the delicious juices. When shopping for lamb, be sure to buy the foreshanks (front), not the short (hind) osso buco cut for this dish.

Wine: California Grenache
Beer: Washington State India pale ale

4 lamb foreshanks (about 1 pound each)
1 teaspoon coarsely ground black pepper
Salt, to taste
3 tablespoons olive oil
6 carrots, peeled and cut into ½-inch pieces
1 onion, halved lengthwise and slivered
1 cup defatted chicken broth, preferably
    homemade
1 cup dry white wine
2 tablespoons clover honey
4 cloves garlic, lightly crushed
2 cinnamon sticks (each 3 inches long)
4 fresh sage leaves
Pinch of ground allspice
1 cup chopped seeded ripe plum tomatoes
1½ cups dried sour cherries

¼ cup chopped fresh flat-leaf parsley
Cooked couscous or white rice, for serving

1. Preheat the oven to 350°F.

2. Sprinkle the lamb well with the pepper and salt.

3. Heat 2 tablespoons of the olive oil in an ovenproof pot over medium heat. Add 2 of the shanks and brown them well on all sides, about 8 minutes per side. Transfer the browned shanks to a plate, and repeat with the remaining 2 shanks.

4. Pour off all the fat in the pot and add the remaining 1 tablespoon olive oil. Add the carrots and onion, and cook over medium-low heat, stirring occasionally, until wilted, 10 to 12 minutes.

5. Return the lamb shanks to the pot, along with any accumulated juices. Add the chicken broth, wine, honey, garlic, cinnamon sticks, sage, and allspice. Bring to a boil, cover, and transfer to the oven. Roast until the meat is tender, 1 hour.

6. Add the tomatoes and cherries, and cook uncovered for 45 minutes.

7. Remove the cinammon stick, stir in the parsley, and serve over couscous or rice.

Serves 4

NOTES ON LAMB

— ❧ —

The delicate flavor and succulent tenderness of lamb makes it a favorite for a wide variety of meals, and an ideal choice for just about any preparation. Although all lamb is highly versatile, some cuts lend themselves especially well to certain kinds of cooking.

A butterflied leg or individual chops are great choices for grilling or broiling, and should be served rare to medium. I prefer loin chops for their tender little noisettes. For the most satisfying eating, get the chops cut at least 1 to 1½ inches thick.

A leg of lamb is well suited to roasting and dry oven heat because it is so tender. A roast rack of lamb (rib chops), with long frenched bones capped by paper frills, makes an instant celebratory meal, a perfect choice for any special occasion. Lamb foreshanks are ideal for braising, resulting in a meltingly tender meat when simmered for 1½ to 2 hours. Ground lamb makes great-tasting burgers and can be substituted for beef in chili recipes.

Lamb takes well to a variety of herbs and spices, including rosemary, basil, bay leaves, cinnamon, curry, garlic, oregano, and freshly ground pepper. Rub a mixture of seasonings on the lamb before broiling or roasting, or mix the herbs into ground lamb for redolent patties.

When selecting fresh lamb, look for meat that is pinkish-red. The lighter the color, the lighter-tasting the meat. Choose deeper-hued cuts if you want a more assertive, meatier flavor.

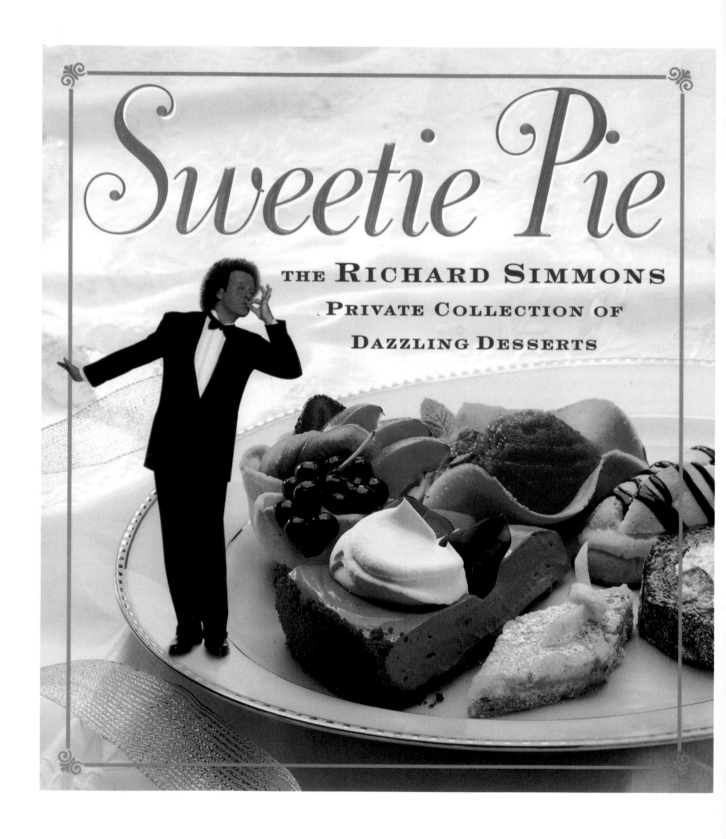

Irrepressible fitness guru Richard Simmons

"After I finished my last book, *Farewell to Fat*, and was traveling around the country making recipes for people and talking about how to lower fat in cooking, I noticed people always wanted to know about desserts. Big surprise, right?"

If you watch late-night talk shows, channel-surf past infomercials, or so much as walk into a bookstore, chances are you'll be seeing Simmons and this book proudly displayed. He's the voice of diet reason to millions, and this dessert volume is bound to appeal to anyone who's ever craved a guilt-free indulgence . . . . as usual, a very large audience indeed.

Smart Cookie ▪ The Cake Walk ▪ Pie in the Sky ▪ The Big Chill ▪ Puddin' on the Ritz ▪ In the Garden of Eden ▪ You Can't Take It with You

FROM THE BOOK

■ DISCOURAGING WORDS
"Repeat after me: Desserts equal fat and sugar, and fat and sugar equal calories. Repeat 10 times."

His last cookbook, *Farewell to Fat*, sold over 600,000 copies.

192 pages, approximately 75 recipes, approximately 125 color photographs, $22. Published by GT Publishing Corporation.

"I'm Late, I'm Late" Carrot Cake

MAKES 9 SERVINGS

PREP: 20 MINUTES

BAKE: AT 350° FOR 40 TO 45 MINUTES

I was one of the late ones to jump on the carrot cake bandwagon. When I first heard of zucchini cake and carrot cake and chocolate-beet cake, I thought, Please—why do we have to put vegetables in a dessert? Let's just leave them on the plate where they're perfectly happy by themselves. But then one afternoon I was walking by a bakery shop on Melrose, and in the window I saw a carrot cake with a creamy white frosting, decorated with little frosting carrots. Okay. Let's see what it's all about, Bugsy. I took a bite, cream cheese frosting and all, and my eyes rolled back in my head and my ears grew long and fuzzy. All I could taste was the delicious natural sweetness from the carrots. I just couldn't believe it! I was converted. In my re-creation here, I don't even add granulated sugar, just a little honey. And— surprise!—I use whole-wheat flour.

Nonstick vegetable-oil cooking spray
3 cups grated carrots (about 9 carrots)
¾ cup all-purpose flour
½ cup whole-wheat flour
1 teaspoon baking soda
1 teaspoon ground cinnamon
½ teaspoon salt
¼ teaspoon ground ginger
Pinch ground cloves
¾ cup honey
¼ cup canola oil
1 large whole egg
2 large egg whites
1 tablespoon fresh lemon juice
⅓ cup dried currants or raisins
Frosting (optional, recipe follows)

1   Preheat oven to 350°. Lightly coat bottom of 8 × 8 × 2-inch square cake pan or 9-inch round layer-cake pan with nonstick cooking spray. Line bottom of pan with waxed paper. Lightly coat paper and sides of pan with nonstick cooking spray.

2   Spread grated carrots between sheets of paper towels and squeeze out excess liquid.

3   In small bowl, stir together both flours, baking soda, cinnamon, salt, ginger, and cloves.

4   In large bowl, with electric mixer on medium speed, beat honey, oil, whole egg, egg whites, and lemon juice, until well blended. By hand, stir in flour mix-

ture, carrots, and currants. Scrape batter into prepared pan, and spread evenly with rubber spatula.

5   Bake in 350° oven until a wooden pick inserted in center of cake comes out clean, 40 to 45 minutes. Cool cake in pan on wire rack for 10 minutes. Turn cake out of pan and cool completely on wire rack. Discard waxed paper.

6   Meanwhile, make frosting, if using, and spread over top of cake. Cut into 9 squares or wedges and serve.

FROSTING

In medium bowl, with electric mixer on medium speed, beat together 4 ounces room-temperature Neufchâtel cream cheese, 2½ tablespoons honey, and 1½ teaspoons pure vanilla extract, until smooth and blended. Cover, and chill until it reaches good spreading consistency.

NUTRIENT VALUE PER SERVING OF MY CAKE, WITHOUT FROSTING

244 calories, 4 g protein, 6 g fat (22% fat; 1 g saturated fat), 44 g carbohydrate, 293 mg sodium, 24 mg cholesterol

WITH FROSTING

296 calories, 5 g protein, 10 g fat (30% fat; 3 g saturated fat), 50 g carbohydrate, 343 mg sodium, 33 mg cholesterol

TRADITIONAL CARROT CAKE WITH FROSTING

650 calories (more than twice the calories), 33 g fat (3⅓ times the fat)

CARROT TOP

Make an additional one-half recipe of frosting. Tint two-thirds orange for carrot decoration, and one-third green for carrot tops. Then spread white frosting over top of cake. Using a pastry bag fitted with a small writing tip, or plastic food-storage bag with ⅛ inch of corner snipped off, pipe on carrots. Then finish with green carrot tops.

Pink Ice Granita

MAKES 6 SERVINGS

PREP: 15 MINUTES, PLUS CHILLING AND FREEZING

Grapefruit are always getting a bum rap. First, there was the broiled grapefruit, looking all wrinkled and tired, in desperate need of a Florida vacation. Then there was the grapefruit diet, where you had to stare at a grapefruit half before each meal. And we all remember when James Cagney pushed a grapefruit half into a woman's face in *Hard to Handle*, 1933. I wanted to take grapefruit to a new plane, so I created this jewel of a dessert.

2 cups fresh grapefruit juice, preferably from ruby red grapefruit (about 2 grapefruit)

¼ cup superfine sugar

2 tablespoons fresh lemon juice

1 Chill 13 × 9 × 2-inch nonaluminum or other nonreactive metal baking pan in freezer, about 30 minutes.

2 In medium bowl, stir together grapefruit juice, sugar, and lemon juice. Refrigerate until very cold.

3 Pour chilled grapefruit mixture into chilled baking pan. Freeze until ice crystals form around edges, about 30 minutes. With a fork, stir edges of ice into rest of mixture to evenly incorporate. Continue to freeze, stirring every 30 minutes, until all the liquid freezes completely, about 3 hours total.

4 Spoon into bowls or hollowed-out orange halves and serve, or scrape into airtight container and store in freezer. If serving from freezer, make sure to let granita soften in refrigerator 20 to 30 minutes so it's not rock hard.

NUTRIENT VALUE PER SERVING OF MY GRANITA

63 calories, 0 g protein, 0 g fat (0% fat; 0 g saturated fat), 16 g carbohydrate, 1 mg sodium, 0 mg cholesterol

ICE CREAM

150 calories (more than 2¼ times the calories), 8 g fat (compared to 0 fat)

is a granita a car?

No, a granita [grah-NEE-ta] is an ice, with absolutely no fat. The French call it a *granité* (grah-nee-TAY) and the Italians, a *granita* (grah-NEE-tah). They're easy to make. Just mix together water, sugar, and a flavoring, and freeze it. To serve, get out your castanets.

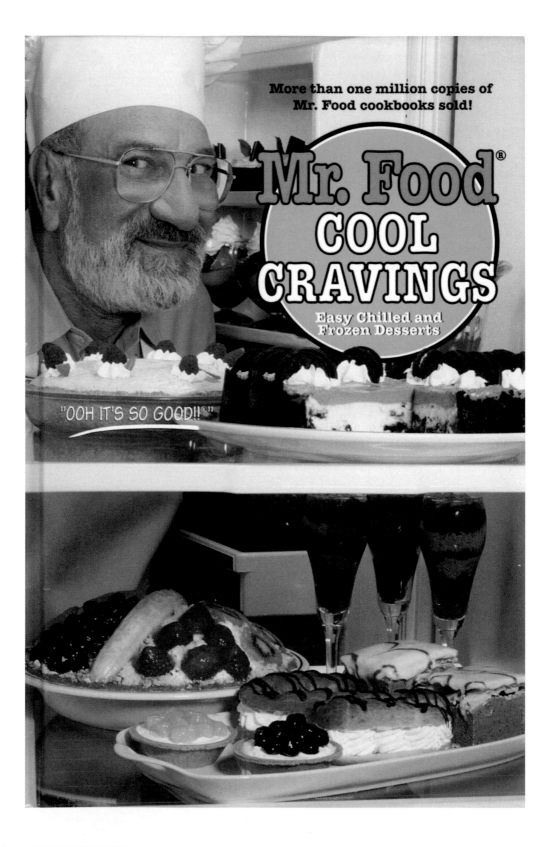

More than one million copies of Mr. Food cookbooks sold!

Mr. Food®
COOL
CRAVINGS
Easy Chilled and
Frozen Desserts

"OOH IT'S SO GOOD!!®"

■ AUTHOR
Art Ginsburg, better known as "Mr. Food®"

"How many times have the kids come home from school, opened the refrigerator, and just stood there looking for something to jump out at them and say, 'Here I am! I'm what you feel like eating!' And how 'bout all those times when, after about an hour or so of sitting in front of the TV, you go to the freezer to see what's in there that can satisfy your desire for something cool and sweet . . . . I guess you're not surprised to find out that a lot of us share this 'gotta have something sweet *now*!' feeling. That's why I want you to have these prescriptions . . . I mean recipes . . . that are guaranteed to do the trick!"

FROM THE BOOK

■ WORDS OF WARNING
"We can make the best-tasting desserts, but if they're not wrapped and stored properly, all the good taste can be overtaken by a stale taste from our refrigerator or freezer . . . not to mention the fact that our frozen goodies can become freezer-burned! Yuck!"

■ WHY IT MADE OUR LIST
With twenty-two books under his belt and more than one million volumes sold, "Mr. Food®" is not to be overlooked. Fans of his syndicated spots and QVC appearances will undoubtedly be craving this latest collection featuring cold goodies, from cakes and pies to banana-split bombes. The recipes are super-simple and many of the ingredients pre-packaged, but when you're sticking your head in the refrigerator looking for something swift and sweet, sometimes that's just what will do it for you.

■ CHAPTERS
Trifles and Parfaits ▪ Puddings and Gelatins ▪ Fruit ▪ Cakes ▪ Cheesecakes ▪ Pies ▪ Frozen Desserts ▪ Frozen Novelties ▪ Scoopable Delights ▪ Cool Creations ▪ Sauces and Toppings ▪ Treats by the Calendar

■ PREVIOUS CREDITS
Ginsburg's "Mr. Food®" books include *One Pot, One Meal*; *Simply Chocolate*; and *Pizza 1-2-3*.

■ SPECIFICS
208 pages, approximately 156 recipes, illustrated, $11.95. Published by William Morrow and Company, Inc.

Frozen Fruit Salad

8 to 10 servings

A refreshing anytime treat, icy-cool fruit salad always goes down easy. And done this way . . . a masterpiece!

1 cup sour cream
1 cup frozen whipped topping,
   thawed
¼ cup sugar
1 teaspoon vanilla extract
1 can (20 ounces) crushed pineapple,
   drained and squeezed dry

1 can (16½ ounces) dark sweet
   cherries, quartered and
   well drained (see Note)
2 medium-sized bananas, cut into
   ¼-inch-thick slices
½ cup chopped walnuts

In a medium-sized bowl, combine the sour cream, whipped topping, sugar, and vanilla. Gently fold in the pineapple, cherries, bananas, and walnuts. Line a 9" × 5" loaf pan with plastic wrap, making sure the plastic wrap extends over the edges. Spoon the fruit mixture into the loaf pan, cover, and freeze overnight. When ready to serve, invert the loaf onto a serving plate and remove the plastic wrap, then slice.

NOTE: After draining the cherries, place them on paper towels until the excess liquid is absorbed.

Chocolate Malted Pops

8 pops

No straws and no blender are needed for this malted. It takes just a few quick strokes, then we pop them in the freezer for solid refreshment.

1 quart vanilla ice cream, softened
¼ cup chocolate malted milk powder
   (see Note)

Eight 5-ounce paper cups
8 nontoxic wooden craft sticks

In a large bowl, combine the ice cream and malted milk powder; stir until well combined. Divide the mixture evenly among the paper cups, then place a wooden stick in the center of each cup. Place in the freezer for at least 3 hours, or until firm. Serve, or wrap each in plastic wrap and keep frozen until ready to serve.

NOTE: Malted milk powder can usually be found next to the cocoa and other drink mixes in the supermarket.

Chapter 4

Vegetarian and Healthy Cooking

A few years ago, the healthy category alone would have been the most crowded in this book. Now, as medical research veers in a different direction, the fervor for low-fat seems, mercifully, to have subsided, and the rush of cookbooks capitalizing on the public zeal has slowed dramatically. On the other hand, more vegetarian cookbooks are on the market than ever before, signaling a clear interest in upping vegetable intake, right in keeping with the latest eating dictums. We've chosen the very best of the batch.

■ **VEGETARIAN COOKING FOR EVERYONE** BY DEBORAH MADISON

Vivid Parsley and Pea Risotto **203**

Spring Vegetable Stew **206**

Winter Citrus Compote in Tangerine Syrup **207**

■ **MOLLIE KATZEN'S VEGETABLE HEAVEN: Over 200 Recipes for Uncommon Soups, Tasty Bites, Side-by-Side Dishes, and Too Many Desserts** BY MOLLIE KATZEN

Jamaican Salsa Salad **210**

Green Salad with Blue Cheese, Walnuts, and Figs **211**

Tunisian Tomato Soup with Chickpeas and Lentils **212**

Santa Fe Stew **214**

■ **THE CHINESE WAY: Healthy Low-Fat Cooking from China's Regions** BY EILEEN YIN-FEI LO

Hot and Sour Soup **218**

Steamed Eggplant with Garlic Sauce **219**

Stir-Fried Sichuan Pork **220**

■ **MARTHA STEWART'S HEALTHY QUICK COOK: *Four Seasons of Great Menus to Make Every Day*** BY MARTHA STEWART

Rustic Gruyère Croutons **229**

Seven-Onion Soup **229**

Curly Endive with Citrus Vinaigrette **229**

Prunes Poached in Armagnac with Enlightened Crème Fraîche **230**

The 1,400 recipes in this book are those that I like to cook. If you're a committed vegetarian, you can prepare every recipe in this book. If you are a vegan, you can cook most of them. If you don't attach a title to your eating style, you can cook everything in this book and serve it with meat, fish, or fowl. This is

Vegetarian Cooking for Everyone

DEBORAH MADISON

AUTHOR OF *THE GREENS COOKBOOK*

Deborah Madison, one of America's most respected vegetarian chefs

■ **WHY SHE WROTE IT**
". . . I know that many vegetarians are reluctant to buy cookbooks centered around meat, as so many are. If they go just to the vegetable section, they're likely to feel that too little of the book pertains to their needs and the slim part that does, fails to answer their basic questions about what's what in the kitchen . . . . What I wanted to write was a compendium of basic information along with a wide range of recipes for those who want to learn to cook well without meat. And this is what this book is meant to be."

■ **WHY IT MADE OUR LIST**
Simple recipes with manageable ingredient lists (not always a hallmark of this writer) and plenty of how-to information make this book a winner. The longest chapter, "Vegetables: The Heart of the Matter," is a mini-cookbook in itself, an A-to-Z guide to vegetable cookery. You don't have to be a vegetarian to want this book—Madison invites you to serve the dishes with meat, chicken, or fish if you wish—but it's a godsend particularly for those intent on meatless meals.

> **FROM THE BOOK**
>
> ■ **A WORD ON FAT**
> *"A highly refined, tasteless oil has the same number of calories and fat grams as a rich-tasting roasted peanut oil, a redolent nut oil, a fruity olive oil, or the sweetest butter. The true flavor of good oil or butter satisfies in a way that tasteless foods don't, and in smaller amounts."*

■ **CHAPTERS**
Becoming a Cook ▪ Foundations of Flavor: Seasonings in the Kitchen ▪ Sauces and Condiments ▪ Greetings from the Cook: Appetizers and First Courses ▪ Sandwiches: A Casual Thing ▪ Salads for All Seasons ▪ Soups from Scratch ▪ Vegetable Stews and Stir-Fries ▪ Gratins and Casseroles: Hearty Dishes for All Seasons ▪ Beans Plain and Fancy ▪ Vegetables: The Heart of the Matter ▪ Pasta, Noodles, and Dumplings ▪ Savory Tarts, Pies, Turnovers, and Pizzas ▪ Grains: Kernels and Seeds of Life ▪ Eggs and Cheese ▪ The Soy Pantry ▪ Breakfast Anytime ▪ Breads by Hand ▪ Desserts: Ending on a Sweet Note

■ **PREVIOUS CREDITS**
The founding chef of San Francisco's Greens restaurant, Madison is the author of *The Savory Way* and *The Greens Cookbook*.

■ **SPECIFICS**
742 pages, 1,400 recipes, 24 color photos plus line drawings, $40. Published by Broadway Books.

Peas

PRECIOUS and fleeting, peas occupy a tiny window in time in late spring and early summer. The minute heat sets in they're finished, but until then they are one of the most delectable treats in the vegetable world. Little need be done except to cook them as soon as you can. Unlike today's corn, their sugars quickly turn to starch once picked.

TYPES OF PEAS:

GOOD PARTNERS FOR
PEAS
*Butter, dark sesame and
   roasted peanut oils
Dill, chives, chervil,
   parsley, basil, mint,
   ginger, garlic
Shallots, onions,
   asparagus, turnips, fava
   beans, scallions*

Pod Peas: Also called *English peas* or *shelling peas*, these are the old-fashioned peas that are shucked from their pods. If they're not starchy, they can be eaten raw.

Snow Peas: Eaten whole, these are the flat, pale green pods sometimes called *Chinese peas*. The peas themselves are barely formed; the pods are tender.

Sugar Snap Peas: A newer variety, these are plump-podded peas that resemble shelling peas, but the pods themselves are sweet, tender, and crisp. They're cooked and eaten whole.

Pea Shoots: Found in Asian markets, these tender vines can be sautéed or stir-fried and eaten right along with the peas.

Winged Peas: Also called *winged beans* or *asparagus peas*, these are another vegetable altogether, but they resemble a small sugar snap pea—with wings. They should be small, no more than 1/2 inch thick. Cook them as you would peas or green beans.

WHAT TO LOOK FOR: Bright green color and a crisp, fresh look is what you want in all peas. Yellowing tells you that they've begun to turn starchy. If you can, bite into one raw to make sure it's tender. While scars may detract from a pea's visual perfection, they usually disappear when cooked.

HOW TO STORE: If you must store them, keep them in a plastic bag in the refrigerator, but try to use them as soon as you can.

HOW TO USE: Peas can be steamed, boiled, stir-fried, made into soups, and tossed shelled and uncooked into salads and pastas. They are so special and their season is so brief that they beg for simple treatments.

SPECIAL HANDLING: Strings should be removed from pods. With a paring knife, cut into the stem end, lift the string that binds the pea like a zipper, and pull down to the blossom end. Turn and pull out the second string on the other side. Very small peas needn't be strung.

QUANTITY: Allow 1 pound pod peas for 1 cup shelled, serving two or three. For edible-pod peas, 1 pound should serve four.

Vivid Parsley and Pea Risotto

2 large bunches parsley, preferably flat-leaf

Salt and freshly milled white pepper

4 to 5 lovage leaves

4 1/2 to 5 cups vegetable stock or water

2 tablespoons butter

1/3 cup diced onion or leek

1 1/2 cups Arborio rice

1/2 cup dry white wine

1 1/2 cups fresh or frozen peas

1/2 cup cream or mascarpone, optional

1/2 cup freshly grated Parmesan

THESE ingredients are so simple, yet the overall effect is stunningly green and fresh tasting. The parsley sauce can be made a day ahead. I always add four or five lovage leaves for their unusual, beguiling flavor.

SERVES 4

With a sharp knife, shave off most of the parsley leaves. Using your fingers, break off the larger stems and use them in the vegetable stock. Measure 3 cups leaves, well packed but not crammed.

Bring 1 1/2 cups water to a boil. Add 1/4 teaspoon salt, the parsley, and the lovage. Boil for 1 minute. Turn off the heat, let stand for 5 minutes, then puree in a blender at high speed until smooth. Taste for salt and season with pepper.

Have the stock simmering on the stove. If the parsley sauce has been refrigerated, bring it to a boil, then turn off the heat.

Melt the butter in a wide pot. Add the onion and cook over medium heat until softened, 3 to 4 minutes. Add the rice and cook, stirring frequently for 1 minute, then pour in the wine and simmer until it's absorbed. Add 2 cups stock, cover, and simmer, stirring occasionally until it's absorbed. Begin adding the remaining stock in 1/2-cup increments, stirring constantly until each addition is absorbed before adding the next. When all has been absorbed and the rice is very nearly done, add the parsley sauce. Raise the heat and cook briskly while stirring until the rice is done and most of the sauce has been absorbed. Add the peas and cream. Taste for salt and season with pepper. Turn off the heat and stir in half the cheese. Serve dusted with the remaining cheese.

Winter Citrus Compote in Tangerine Syrup *page 207*

FACING PAGE: Spring Vegetable Stew *page 206*

Spring Vegetable Stew

COOKING the vegetables separately, then combining them, makes it possible to have everything ready in advance. Radishes and broccoli stems may be surprising, but they really give this dish an exceedingly fresh spring look.

While popovers or fresh herb noodles are good accompaniments, I sometimes add some potato gnocchi or cheese tortellini at the end for a soft, surprising mouthful.

SERVES 4

Salt and freshly milled pepper

12 baby carrots, or 2 carrots, peeled and thinly sliced

½ cup snow peas

6 radishes, including ½ inch of the stems, halved

18 3-inch asparagus tips

6 scallions, including the stems, cut into 3-inch lengths

2 broccoli stems, thickly peeled and sliced diagonally

4 small turnips, or 2 rutabagas and 2 turnips, peeled and cut into sixths

4 tablespoons butter

4 thyme sprigs, preferably lemon thyme

1 tablespoon fresh lemon juice

10 sorrel leaves, sliced into ribbons, optional

1 tablespoon snipped chives

2 teaspoons finely chopped parsley

1 teaspoon chopped tarragon

Bring 3 quarts water to a boil and add 1 tablespoon salt. One type at a time, blanch the vegetables until barely tender, then remove to a bowl of cold water to stop the cooking. When all are blanched, reserve 1 cup of the cooking water. Drain the vegetables. (This can be done ahead of time.)

In a wide skillet, melt the butter with the thyme sprigs and reserved liquid. Add the vegetables and simmer until they're warmed through. Add the lemon juice and season with salt and pepper. Add the sorrel and herbs and cook for 1 minute more. Serve at once.

Blanching

Sometimes it's preferable to cook some of the ingredients separately to preserve their fresh color and texture. Blanching one or more vegetables gives you some control over how your final dish will look since they're cooked separately, then added at the last minute. But don't be afraid to allow at least some of the vegetables to soften—that's often when they taste best. One of the best vegetable braises I've ever eaten was in a Roman restaurant one spring. Asparagus, peas, and fava beans were cooked to nearly a jamlike consistency. By American standards the dish was impossibly overcooked, but it was over the top in terms of sheer flavor.

With practice you'll be able to judge how long individual vegetables take to cook when added to the stew. Start with those that take the longest cooking time and proceed with those that take the shortest time, ensuring that everything will be cooked perfectly at the end.

Winter Citrus Compote in Tangerine Syrup

¾ cup fresh tangerine juice or a mixture of tangerine and orange juices

3 tablespoons sugar

6 large kumquats, sliced into rounds

2 tablespoons zest removed from any of the citrus below

1 teaspoon orange flower water

3 small pink grapefruit

3 navel oranges or tangelos

3 blood oranges

3 tangelos, Honeybells, or other citrus

Sprigs of mint leaves

THIS cheerful-looking compote makes a perfect end to a winter meal or beginning to a festive brunch. You can be very extravagant and use every conceivable variety of citrus fruit or just a few kinds. Following are some suggestions— improvise with what you have. Some special fruits to keep your eye out for are small pink Texas grapefruit, blood oranges, Honeybells, Satsumas, and kumquats.

SERVES 6

Bring the juice and sugar to a boil in a small saucepan. Add the kumquats and zest, then lower the heat and simmer for 10 minutes. Stir in the orange flower water and set aside.

Peel the grapefruit, oranges, and tangelos. If the grapefruits are small ones, slice them into rounds; otherwise section them. Slice the remaining fruits into rounds about ⅓ inch wide. Place the fruit and juices in a serving bowl or deep platter. Pour the syrup with the kumquats and zest over the fruit and chill until ready to serve. Serve garnished with sprigs of mint.

> *Variations:* Other fruits happily complement citrus and add to the luster of this dish. Add thinly sliced small star fruits or kiwifruit, or drizzle the contents, seeds and all, of one or two passion fruits over the compote.

Compotes and Poached Fruits

Mixtures of fruits sweetened and suspended in syrups, compotes are one of the best ways of presenting both perfect fruit and those that don't have quite the flavor or sweetness to stand on their own. Compotes provide us with desserts that avoid added crusts, fillings, and creams. Just a spoonful of crème fraîche or whipped cream sets off the fruit beautifully. Most compotes are best chilled, accompanied, if at all, with a simple cookie or a slice of cake. Leftovers are wonderful for breakfast or brunch.

Many compotes leave a residue of tinted fruit-flavored syrup. It keeps more or less indefinitely, refrigerated, and can be used to sweeten iced tea, mixed with club soda or champagne, or spooned around a scoop of vanilla ice cream or yogurt.

Mollie Katzen's
VEGETABLE
HEAVEN

*Over 200 recipes for uncommon soups, tasty bites,
side-by-side dishes, and too many desserts
by the celebrated author of*
Moosewood Cookbook, The Enchanted Broccoli Forest,
and Still Life with Menu

Features
recipes from
*Mollie Katzen's
Cooking Show:
Vegetable Heaven*
on Public
Television

Celebrated vegetarian and *Moosewood Cookbook* author Mollie Katzen

■ **WHY SHE WROTE IT**

As a companion to her PBS cooking series, *Mollie Katzen's Cooking Show: Vegetable Heaven.*

■ **WHY IT MADE OUR LIST**

Even vegetarians have lightened their food. The heavy, complicated recipes that filled *The Moosewood Cookbook* twenty years ago have given way in Katzen's latest collection to simpler, often boldly seasoned dishes that keep the number of ingredients to a minimum. Instead of a big stodgy main dish with side dishes, she recommends two or three smallish "side-by-side" dishes to make a meal. Katzen's relaxed, engaging style and light-hearted paintings of vegetables add to the pleasure of using the book.

■ **CHAPTERS**

Openers, Cleansers, and Sparklers: Appetizers and Salads ▪ Uncommon Everyday Soups ▪ A Dozen Tasty Bites ▪ Side-by-Side Dishes: Beans, Grains, and Vegetables ▪ Tidy Little Main Dishes: Lunch, Brunch, and Supper ▪ On Top of Spaghetti: Pastas for Real Life ▪ Never a Bland Moment: Condiments and Sauces ▪ Too Many Desserts

■ **PREVIOUS CREDITS**

Among Katzen's other odes to vegetables are *The Enchanted Broccoli Forest* and *Still Life with Menu.*

■ **SPECIFICS**

224 pages, more than 200 recipes, 55 color paintings, $27.50. Published by Hyperion.

FROM THE BOOK

■ **RECENT HISTORY LESSON**

"Sometime during the 1980s, unusual ingredients and unconventional combinations became an obsession for many young chefs . . . . (A friend of a friend from New York returned from a much-hyped California restaurant complaining about her meal there, Pasta with Salami and Peaches. When asked why she had ordered it, she explained that it had been the simplest dish on the menu.)"

JAMAICAN SALSA SALAD

It looks like a colorful, chunky guacamole at first glance, but you'll know it's something far more interesting and exotic as soon as it hits your mouth.

½ cup minced red onion

6 tablespoons fresh lime juice

1 to 2 small serrano chiles (2½ inches long), seeded and very finely minced

4 small, ripe avocados, peeled and diced (save the pits)

1 ripe mango, cut into small dice

1½ cups minced fresh pineapple

1½ cups minced jicama

2 teaspoons minced garlic

½ to ¾ teaspoon salt

3 tablespoons minced fresh cilantro

3 tablespoons minced fresh mint

½ teaspoon ground cumin

Put up about a quart of water to boil. Meanwhile, place the onion in a strainer or colander over a large bowl or in the sink. Pour the boiling water over the onion and let it stand while you prepare the other ingredients. (This slightly cooks the onion, softening its sharp edge.)

Combine the lime juice and minced chiles in a medium-sized bowl. Add the avocados, mango, pineapple, jicama, garlic, salt, herbs, and cumin, along with the onion. Mix everything together gently but thoroughly.

Place the avocado pits in the salad. (This helps the avocados retain their gorgeous color.) Cover tightly, and chill for about 2 hours. Remove the pits before serving.

Yield: 6 cups
Preparation time: 20 to 25 minutes, plus time to chill

⋆ Serve this as you would either a salsa or a salad. Scoop it up with chips before a summer meal, or use it as a terrific sandwich filling.

⋆ Jamaican Salsa Salad is also a perfect addition to a dinner of plain beans and rice.

⋆ This tastes best soon after it is made. It doesn't keep very well beyond the first day.

⋆ If you don't have access to fresh chiles, substitute red pepper flakes to taste.

GREEN SALAD

WITH BLUE CHEESE, WALNUTS, AND FIGS

Fresh figs are sublime, but dried figs are quite delicious as well. You can successfully make this rich-tasting salad with either kind any time of year.

Place the greens in a large bowl. Drizzle in the oil, sprinkle in the salt, and toss until well coated.

Add the figs, blue cheese, and walnuts, and toss gently but thoroughly. Grind in some black pepper.

Serve immediately, and pass a dish of lemon wedges for squeezing over the top of each serving.

Yield: 4 to 6 servings
Preparation time: 10 minutes

½ pound fresh salad greens, cleaned, dried, and chilled

3 to 4 tablespoons walnut oil

A scant ¼ teaspoon salt

4 ripe fresh figs (or 4 to 6 dried figs), sliced

¼ cup crumbled blue cheese

¼ cup minced walnuts, lightly toasted

Freshly ground black pepper

2 lemons, cut into squeezable wedges

⭐ *Some walnut oils are far more flavorful than others. I find the imported French brands to have the deepest, toastiest flavor. Experiment around to find a good walnut oil, and keep it refrigerated so you can use it over time. (A little bit goes a long way.)*

⭐ *If you don't have walnut oil on hand, go ahead and make this salad with extra virgin olive oil. It will still taste fine.*

TUNISIAN TOMATO SOUP
WITH CHICKPEAS AND LENTILS

- I cup uncooked chickpeas, soaked overnight (or I to 2 15-ounce cans chickpeas)
- I cup uncooked lentils (any kind), rinsed and picked over
- I cinnamon stick
- 2 tablespoons olive oil
- 4 cups minced onion
- 2 tablespoons minced garlic
- 2 teaspoons salt
- I teaspoon turmeric
- 1½ teaspoons cumin seeds
- 2 teaspoons ground cumin
- 2 to 3 bay leaves
- I 28-ounce can crushed tomatoes
- Black pepper and cayenne to taste
- 3 tablespoons fresh lemon juice (or to taste)

OPTIONAL TOPPINGS:

- Yogurt
- Minced fresh parsley or mint
- A few currants

⭐ *Streamline the preparation time by chopping the onions, mincing the garlic, and sautéing them with the seasonings while the legumes cook.*

⭐ *This soup freezes well if stored in an airtight container.*

It seems like an ordinary list of ingredients, but when they are combined in this very satisfying soup, the flavors transcend the sum of their parts.

Place the soaked, uncooked chickpeas in a large pot and cover with water by 3 inches. Bring to a boil, lower heat to a simmer, partially cover, and cook for 1 hour. (If you're using canned chickpeas, rinse and drain them, and set them aside.)

Add the lentils and cinnamon stick, partially cover again, and cook for another 30 minutes, or until the chickpeas and lentils are perfectly tender, but not mushy. (If you're using canned chickpeas, just cook the lentils with the cinnamon stick in 7 cups water until tender—about 30 minutes.) Remove and discard the cinnamon stick, and drain the legumes, saving the water, if any is left.

Meanwhile, heat the oil in a soup pot or Dutch oven. Add the onion, garlic, salt, turmeric, cumin seeds, ground cumin, and bay leaves, and sauté over medium heat for 5 to 8 minutes, or until the onions are soft.

Add 6 cups of water (including the reserved cooking water from the lentils, if any) and the tomatoes, and bring to a boil. Lower the heat to a simmer, partially cover, and cook for another 15 minutes or so. (The timing does not need to be exact.) Fish out and discard the bay leaves.

Stir in the chickpeas and lentils, and cook for only about 5 minutes longer, so the legumes won't become mushy. Season to taste with black pepper, cayenne, and lemon juice.

Serve hot, topped with some yogurt, a sprinkling of parsley or mint, and currants, if desired.

Yield: 6 servings (maybe a little more)
Preparation time: About 80 minutes with dried chickpeas; 50 minutes with canned chickpeas (25 minutes of work either way)

SANTA FE STEW

Brimming with more spunk than you can shake a stick at, this great stew goes well with warmed corn tortillas (the thick kind, if possible). You probably won't want anything else.

2 tablespoons olive oil

3 cups chopped onion

2 teaspoons salt

2 teaspoons cumin seeds

1/2 teaspoon cinnamon

4 to 5 tablespoons garlic, minced

2 medium-sized Anaheim chiles, minced

2 medium-sized poblano chiles, minced

2 tablespoons chile powder

2 cups water

1 medium-sized (2-pound) butternut squash, peeled, seeded, and chopped (about 5 cups)

4 to 5 tablespoons lime juice (possibly more, to taste)

1 1/2 to 3 cups cooked pinto beans (1 or 2 15-ounce cans, rinsed and drained)

OPTIONAL TOPPINGS:

Sour cream or Chipotle Cream (opposite page)

Lightly toasted pepitas (aka pumpkin seeds)

Minced fresh cilantro and/or parsley

✷ *You can make this more or less "beany" by adding anywhere from 1/2 to 3 cups of cooked beans (1 or 2 15-ounce cans).*

✷ *This recipe calls for a combination of fresh Anaheim and poblano chiles. If you can't find these, substitute 2 bell peppers and a 7-ounce can of diced green chiles.*

Heat the oil in a large, deep skillet or Dutch oven. Add the onion, 1 teaspoon of the salt, cumin, and cinnamon. Cook over very low heat until the onion is soft (about 10 minutes), stirring frequently.

Stir in the garlic, chiles, and chile powder. Cover, and cook for about 5 minutes over medium-low heat, stirring occasionally. Add the water, cover, and cook another 15 minutes.

Stir in the squash, the remaining teaspoon of salt, and the lime juice. Cover, and cook over low heat for 15 minutes longer, or until the squash is perfectly tender, but not mushy.

Gently stir in the beans, cover, and cook for only about 5 more minutes. Taste to see if it needs more lime juice.

Serve hot, topped with a little sour cream or Chipotle Cream, a generous sprinkling of lightly toasted pepitas, and a little bit of minced cilantro or parsley, if desired.

Yield: 4 to 6 servings
Preparation time: 1 hour (15 minutes of work)

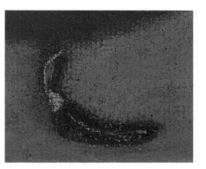

CHIPOTLE CREAM

Chipotle chiles are smoked dried jalapeños. They most commonly come in cans, packed in a tomato-vinegar preparation called adobo sauce. A little bit of canned chipotles-in-adobo goes a very long way, both in terms of heat and powerful smoky essence. In this sauce, sour cream and/or yogurt create a soothing, luxurious vehicle for the wild chipotle flavor.

Place the sour cream and/or yogurt in a small bowl and whisk until smooth.

Whisk in ½ teaspoon minced chipotle chiles, and let it sit for about 10 minutes, so the flavor can develop. Taste to see if it needs more chipotles, and adjust, as desired.

Store in a tightly covered container in the refrigerator. Bring to room temperature before serving.

Yield: 1 cup
Preparation time: 5 minutes

1 cup sour cream or yogurt
  (or a combination)
½ to 1 teaspoon canned chipotle
  chiles, finely minced

....

Serve this wherever it seems appropriate—on any egg dish, with beans, rice, or cornmeal preparations, or drizzled onto soups.

After you open the can of chiles and take out what you need, store the remainder in a tightly lidded jar. They will last indefinitely.

THE CHINESE WAY

Healthy Low-fat Cooking from China's Regions

Eileen Yin-Fei Lo

Eileen Yin-Fei Lo, authority on Chinese cooking

"All of us have been subjected in recent times to low-fat recipe books that mask blandness with presentation, and substitute parades of spices for true and natural flavors . . . . In this book I am bringing balance and flavor to foods so that you who follow the recipes, cook the foods, and eat them will be happy and satisfied."

FROM THE BOOK

■ CULINARY OBSERVATION

"Let me make the point first that Chinese low-fat cooking is virtually redundant; proper Chinese cooking, that is. In those corner neighborhood Chinese restaurants with which most Westerners have grown up, there has always been an extensive use of fats and heavy oils. This is not proper Chinese cooking."

■ WHY IT MADE OUR LIST

With its authentic Chinese recipes (many of them for home-style dishes not found on restaurant menus), time-honored techniques, and irresistible flavors, this is like no "diet book" we've ever seen. It will be as interesting to those who admire the Chinese way of steaming, stir-frying, and blanching as to those who watch their waistlines. The latter, however, should take heart from the experience of Lo's husband, Fred, who lost over fifty pounds while taste-testing the recipes she was developing—and has kept them off.

■ CHAPTERS

My Special Preparations ▪ Rice and Noodles ▪ Foods from the Water ▪ The Versatile Chicken and Other Poultry ▪ Foods from the Land ▪ To Confucius Meat Was Pork ▪ Soups, Glorious Soups ▪ Tong Soi and Other Sweets

■ PREVIOUS CREDITS

From the Earth: Chinese Vegetarian Cooking is the most recent of Lo's several earlier books.

■ SPECIFICS

326 pages, 200 recipes, illustrated, $24.95. Published by Macmillan.

酸辣湯 Hot and Sour Soup

Seun Lot Tong

Is there a more familiar soup than this in the Chinese kitchen? I suppose not. It would be difficult to find anyone who does not know about, or has not tasted, some version of this soup with its origins in China's north and west. This version uses no oil in the preparation, and the flavor remains absolutely true to the soup's tradition.

5 cups Chicken Stock (page 221)

1 slice ginger, ½ inch thick, lightly smashed

40 tiger lily buds, soaked in hot water 30 minutes, washed, hard ends removed, cut in half

2 tablespoons cloud ears, soaked in hot water 30 minutes, washed three times to remove grit

½ cup bamboo shoots, julienned

¼ teaspoon salt

1½ teaspoons Hot Pepper Flakes (page 224)

3 tablespoons red wine vinegar

4 ounces lean pork loin, shredded

3 tablespoons cornstarch mixed with 3 tablespoons cold water

2 large eggs, beaten

1½ teaspoons dark soy sauce

2 cakes fresh bean curd (8 ounces), cut into ⅓-inch strips

2 tablespoons finely sliced scallion greens

Yield:
6 servings

1. In a large pot place stock, ginger, tiger lily buds, cloud ears, bamboo shoots, and salt. Cover pot and bring to a boil over high heat. Lower heat and simmer for 10 minutes. Add Hot Pepper Flakes and vinegar and stir in. Turn heat back to high and return soup to a boil. Boil for 2 minutes. Add pork, stir and cook for 2 minutes more.

2. Stir cornstarch mixture and pour into soup, stirring to combine thoroughly. Add beaten eggs in the same manner. Add soy sauce and mix well. Add bean curd strips, stir and bring soup back to a boil. Turn off heat, transfer to a heated tureen, sprinkle with sliced scallions, and serve. (If you wish soup to be hotter, you may add another ½ teaspoon of Hot Pepper Flakes before transferring to tureen.)

Nutrition per serving: 173 Calories; 5.5g Fat; 27% calories from fat; 2.5g Carbohydrates; 87mg Cholesterol; 361mg Sodium.

Steamed Eggplant with Garlic Sauce

Sun Yung Ai Guah

This dish has its roots in Sichuan and Hunan. As it is customarily prepared, the eggplant is deep-fried, then stir-fried. I have lessened the fat content considerably by steaming the eggplant instead. However, the flavors remain defined and intense.

I pound eggplant, peeled and sliced lengthwise into ½-inch strips

SAUCE

I tablespoon dark soy sauce

½ teaspoon Hot Pepper Flakes (page 224)

2 teaspoons sugar

2 teaspoons oyster sauce

I teaspoon white vinegar

¼ teaspoon salt

I teaspoon cornstarch mixed with I tablespoon Vegetable Stock (page 222)

½ teaspoon Shao-Hsing wine or sherry

TO COMPLETE THE DISH

I½ teaspoons peanut oil

2 teaspoons minced garlic

I½ tablespoons Vegetable Stock (page 222)

Yield:
4 servings

1. Lay strips of eggplant in a steam-proof dish. Steam for 12 to 15 minutes until very soft. Turn off heat. Remove from steamer and reserve.

2. Combine sauce ingredients and reserve.

3. Heat wok over high heat for 30 seconds. Add peanut oil to coat wok. When a wisp of white smoke appears, add garlic, stir until garlic turns light brown, about 10 seconds. Add eggplant and mix well. Add stock and stir to mix, cooking until eggplant begins to come apart. Make a well in the mixture, stir sauce, pour in. Cook and mix until sauce begins to bubble. Turn off heat, transfer to a heated dish, and serve.

Nutrition per serving: 58 Calories; 1.5g Fat; 23% calories from fat; 9g Carbohydrates; 0mg Cholesterol; 440mg Sodium.

Stir-Fried Sichuan Pork

Sei Cheun Chau Yuk See

There is a mistaken belief that all Sichuan cooking is excessively oily. It is true that a good deal of oil is used, and that some dishes are quite high in oil, but the key word is some. *It is possible to maintain true Sichuan tastes by blanching in water instead of in oil.*

¾ cup Chicken Stock (opposite page)

8 ounces lean pork loin, julienned

I small carrot, julienned

SAUCE

½ teaspoon Hot Pepper Flakes (page 224)

I teaspoon soy sauce

2 teaspoons oyster sauce

¾ teaspoon sugar

2 teaspoons Shao-Hsing wine or sherry

⅛ teaspoon salt

Pinch white pepper

2 teaspoons cornstarch

¼ cup Chicken Stock (opposite page)

TO COMPLETE THE DISH

2 teaspoons Garlic Oil (page 223)

I teaspoon minced ginger

I teaspoon minced garlic

½ medium red bell pepper, julienned

½ medium green bell pepper, julienned

3 scallions, trimmed, cut into 2-inch lengths, white portions quartered
    lengthwise

¼ cup bamboo shoots, julienned

I. Heat wok over high heat. Add stock, bring to a boil. Add pork and carrot, stir to separate. Cook for 30 to 40 seconds, or until pork turns white. Turn off heat, remove pork and carrot, reserve. Remove poaching stock from wok, reserve.

2. Combine the sauce ingredients. Reserve.

3. Wipe off wok and spatula. Heat wok over high heat for 30 seconds, add Garlic Oil and coat wok. When a wisp of white smoke appears, add ginger and garlic, stir briefly. Add peppers, scallions, and bamboo shoots and stir-fry together for 1 minute. Add 2 tablespoons of poaching stock and stir-fry for 1 more minute. Add pork and carrot, stir together thoroughly, for 1 more minute until very hot. Make a well in the mixture, stir sauce, pour in. Mix well. When sauce begins to bubble, turn off heat, transfer to a heated dish, and serve.

Nutrition per serving: 163 Calories; 5.5g Fat; 28% calories from fat; 2.5g Carbohydrates; 37mg Cholesterol; 202mg Sodium.

鶏
上
湯 Chicken Stock

2 whole chickens (8 pounds), fat removed, washed, also wash giblets. Cut each chicken into 4 pieces

10 cups water

4½ quarts cold water

¼ pound fresh ginger, cut into thirds, lightly smashed

6 whole garlic cloves, peeled

1 bunch scallions, trimmed, washed, cut into thirds

4 medium onions, quartered

¼ pound coriander, cut into thirds (1 cup)

½ cup Fried Scallions (page 223)

½ teaspoon white peppercorns

Salt to taste

1. In a large stockpot bring 10 cups of water to a boil. Add chicken and giblets, allow to boil for 1 minute. This will bring blood and meat juices to the top. Turn off heat. Pour off water, run cold water into pot to rinse chicken. Drain.

2. Place chicken and giblets back into pot. Add 4½ quarts cold water and all remaining ingredients. Cover pot and bring to a boil over high heat. Lower heat to simmer, leave a small opening at the cover and simmer for 4 hours.

3. Turn off heat. Allow to cool for 10 to 15 minutes. Strain and pour into containers. The stock will keep refrigerated for 4 to 5 days. It may be frozen. It will keep up to 6 months.

Nutrition per serving (per tablespoon): 1.5 Calories; less than 1g Fat; 0 Carbohydrates; 0 Cholesterol; 26mg Sodium.

Note: You may eat the chicken used to make this stock if you wish. It will, unfortunately, be quite bland, for all of its flavor will have gone into the stock.

齋
上
湯

Vegetable Stock

4 quarts cold water

1 pound carrots, peeled and cut into thirds

2 pounds onions, quartered

2 bunches scallions, trimmed and cut into thirds

1/2 pound fresh mushrooms, cut into thirds

8 stalks celery, halved

1/4 pound fresh coriander (cilantro), cut into thirds (1 cup)

1/4 cup Chinese preserved dates, soaked in hot water 30 minutes and washed (or 4 preserved figs)

2 tablespoons boxthorn seeds, soaked in hot water 30 minutes and washed (or 4 pitted sweet dates)

1 teaspoon white peppercorns

3 ounces fresh ginger, lightly smashed

1/2 cup Fried Scallions (opposite page)

Salt to taste

**Yield:
3 to 3½
quarts**

1. In a large pot bring water to a boil. Add all ingredients to the boiling water, reduce heat, and simmer at a slow boil in a partially covered pot for 5 hours.

2. When the stock is cooked, remove from the heat and strain the liquid. Discard the solids. Store stock in a plastic container until needed. The stock will keep, refrigerated, for 4 to 5 days, or it can be frozen for up to 6 months.

Nutrition per serving (per tablespoon): 2.2 Calories; less than 1g Fat; 1g Carbohydrates; 0 Cholesterol; 26mg Sodium.

Note: Preserved dates come in 1-pound plastic packages labeled either "red dates" or "dates" and can be found in Chinese and Asian markets. After opening the package, the dates should be placed in a glass jar, covered, and stored in a cool place. They will keep for 6 months. Boxthorn seeds, so labeled, come in ½-pound to 1-pound packages. Store likewise.

葱
油

Scallion Oil

Scallion oil is used widely in this book, as you will see. The fried scallions that remain after the oil has been made are perfect ingredients for stocks, or even as additions to stir-fried dishes.

1 cup peanut oil

5 scallions, cut into 2-inch sections, white portions smashed

Yield:
¾ cup

Heat wok over medium heat. Add peanut oil, then scallions. When the scallions turn deep brown, the oil is done. With a strainer remove the scallions. Strain the oil through a fine strainer into a bowl and allow to cool to room temperature. Pour oil into a glass jar, seal and store in a cool place until needed. Do not refrigerate.

蒜
油

Garlic Oil

The crisp garlic that results from this infusion is used in my seafood stock, in soups, and in other recipes in this book. My husband thinks it makes a great snack food.

¾ cup of garlic (2 bulbs) peeled, thinly sliced

¾ cup peanut oil

Yield:
¾ cup

Heat wok over high heat for 30 seconds. Add peanut oil and garlic. Stir to separate. Cook for 3 minutes. Lower heat to low and cook for 8 minutes more or until garlic turns light brown. Turn off heat. Strain oil into a bowl and allow to cool to room temperature. Pour into a glass jar and seal. This will keep for 1 month at room temperature, or 6 months refrigerated.

辣 # Hot Pepper Oil

The hot pepper flakes that remain after this infusion should be kept with the oil. They will rest at the bottom of the storage jar and will be used in various recipes in this book.

油

½ cup hot red pepper flakes
⅓ cup sesame oil
½ cup peanut oil

**Yield:
1⅓ cups**

Place all the ingredients in a large jar and mix well. Close the jar tightly and place in a cool, dry place for 2 weeks. The oil will then be ready for use. The longer it is stored, the more potent it becomes. Because the heat of hot pepper flakes varies, the oil may be ready for use in 1 week instead of 2. Taste it.

Alternately: Place the hot pepper flakes in a mixing bowl. Bring the peanut and sesame oils to a boil and pour over the flakes. (I caution you not to have your face over the bowl, for the fumes may cause discomfort and coughing.) After the oil cools, it is ready for use. Store as above.

Techniques

炒 # Stir-Frying

This is surely the most well known of all Chinese cooking techniques. It is fascinating to watch finely sliced and chopped foods being whisked through a bit of oil and tossed with a spatula. The hands and arms move as the wok is often tipped back and forth. Stir-frying is all movement and rhythm. What leads to it is organized preparation.

The object of stir-frying is to cook foods precisely to the point at which they retain their flavor, color, texture, and nutritive value. All foods, evenly cut, must be next to the wok, ready to be put into the heated oil. This is simply organization, so that as you cook you will have everything within reach, and the rhythm of stir-frying will not be interrupted. The best stir-fried foods are those that retain their natural characteristics while absorbing and retaining the heat from the wok.

When I stir-fry I heat the wok for a specific time, usually from 30 seconds to 1 minute. I pour oil into the wok and coat its sides by spreading it with a spatula. I drop some minced or sliced ginger into the oil; when it becomes light brown, the oil is ready. I usually add a bit of salt to the oil, place the food in the wok and begin tossing it through the oil—1 to 2 minutes for soft vegetables such as bok choy and scallions, about a minute longer for firmer vegetables such as cabbage, carrots, and broccoli. I usually poach meats and seafood in stock before stir-frying them later. This is particularly advantageous in low-fat cooking because poaching in stock imparts flavor and allows one to stir-fry with far less oil.

If vegetables are too wet they will not stir-fry well, so they should be patted dry with paper towels. If they are too dry, however, you may have to add a bit of stock, perhaps 1 to 2 tablespoons, to the wok while cooking. When stock is added in this manner, steam is created, which aids the cooking process.

Stir-frying may initially appear as a rather frenzied activity, but it is not. The more you do it, the more you will realize that it is simply establishing a cooking rhythm.

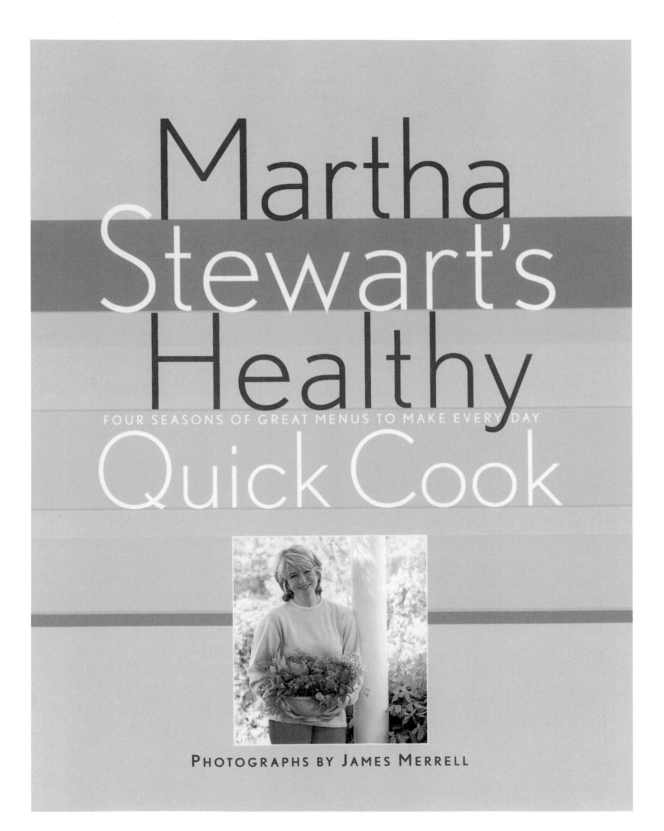

Martha Stewart's
Stewart's
Healthy
FOUR SEASONS OF GREAT MENUS TO MAKE EVERY DAY
Quick Cook

PHOTOGRAPHS BY JAMES MERRELL

Doyenne of domesticity Martha Stewart

"So much has happened in the world of food and in my cooking and eating habits since I wrote *Quick Cook, Quick Cook Menus*, and *Menus for Entertaining*. I still use many of those recipes and love the results, but things change and this book is a reflection of how much things change. I still use butter and oils, and I still eat meats, fish, milk, and eggs. However, I eat more sparingly of rich ingredients and cook with a lighter but equally flavorful touch."

There's no denying that over the last decade, Martha Stewart has been one of the major influences on the way Americans entertain. Here, she offers fifty-two menus arranged by season, complete with preparation tips, serving suggestions, and advice on table settings. Her "quick" may not be the same as yours (some menus take more than an hour), and not everyone has "opalescent blown-glass dessert bowls" or "Victorian sterling silver spoons" for serving—but that's just Martha being Martha.

FROM THE BOOK

■ ON ASIAN IMPACT
"Asian influences and ingredients and the cuisines of Japan, China, Vietnam, and Thailand now are very important to me . . . . I love the taste of fresh cilantro, delicate tofu, soba and udon noodles, and wasabi. Spices, such as strong curry and tandoori, hot peppers, and highly flavored mushrooms are much more important to me than sugar or butter or cream."

Spring ▪ Summer ▪ Fall ▪ Winter

The ubiquitous Stewart is the author of twelve books and the publisher and editorial director of *Martha Stewart Living*.

224 pages, more than 175 recipes, 150 color photos, $32.50. Published by Clarkson N. Potter, Inc.

MENU · **RUSTIC GRUYÈRE CROUTONS** · SEVEN-ONION SOUP · **CURLY ENDIVE WITH CITRUS VINAIGRETTE** · PRUNES POACHED IN ARMAGNAC WITH ENLIGHTENED CRÈME FRAÎCHE · SERVES 4

I love French onion soup, but the long cooking time and gobs of cheese characteristic of the classic version no longer appeal to me. My version—deconstructed, if you will—achieves the same full flavor of the traditional soup from dried porcini mushrooms and a bit of marsala wine. The croutons need only thin shavings of assertively flavored cheese to satisfy. I use Gruyère, but Emmental and Beaufort are excellent, too.

Rustic Gruyère Croutons

½	small loaf whole-grain bread, broken into 4 rough pieces
2	ounces Gruyère cheese, shaved into paper-thin slices
	Kosher salt and freshly ground black pepper

MAKES 4 CROUTONS

Toast the bread on both sides. Top each piece of bread with a slice of Gruyère and slide under the broiler until the cheese bubbles. Season with salt and pepper and serve.

Seven-Onion Soup

2	tablespoons extra-virgin olive oil
2	red onions, coarsely chopped
2	white onions, coarsely chopped
2	yellow onions, coarsely chopped
12	fresh pearl onions or 10 ounces frozen
3	shallots, coarsely chopped
2	leeks, washed and cut into ¼-inch rings
4	medium bunches of chives, coarsely chopped
¼	cup marsala wine
6	cups beef stock or low-sodium canned broth
2	tablespoons coarsely chopped dried porcini
1	tablespoon fresh thyme leaves, plus 4 sprigs of thyme

SERVES 4

In a 4-quart soup pot over medium heat, combine the olive oil, red, white, yellow, and pearl onions, and the shallots and sauté until golden brown and soft. Add the leeks and chives and cook until the onions turn a deep golden brown, about 5 minutes. Add the wine and cook, stirring, 2 minutes more, or until the mixture begins to bubble. Add 2 cups of stock every 15 minutes for the next 45 minutes, allowing the liquid to reduce by one fourth after each addition. Add the mushrooms and thyme leaves with the last 2 cups of stock. The soup will be a very deep brown. Ladle into deep soup bowls and garnish with the thyme sprigs.

Curly Endive with Citrus Vinaigrette

1	large head of curly endive, washed, dried, and torn into bite-size pieces
¾	cup Citrus Vinaigrette (next page)
	Kosher salt and freshly ground black pepper

SERVES 4

In a large salad bowl, place the endive. Drizzle the vinaigrette over the greens and toss to coat. Season to taste with salt and pepper.

OPPOSITE *Seven-Onion Soup with Rustic Gruyère Croutons is as flavorful as classic French onion soup—without all the fat.* **LEFT** *While not traditional, I eat lacy-edged curly endive with the onion soup—not before or after.*

ABOVE *The blue-gray hue of my ironstone soup terrine showcases beautifully the rich mahogany broth in Seven-Onion Soup.* RIGHT *Poaching prunes, or most any whole fruit— pears, apricots, or bananas—is foolproof.*

Prunes Poached in Armagnac with Enlightened Crème Fraîche

16	pitted prunes
¼	cup dried cranberries
1½	cups cranberry juice
2	tablespoons Armagnac or orange juice
2	tablespoons sugar
½	cup Enlightened Crème Fraîche (below)

In a large saucepan over medium heat, combine all of the ingredients except the Enlightened Crème Fraîche and cook, stirring occasionally, until the sauce is thick enough to coat the back of a spoon, about 15 minutes. Spoon 4 prunes and some of the sauce onto each of 4 dessert plates and drizzle 2 teaspoons of Enlightened Crème Fraîche over each.

Enlightened Crème Fraîche

½	cup buttermilk
½	cup heavy cream

MAKES 1 CUP

Combine the ingredients in a plastic container. Set the mixture aside in a warm place for 24 to 36 hours, until thickened. Refrigerate immediately. Whip until thickened before serving. This will keep, tightly covered, for about 4 days in the refrigerator.

Note: This "enlightened" version of crème fraîche has a higher ratio of low-fat buttermilk to high-fat cream.

Citrus Vinaigrette

1	teaspoon white wine vinegar
1	tablespoon lemon juice
1	tablespoon honey
½	cup grapefruit juice
2	tablespoons canola oil
1	large grapefruit, peeled, pith removed and cut into sections
	Kosher salt and freshly ground black pepper

MAKES ¾ CUP

In a small bowl, whisk together the vinegar, lemon juice, honey, grapefruit juice, and canola oil. Add the grapefruit sections and season with salt and pepper. The vinaigrette will keep, tightly covered, in the refrigerator for up to 3 days.

Chapter 5
Special Topics

Not all books are easily categorized, and this final chapter is something of a grab bag. Trend-spotters may note that there are two books about preparing fish quickly, two about baking your own bread, and four focusing on American cooking, with an accent on nostalgia. A book on the science of cooking—a topic that is infinitely more entertaining than it sounds—rounds out the group.

■ **GREAT FISH, QUICK** BY LESLIE REVSIN

Grilled Sea Scallops with Olives in Olive Oil **236**

Steamed Mussels with Mustards **238**

Grilled Mahi Mahi with Wilted Escarole, Spinach, and Basil **240**

■ **QUICK FROM SCRATCH: FISH AND SHELLFISH** EDITED BY JUDITH HILL

Thai Hot-and-Sour Fish Soup **245**

Shrimp, Jicama, and Mango Salad **247**

Orange Roughy with Gremolada Bread Crumbs **249**

■ **THE AMERICAN CENTURY COOKBOOK** BY JEAN ANDERSON

Avocado and Grapefruit Salad **252**

French Onion Soup Gratinée **252**

Mississippi Mud Cake **254**

Louis Diat's Carpet-Bag Steak **255**

■ **NEW RECIPES FROM QUILT COUNTRY:** More Food & Folkways from the Amish & **Mennonites** BY MARCIA ADAMS

Amish Roast Chicken and Potatoes with Garlic **259**

Soft Orange-Frosted Cookies 259

Buttered Toffee Apple Pie 260

■ **STEWS, BOGS & BURGOOS: Recipes from the Great American Stewpot** BY JAMES VILLAS

New England Pork and Clam Stew 264

Columbia County Applejack Beef Stew 265

Tigua Green Indian Chili 266

■ **LATIN AMERICAN COOKING ACROSS THE U.S.A.** BY HIMILCE NOVAS AND ROSEMARY SILVA

Tortilla Soup 270

Mussels in *Salsa Caribe* and White Wine 272

Curried Goat or Lamb 274

■ **WHAT YOU KNEAD** BY MARY ANN ESPOSITO

Nonna's Sponge Dough 278

Straight Dough 281

Pumpkin Seed, Sage, and Pancetta Bread 283

Tangy Tomato Logs 284

Grissini Rustici/Country Breadsticks 285

■ **THE BEST BREAD EVER: Great Homemade Bread Using Your Food Processor** BY CHARLES VAN OVER

The Best Bread Ever 288

■ **COOKWISE: The Hows & Whys of Successful Cooking** BY SHIRLEY O. CORRIHER

Chicken Stock 296

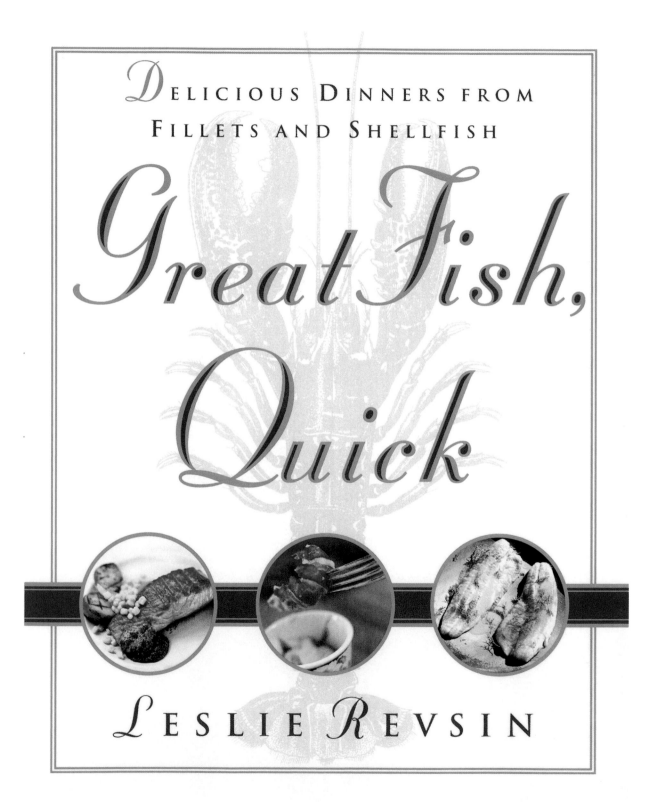

DELICIOUS DINNERS FROM
FILLETS AND SHELLFISH

Great Fish, Quick

LESLIE REVSIN

AUTHOR

Former New York City chef Leslie Revsin

WHY SHE WROTE IT

"This book is dedicated to the proposition that fish fillets and steaks, and all varieties of shell-fish, are just as quick and easy to cook as chicken breasts—and much more versatile as well."

WHY IT MADE OUR LIST

In this exceptionally easy-to-use book, Revsin takes the fuss out of fish. The preparations are fairly basic—mostly baked, grilled, sautéed, or roasted fish with a simple sauce or topping, no filleting or stuffing required. The fish and shellfish are arranged alphabetically within groups, followed by their recipes. And an appendix lists all the recipes that take less than thirty minutes, making it no trouble to find the quickest of the quick.

> **FROM THE BOOK**
>
> ■ **CULINARY OBSERVATION**
>
> *"Chicken breasts will always taste like 'you know what' even when they're all dressed up . . . but 'chickens of the sea' taste like buttery salmon; or sweet, lightly rich red snapper; or delicate, milky cod; or juicy, meaty swordfish."*

CHAPTERS

Delicate White Fleshed Fillets ▪ Darker Fleshed Fillets with Richer Flavor ▪ Sea Animals with Shells and Armor ▪ Recipes with a Combination of Sea Animals

SPECIFICS

308 pages, more than 100 recipes, 12 color photographs, $27.50. Published by Doubleday.

Grilled Sea Scallops with
Olives in Olive Oil

4 servings

PREP AND
COOKING
TIME
25–30
minutes

If you're an olive freak as I am, this will be right up your alley. Rich, deeply sweet—almost musky—sea scallops grill beautifully when they're big, big, big. They get golden and smoky, and are right at home luxuriating in fruity olive oil with chopped green and purple/black Mediterranean olives, coarse black pepper, ground coriander, and herbs. Thread the scallops through their sides with wooden skewers so they'll lie flat on the grill, and then you can do a lot easily. Toss any leftovers with the olives in oil and have them cold. Try the recipe with lobster tails, shrimp, stir-fried calamari, salmon fillets, or with swordfish, tuna, or shark steaks.

6 tablespoons full-flavored, fruity olive oil

3 tablespoons mixed black and green chopped, pitted olives (such as
purple/black kalamata, Gaeta, or niçoise, and green Amfissa, Atalanti,
or Sicilian)

$^1/_8$ teaspoon somewhat coarsely ground fresh black pepper, + more to taste

Salt to taste

1 teaspoon fresh thyme leaves, very lightly chopped

$^1/_8$ teaspoon very finely chopped fresh rosemary leaves

1 teaspoon chopped fresh sage leaves

1 teaspoon coarsely chopped fresh (flat-leaf or curly) parsley

$^1/_2$ teaspoon ground coriander

Pinch of crushed red pepper flakes

$1^1/_2$ pounds sea scallops, at least 1″ in height

Wooden skewers, soaked in water for at least 30 minutes before using

TO PREPARE: Start a medium-hot fire in the grill (or preheat the oven broiler). Fifteen minutes before you're going to grill the sea scallops, put the grill grate 5″ to 6″ above the glowing coals if it isn't already there. (I also like to brush the top of the grate with vegetable oil just before grilling to help prevent sticking.)

Place 4 tablespoons of the olive oil in a small mixing bowl and stir in the chopped olives, $^1/_8$ teaspoon of the pepper, and all the seasonings. Set it aside while you prepare the scallops. The olives in olive oil can be made up to 2 weeks ahead, adding the parsley at the last minute to preserve its color, and refrigerated. Just be sure to let the mixture come to room temperature before serving it.

Clean the scallops by peeling off and discarding the little strip of muscle that is attached to one side. (If your scallops are somewhat old, the muscle strip may not be there.) Place the scallops in a colander and wash them well under cold running water—keep an eye open for specks of dark sand. Drain the scallops and roll them in paper towels to dry them thoroughly.

Place the scallops in a large mixing bowl, drizzle them with the remaining 2 tablespoons of olive oil, and season them with salt and pepper. Toss them gently but thoroughly with a rubber spatula.

Remove the wooden skewers from the water and thread the scallops onto the skewers through their sides. (If you push the skewer through their ends, there's a good chance they'll split, plus they won't lie flat on the grill.) Leave about $1/4''$ space between scallops (so they cook all around) and at least $1/2''$ at each end so you can handle the skewers.

Place the skewers over the coals (or in the broiler) and grill the first side golden brown, 4 to 5 minutes. Turn the skewers over and grill (or broil) the scallops for 1 to 2 minutes more, or until they're springy-firm when gently squeezed on their sides, or slightly translucent in the center when cut with a knife. They'll be medium at this point. For well done, cook for another minute or two.

TO SERVE: Push the scallops off the skewers onto warm dinner plates and spoon the olives in olive oil over them. Serve right away.

Steamed Mussels
with Mustards

4 main course
or 8 to 10
appetizer
servings

PREP AND
COOKING
TIME
25–30
minutes

*M*ake a vinaigrette with 3 different mustards—whole-grain, Dijon, and English-style dry. Then simply steam the mussels in the water that clings to their shells after they've been rinsed. Pile them into bowls with some of their natural juices, and drizzle them with the vinaigrette—the sweet, unadorned mussel flavor predominates, highlighted by mini-mustard bursts in your mouth. You can serve the mussels as a first course, or serve the vinaigrette with almost any fillet or shellfish you can think of.

4 pounds cultivated mussels

$1^1/_2$ teaspoons + $^1/_4$ cup olive oil

$^1/_3$ cup mixed green and red bell peppers, cut into $^1/_4$″–$^1/_3$″ dice

Salt and freshly ground black or white pepper to taste

Generous $^1/_4$ teaspoon dry mustard

$1^1/_2$ tablespoons fresh squeezed lemon juice

1 tablespoon Dijon mustard, preferably French (see Note)

$1^1/_2$ teaspoons whole-grain mustard, preferably Pommery from France; *or* $4^1/_2$ teaspoons Dijon only

TO PREPARE: Rinse the mussels well (scrub them if they look muddy), clip off any beards with small scissors, and soak the mussels in a bowl of cold water to cover while you prepare the vinaigrette. Or soak them in a diluted paste of cornmeal or flour in the refrigerator overnight.

In a small skillet, heat $1^1/_2$ teaspoons of the olive oil over low to medium heat and add the diced peppers. Sauté them, stirring occasionally, until they're crisp-tender, 3 to 4 minutes. Season them with salt and pepper and set them aside on a small plate to cool.

Place the dry mustard in a small bowl and stir in about $^1/_2$ teaspoon of the lemon juice to make a smooth mixture. Stir in the remaining lemon juice and the Dijon and Pommery mustards.

In a slow stream, gradually whisk the $^1/_4$ cup of olive oil into the mustards—the dressing will emulsify and thicken lightly. Stir in the cooled peppers, season well with salt and pepper, and set the dressing aside while you steam the mussels. Or make and refrigerate the dressing up to a week ahead—it will probably separate, so stir or vigorously shake it together right before serving. Be sure to serve it at room temperature.

Pour the mussels into a colander, shaking it to drain any excess water. Pour them into a large pot (or 2 medium)—filling it by no more than half—and cover the pot tightly. Steam the mussels over high heat until they've all *just* opened, 3 to 6 minutes, stirring them up from the bottom of the pot once or twice during cooking. Discard any mussels that haven't opened, taste the juices, and adjust the seasoning with salt and pepper.

TO SERVE: Pile the mussels into warm soup plates or deep soup bowls, adding ¼ cup of broth to each bowl. (You'll have broth left—cool and refrigerate or freeze it for another use, or eat more of it!) Drizzle 2 tablespoons of mustard vinaigrette over each portion, and serve right away.

NOTE: You may wonder why I keep suggesting *French* Dijon. There are two reasons: First, it's the real thing—Dijon mustard originated in France—Dijon, France, of all places! And its flavor is what Dijon mustard should be. And second, it has wonderful thickening ability, holding oil in emulsion better than American mustard marketed with a "Dijon" label.

Grilled Mahimahi with
Wilted Escarole, Spinach, and Basil

4 servings

PREP AND
COOKING
TIME
45–50
minutes

If you can be in the kitchen wilting the greens while a designated-someone is on the patio grilling the mahi, it's an ideal division of labor! But if there's no one around to help, you can sauté or broil the mahi just as well. Be sure to cook the mahi over low to moderate heat—high heat tends to tighten and dry it out, even when you swear you haven't overcooked it. Try these greens with salmon, swordfish, grouper, catfish, or sea trout fillets too.

2 small bunches spinach, *or* one 10-ounce bag fresh spinach

1 bunch fresh basil

1 small head escarole

Four 7-ounce mahimahi fillets, each ³/₄″–1″ thick

Salt and freshly ground black or white pepper to taste

5 tablespoons olive oil, preferably extra-virgin

1 tablespoon finely chopped garlic

Lemon wedges

TO PREPARE: Start a low fire in the grill. Fifteen minutes before you're going to grill the mahi fillets, put the grill grate 6″ or 7″ above the glowing coals if it isn't already there. (I also like to brush the top of the grate with vegetable oil just before grilling to help prevent sticking.)

Cut or break the spinach leaves from their stems and discard the stems. Measure 4 cups, somewhat packed, and save the remainder for another preparation. Fill a *very* large bowl (or your sink) with cold water and put the spinach leaves in it. Pick the basil leaves from their stems and measure 1 cup, somewhat packed. Add the basil leaves to the spinach. Wash the leaves by pushing them up and down in the water several times. Then let the leaves remain undisturbed for a minute or two, long enough to let any sand that got stirred up settle on the bottom. Scoop the leaves out without stirring up the sediment. If there's a good amount of sand in the bottom of the bowl, empty the water and repeat the process until the water has no sand. Dry the leaves very well in a salad spinner or roll them between layers of paper towels and set them aside. You can do this up to a day ahead and refrigerate them.

Snap off the leaves of escarole and wash and dry them if they're dirty (sometimes, when fortune smiles, the ribs only need to be wiped clean with a damp paper towel—but check the green of the leaves carefully). Cut enough of the leaves crosswise into 1″ pieces to measure 3¹/₂ cups, and set them aside separate from the spinach-basil, or refrigerate them for up to 2 days. Reserve the rest for another use.

Season the fillets with salt and pepper and rub them all over with a tablespoon of the olive oil.

Place them, round side down, over the coals and grill them, turning once, until they're lightly browned and just cooked through, 7 to 10 minutes. To check, make a cut in the thickest part of one fillet to see if it's opaque all the way through. When they're done, remove the fillets from the grill and keep them warm briefly while you wilt the greens. (If you're comfortable with the timing, and you have a "designated-someone," you can start the greens 2 minutes before the fillets are done.)

Place 3 tablespoons of the olive oil in a wok, or a very large skillet set over high heat. When the oil is very hot and just *starting* to smoke, add the escarole and stir-fry it for 1 to 2 minutes, until the green of their leaves has wilted. Add the spinach-basil mixture and the garlic and stir-fry them until the spinach starts to wilt, about 30 seconds. Turn off the heat—the retained heat of the wok will continue wilting the greens. At this point, all the greens should be collapsed but still quite crunchy. Adjust the seasoning with salt and pepper.

TO SERVE: Distribute the greens over warm dinner plates, place a fillet on top, and drizzle the fish with the remaining tablespoon of olive oil. Garnish the plates with lemon wedges and serve right away.

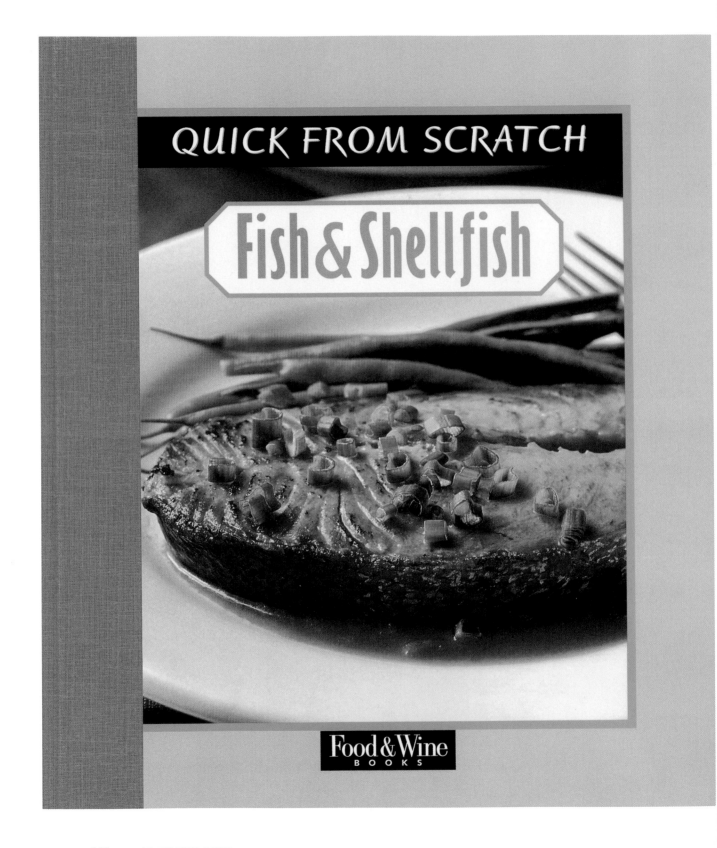

QUICK FROM SCRATCH

Fish & Shellfish

Food&Wine
BOOKS

■ EDITOR
Judith Hill, editor in chief of Food & Wine Books

■ WHY WE WROTE IT
"You, our readers who have enjoyed other books in this series, have told us that you want this particular volume—that you'd like to serve fish but don't quite feel comfortable with it as an ingredient and need some good ideas for cooking it. Your requests launched us, and we have had more fun writing this book than any other that Food & Wine Books has published so far."

■ WHY IT MADE OUR LIST
No false modesty for us; we think our book can stand proudly with the best of the year. The recipes are easy but elegant, they take very little time to make, they've been thoroughly tested, and, of course, they're delicious. Each recipe is accompanied by a wine recommendation and a full-page color photograph, and virtually all list fish alternatives so you can use whatever you find at the market. These are new, never-before-published recipes.

FROM THE BOOK

■ CULINARY ADVICE
"There's nothing like fresh-ground pepper. If you've been using preground, buy a pepper mill, fill it, and give it a grind. You'll never look back."

■ CHAPTERS
Soups & Stews ▪ Roasted & Baked ▪ Grilled & Broiled ▪ Sautéed & Fried ▪ Braised, Steamed, Boiled & Poached ▪ Pasta, Rice & Couscous

■ PREVIOUS CREDITS
Other entries in the *Quick from Scratch* series include *Pasta*, *Chicken*, *Italian*, and *One-Dish Meals*.

■ SPECIFICS
192 pages, 75 recipes, 75 color photographs, $25.95. Published by American Express Publishing Corporation.

THAI HOT-AND-SOUR FISH SOUP

In our hot-and-sour soup, lemon and lime zest, lime juice, and fresh ginger replace the traditional lemongrass, kaffir lime leaves, and galangal, which can be difficult to find. To change the heat level, adjust the number of jalapeños up or down to your taste.

WINE RECOMMENDATION

The strong flavors here suggest a light white without too much taste of its own. A pinot grigio from Italy will do fine—unless you increase the heat with more jalapeños. Then serve a cold beer.

SERVES 4

1½ tablespoons cooking oil

3 shallots, cut into thin slices

1 tablespoon chopped fresh ginger

5 jalapeño peppers, seeds and ribs removed, peppers cut into thin slices

1 quart canned low-sodium chicken broth or homemade stock

2 cups water

Grated zest of 2 lemons

Grated zest of 3 limes

½ pound mushrooms, quartered

5 tablespoons lime juice (from about 3 limes)

¼ cup Asian fish sauce (nam pla or nuoc mam)*

2 pounds swordfish steaks, skinned, cut into approximately 2-by-1-inch pieces

2 tomatoes, cut into large dice (optional)

⅓ cup cilantro leaves (optional)

*Available at Asian markets and many supermarkets

1. In a large pot, heat the oil over moderately low heat. Add the shallots, ginger, and jalapeños; cook, stirring occasionally, for 3 minutes. Add the broth and water; bring to a boil. Reduce the heat and simmer for 5 minutes. Stir in the zests and mushrooms; simmer 5 minutes longer.

2. Add the lime juice, fish sauce, and swordfish to the soup. Cook until the fish is just done, about 2 minutes. Serve sprinkled with the tomatoes and cilantro, if using.

FISH ALTERNATIVES

Thai Hot-and-Sour Soup is often made with shrimp. Or, use any moderately firm, skinless steaks or fillets, such as catfish, black sea bass, or pompano, in place of the swordfish.

ASIAN FISH SAUCE

Fish sauce is used as a condiment, much like soy sauce. Either the Thai version (nam pla) or the Vietnamese (nuoc mam) will add great depth of flavor to quick dishes.

SHRIMP, JICAMA, AND MANGO SALAD

The crunchy jicama and the soft, sweet mango provide lively counterpoints to the shrimp in both flavor and texture. Tossed with a lemony vinaigrette and a generous amount of cilantro, the salad is ideal for a warm summer evening.

WINE RECOMMENDATION

Mango, lemon juice, and cilantro invite a light-bodied, acidic white, such as an Orvieto from Italy or a Muscadet de Sèvre-et-Maine from France.

SERVES 4

- ¾ cup water
- 2 teaspoons salt
- 1½ pounds large shrimp, shelled
- 1 small jicama (about ¾ pound), peeled and cut into ¼-inch dice
- 1 mango, peeled and cut into ¼-inch dice
- ½ cup chopped cilantro or flat-leaf parsley
- 6 tablespoons lemon juice
- ½ teaspoon Dijon mustard
- ¼ teaspoon fresh-ground black pepper
- ¼ cup olive oil

1. In a large frying pan, bring the water and ¾ teaspoon of the salt to a boil. Add the shrimp, cover, and bring back to a boil. Cook, covered, over moderate heat for 1 minute. Stir. Continue cooking until the shrimp are just done, about 2 minutes longer. Drain. When the shrimp are cool enough to handle, cut each one in half lengthwise and then in half crosswise.

2. Put the shrimp in a large glass or stainless-steel bowl and add the jicama, mango, and cilantro.

3. In a small glass or stainless-steel bowl, whisk together the lemon juice, the mustard, the remaining 1¼ teaspoons of salt, and the pepper. Add the oil slowly, whisking. Just before serving, add this vinaigrette to the shrimp mixture and toss.

SHELLFISH ALTERNATIVES

Crabmeat, though expensive, is delicious in this salad and is a time-saver, too, since it's usually already cooked. (For that matter, you can use precooked shrimp instead of boiling uncooked ones.) If you really want to splurge, try the salad with lobster.

ORANGE ROUGHY WITH GREMOLADA BREAD CRUMBS

Breaded fish never crisps well in the oven. Here the bread-crumb topping is prepared on the stovetop and sprinkled over the fish when it's already on the plate. Be sure to spoon the pan juices around, and not over, the fish so the crumbs stay crunchy.

WINE RECOMMENDATION

One of the new, clean-as-a-whistle white wines from Spain or the south of France will pair nicely with the Mediterranean flavors of garlic and olive oil. Look for the Spanish albariño or a Côtes de Gascogne from France.

SERVES 4

2 pounds orange-roughy fillets, cut to make 4 pieces

Salt

Fresh-ground black pepper

¼ cup dry white wine

¼ cup plus 2 tablespoons olive oil

½ cup dry bread crumbs

2 cloves garlic, minced

Grated zest of 1 lemon

2 tablespoons chopped fresh parsley

1. Heat the oven to 400°. Season the orange-roughy fillets with ¼ teaspoon of salt and ⅛ teaspoon of pepper. Put the fish fillets in a glass or stainless-steel baking dish and add the wine and the ¼ cup oil to the dish. Bake the fish until just done, about 12 minutes for ¾-inch-thick fillets.

2. Meanwhile, in a small frying pan, toast the bread crumbs over low heat, stirring, until they're light brown and fragrant, about 4 minutes. Stir in the garlic, lemon zest, and parsley and cook 1 minute longer. Remove from the heat and stir in ⅛ teaspoon each salt and pepper and the remaining 2 tablespoons oil.

3. Transfer the fish to plates. Sprinkle with the bread crumbs and spoon the pan juices around the fish.

FISH ALTERNATIVES

Any mild white-fleshed fish will work equally well here. Try flounder, sole, pike, or catfish fillets.

VARIATION

ORANGE ROUGHY WITH ORANGE GREMOLADA BREAD CRUMBS

Substitute the grated zest of ½ orange for the lemon zest in the bread-crumb mixture.

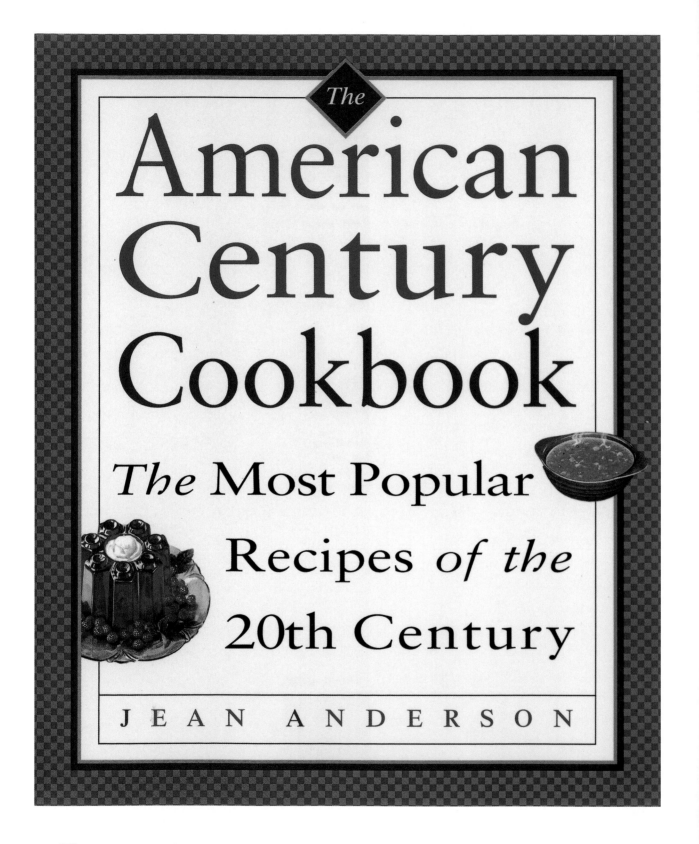

The American Century Cookbook

The Most Popular Recipes *of the* 20th Century

JEAN ANDERSON

Well-known food writer and cookbook author Jean Anderson

■ WHY SHE WROTE IT

"For the past ten years, I have been traveling backward in time. Back across the decades to 1900 and beyond. My quest: To trace this century's role in our culinary coming of age. To track the recipes, foods, food trends, food people, appliances, and gadgets that have had an impact on our lives from 1900 onward."

■ WHY IT MADE OUR LIST

This delightful collection of recipes, anecdotes, historical tidbits, and vintage advertisements is pretty irresistible; once you start leafing through the pages, it's hard to stop. The recipes—some written by Anderson, some taken from old cookbooks and magazines, from the test kitchens of food companies, and from chefs and cooking teachers—range from old favorites to those we'd like to forget (care for some Coca-Cola Salad?) Timelines listing great moments in food ("1927: A Nebraska chemist concocts Kool-Aid") and boxes on the origins of such cultural necessities as Tang, Spam, and Fritos add to the kitschy fun.

■ CHAPTERS

Appetizers & Snacks ▪ Soups ▪ Meats, Fish & Fowl ▪ Casseroles ▪ Eggs, Cheese, Pasta & Grains ▪ Vegetables ▪ Salads & Salad Dressings ▪ Breads & Sandwiches ▪ Puddings, Pies & Other Desserts ▪ Cakes & Frostings ▪ Cookies & Candies

■ PREVIOUS CREDITS

Anderson is the author of more than twenty cookbooks, including *Food of Portugal* and the *Doubleday Cookbook* (with Elaine Hanna).

■ SPECIFICS

548 pages, more than 500 recipes, approximately 60 black-and-white photographs and 285 illustrations, $32.50. Published by Clarkson N. Potter, Inc.

FROM THE BOOK

■ ON THE NEXT CENTURY

"What does the twenty-first century promise? Perhaps more light will be shed on the cooking of Africa, in particular on that of Egypt, Angola, and South Africa. Perhaps there will be an upsurge of interest in the cuisines of Argentina, Brazil, Chile, Colombia and Venezuela. Perhaps robots will be running our kitchens."

Avocado and Grapefruit Salad

Makes 6 to 8 Servings

✻

AVOCADOS, INDIGENOUS to Central and South America, were first planted in Florida in 1833 and fifteen years later in California just east of Los Angeles (today most of our crop comes from California). Only in the 1950s, however, did "alligator pears," as avocados used to be called, become trendy salad ingredients. Two classic combos are given here: grapefruit and avocado and orange and avocado. The recipes were adapted from ones developed by the California Avocado Advisory Board (now the California Avocado Commission) for its booklet, *The Avocado Bravo.*

SALAD

3 ripe medium California avocados, pitted, peeled, and sliced
3 medium grapefruits, peeled, sectioned, and seeded
1 head Bibb lettuce, separated into leaves, washed and patted dry
3 to 5 sprigs watercress

DRESSING

⅓ cup vegetable oil
¼ cup tarragon vinegar
¼ cup fresh grapefruit juice
1 tablespoon fresh lemon juice
1 teaspoon sugar
½ teaspoon salt
½ cup crumbled Roquefort cheese (optional)

1. SALAD: Fan avocado slices and grapefruit sections out on bed of lettuce in large bowl, alternating the fruits.

2. DRESSING: Whisk together oil, vinegar, grapefruit juice, lemon juice, sugar, and salt until creamy; mix in Roquefort, if desired.

3. Spoon dressing evenly over salad, garnish with watercress, and serve.

——— VARIATION ———

AVOCADO AND ORANGE SALAD: Prepare as directed, substituting 3 cups orange or mandarin orange segments for grapefruit; in dressing, use orange juice in place of grapefruit juice. Makes 6 to 8 servings.

French Onion Soup Gratinée

Makes 6 Servings

✻

ALTHOUGH THIS soup was known early this century, and perhaps somewhat earlier, it was hardly a "household name" until after World War II when GIs came home from France with a taste for it. I first dipped into French Onion Soup when I was an undergraduate at Cornell in the 1950s. Today's sophisticated cooks may consider it a cliché. Still, nothing beats it for warming up a wintry day.

¼ cup (½ stick) butter
4 large yellow onions (about 2 pounds), peeled and thinly sliced
6 cups rich brown stock or broth, preferably homemade
½ teaspoon salt (or to taste)
¼ teaspoon black pepper (or to taste)
12 (½-inch-thick) slices French bread (about 1 medium loaf)
¾ cup coarsely shredded Gruyère cheese
¼ cup freshly grated Parmesan cheese

1. Preheat oven to 300° F. Melt butter in large heavy saucepan over moderately low heat, add onions, and cook, uncovered, stirring occasionally, until golden brown, 15 to 20 minutes.

2. Add stock, salt, and pepper and simmer, uncovered, stirring occasionally, about 15 minutes.

3. Meanwhile, spread bread slices on ungreased baking sheet and toast until crisp and golden, about 15 minutes. Remove toast from oven and preheat broiler.

4. Taste soup and adjust salt and pepper as needed. Arrange 2 slices of toast in each of six 8- to 10-ounce flameproof soup bowls, ladle in soup, and sprinkle with Gruyère, then with Parmesan, dividing all amounts evenly.

5. Place bowls on heavy-duty baking sheet, set 4 inches from broiler unit, and broil just until cheese melts and is tipped with brown, about 2 minutes. Serve at once.

GUACAMOLE

In *The Dictionary of American Food and Drink* (Revised Edition, 1994), food writer John Mariani pinpoints 1920 as the date of the first American (English-language) reference to this avocado dip. My own research has turned up nothing earlier than 1942. Even Artemis Ward's exhaustive *Encyclopedia of Food* (1923) makes no mention of guacamole despite two pages on the avocado. This is, he says, "primarily a salad fruit to be served in halves or sections to be eaten with salt (and pepper and vinegar if desired), or with a little lime, or lemon juice and sugar . . . . It is also combined in soups and cooked as a vegetable."

A starchy man, Ward goes on to say that "the title 'alligator pear' is deservedly losing ground. It is, under present conditions, a misleading misnomer and should be consigned to oblivion. The smooth skin of the fruit conveys no suggestion of an alligator or its skin." Clearly the leathery, black-skinned Haas and Fuerte avocados of California were unknown to Ward; he wrote only of the giant, smooth, green-skinned Florida variety, which had been introduced in the 1830s. Ward further says that "the word 'avocado' is . . . merely a development of a phonetic substitute for '*ahuacatl*,' the Aztec name for the fruit." Most etymologists agree. They also agree that *guacamole* descends from *ahuacamolli*, the Indian name for "avocado sauce."

The first mention (and recipe) for guacamole I've located after digging through scores of late-nineteenth- and early-twentieth-century cookbooks appears in *The Good Housekeeping Cook Book* (1942). The next year, Irma Rombauer included "Avocado Spread (Guacamole)" in the *Joy of Cooking*. But her recipe would hardly pass for *guacamole* today. It directs the cook to mash the pulp of one or two avocados, to mix with onion juice, lemon juice, and salt (no quantities given), then to "heap on small crackers or toast" and "garnish with paprika and parsley." Irma goes on to say that "a good holiday touch is a bit of pimiento or a slice of stuffed olive."

That same year *Sunset* magazine's "Kitchen Cabinet" column ran a recipe for a spicier "Huacamole" made with chopped tomato, onion, and garlic plus mayonnaise, salad oil, sugar and "2 teaspoons (or more) chili powder."

Helen Evans Brown (*West Coast Cook Book*, 1952) also dishes up an unorthodox guacamole:

You'll want very ripe avocados for this—never mind the blemishes; they are easily cut out. Mash a large one in a bowl that has been rubbed with garlic, and season it with ¼ teaspoon each of salt and chili powder, and a teaspoon of lemon juice. Add 2 teaspoons of very finely minced onion. Now taste it and add more salt if need be, and a little more chili powder, if that's the way you like it. The flesh part of ripe tomatoes, cut in dice, may be added, or small piece of canned green chilis, or sliced ripe olives, or crisp and crumbled bacon. Mix well and put in a bowl, covering the top with a thin layer of mayonnaise—this to keep the mixture from blackening.

In *Elena's Secrets of Mexican Cooking* (1958), Elena Zelayeta, who for years ran a successful San Francisco restaurant, is the first cookbook author I've found to suggest chopped fresh coriander (cilantro) as a seasoning—a thoroughly Mexican touch. And why not? Elena was born in Mexico, the daughter of innkeepers. Most 1990s cooks, now aiming for authenticity, do add cilantro to their guacamole along with chopped jalapeños. And many prefer lime juice to lemon.

In big-city restaurants, the making of guacamole has been elevated to high art. Take New York City's Rosa Mexicano, for example. Here, all ingredients are trundled to your table, then the guacamole is ceremoniously prepared before your eyes in stone *metates*—tailored, you might say, to your own taste.

"More garlic?" . . . "More onion?" . . . "More jalapeños?" . . . "More cilantro?" You've only to speak up.

COBB SALAD

About the time mass America became motorized, architects had a field day designing restaurants in the shape of hot dogs, chickens, pigs, even hoopskirted plantation cooks. But none caught America's fancy like The Brown Derby, which opened in 1926 directly across Wilshire Boulevard from the Ambassador Hotel.

Why a Derby? There are several legends. According to Betty Goodwin (*Hollywood du Jour*, 1993), "the Derby was chosen as a classy symbol for the newly moneyed and sophisticated folk of Hollywood." Or it might have been because restaurant cofounder Wilson Mizner liked "the hat worn by Al Smith, governor of New York, on a visit to Los Angeles." Soon the Derby was packing in the celebrities—John Barrymore, Charlie Chaplin, W.C. Fields—who liked the fact that they could hang out there until four in the morning.

A second Brown Derby opened three years later at the corner of Hollywood and Vine. And though of more conventional design, it was even more popular thanks to its proximity to major movie studios

and to such star-power "regulars" as the two Joans (Bennett and Crawford), Jean Harlow, Katharine Hepburn, and William Powell. Robert Cobb bought the Derbies in 1934, and before long there were two more—one in Beverly Hills and another in Los Feliz.

Like so many classic recipes, Bob Cobb's salad was tossed together out of odds and ends. Arthur Schwartz, *New York Daily News* columnist, says the year was 1937 and that it happened one midnight when Cobb needed to rustle up something for his good buddy Sid Grauman (of Grauman's Chinese Theater). Cobb opened the huge restaurant refrigerator and "pulled out this and that: a head of lettuce, an avocado, some romaine, watercress, tomatoes, some cold breast of chicken, a hard-boiled egg, chives, cheese, and some old-fashioned French dressing. He started chopping. Added some crisp bacon—swiped from a busy chef." Grauman liked Cobb's spur-of-the moment salad so much he ordered it the next day for lunch and pretty soon studio boss Jack Warner was sending his chauffeur over for takeout. "Since 1937," Schwartz adds, "more than four million Cobb Salads have been sold at Brown Derby restaurants."

Mississippi Mud Cake

Makes a 13 × 9 × 2-inch Loaf Cake, 24 Servings

✱

THIS HAS to be the richest cake in all creation, a chocoholic's idea of bliss. I first encountered Mississippi Mud Cake in the 1970s in Jackson, Mississippi, but I'm told it's popular up and down the Mississippi, particularly from St. Louis south. This recipe is adapted from *Martha White's Southern Sampler* (1989). Southerners all know Martha White, the soft Tennessee flour they've depended on for tender biscuits and cakes for nearly a hundred years (company founder

Richard Lindsey named his finest flour after his three-year-old daughter Martha White Lindsey). Founded in Nashville in 1899 as the Royal Flour Mill, the company name officially became Martha White when new owners took over in 1941. Martha White's test kitchens were active almost from the start, developing many of the recipes now considered Southern classics. Note that this cake has no leavening.

CAKE

- 1½ cups sifted all-purpose flour
- ⅓ cup unsweetened cocoa powder
- ½ teaspoon salt
- 1 cup vegetable shortening
- 1½ cups granulated sugar
- 4 eggs
- 2 teaspoons vanilla extract
- 1 cup coarsely chopped pecans
- 2 cups miniature marshmallows

ICING

- 1 cup (2 sticks) butter or margarine, melted
- ⅓ cup unsweetened cocoa powder
- ½ cup evaporated milk
- 4 cups sifted confectioners' (10X) sugar (about 1 pound)
- 1 teaspoon vanilla extract
- ½ cup coarsely chopped pecans

1. CAKE: Preheat oven to 325°F. Grease and flour 13 × 9 × 2-inch baking pan; set aside.

2. Sift flour with cocoa and salt onto wax paper and set aside.

3. Cream shortening and granulated sugar in large mixing bowl at moderate speed until fluffy-light, 6 to 7 minutes. Add eggs, one at a time, beating well after each addition. Beat in vanilla. Mix sifted dry ingredients into batter, then fold in pecans.

4. Scrape into pan, spreading to corners, and bake 30 to 35 minutes, until cake begins to pull from sides of pan and toothpick inserted in center comes out clean.

5. Remove pan from oven and scatter marshmallows evenly over cake. Return to oven and bake 10-minutes more or until marshmallows melt.

6. Cool cake in pan on wire rack. Cake will sink as it cools but this is what gives it its "Mississippi mud" texture.

7. ICING: Blend butter and cocoa in medium mixing bowl. Beat in evaporated milk, then gradually mix in 10X sugar and beat until smooth. Stir in vanilla and pecans. Spread smoothly over cake and let harden before cutting into bars. Make the pieces small; this cake is rich.

VINTAGE RECIPE

Carpetbag Steak

THOUGH POPULAR in Australia, this unusual steak stuffed with oysters is apparently of American origin. It takes its name from the cloth satchel travelers used around the time of the Civil War. Just before the turn of the century, when broiled steaks were coming into vogue, a popular way to serve them was under a coverlet of oysters. This recipe simply takes that late-nineteenth-century recipe one step further. Who's responsible? Perhaps Chasen's restaurant, which opened in Hollywood in 1936 (and closed in 1995). Carpetbagger Steak, as Chasen's called it, was a house specialty. Or was Louis Diat the creator? He includes this recipe for it in *Cooking à la Ritz* (1941):

LOUIS DIAT'S CARPET-BAG STEAK

HAVE butcher cut steak from the sirloin 1½ to 2 inches thick, and then cut through the center to make a pocket. Stuff this pocket with raw oysters, seasoned with salt and pepper. Then sew the edges of pocket together. Broil about fifteen minutes on each side. Serve with any desired potatoes.

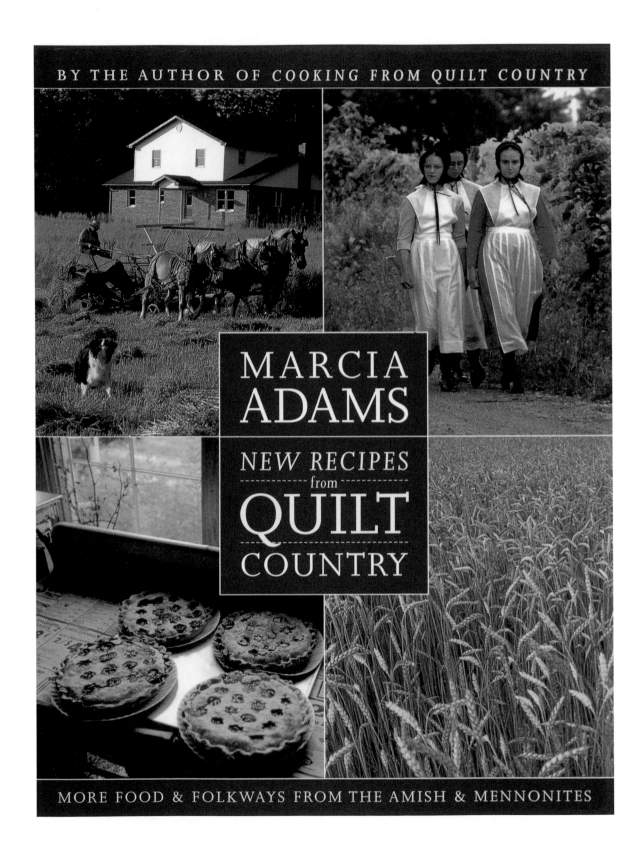

BY THE AUTHOR OF COOKING FROM QUILT COUNTRY

MARCIA ADAMS

NEW RECIPES
from
QUILT
COUNTRY

MORE FOOD & FOLKWAYS FROM THE AMISH & MENNONITES

Marcia Adams, who visited these parts before in *Cooking from Quilt Country*

■ WHY SHE WROTE IT

". . . with my interest—indeed, passion—for saving old recipes for posterity, I did want to save these old, unusual recipes that I discovered, as strange as some of them may sound to our English ears . . . . I hope that by preparing them for your family and loved ones you may create in your home the comforting sense of tradition, harmony, and the love of the land that is such a palpable presence in every Amish and Mennonite home I've visited."

■ WHY IT MADE OUR LIST

Adams' first collection of authentic Amish and Mennonite recipes was a surprise hit in 1989, and is still popular, with 250,000 books in print. These are homey, hearty dishes, without a speck of concern for fat grams or calorie counts (and if, as Adams reports, an Amish farmer burns 8,000 calories a day and his wife, 4,000, it's no wonder). The tasty recipes, serene photographs, and evocative text may have you yearning for a simpler way of life—or at least for a piece of one of those pies.

FROM THE BOOK

■ CULTURAL OBSERVATION

"I have never interviewed an Amish woman alone; there were always other female members of the family, either in the kitchen working or passing in and out as they attended to other household duties. It is a supportive, warm, and practical way for Amish women to live. And they never have to hire a baby-sitter."

■ CHAPTERS

Family Breakfast ▪ Baking Day ▪ The School Lunch Bucket ▪ Lady Food ▪ Noon Meals ▪ Auction Day ▪ Roadside Stand ▪ The Harvest Cellar ▪ Casseroles and Carry-Ins ▪ Family Milestones ▪ Growing Up Amish ▪ Changing Times, Familiar Favorites ▪ The Basics

■ SPECIFICS

294 pages, more than 250 recipes, approximately 110 color photographs, $30. Published by Clarkson N. Potter, Inc.

Amish Roast Chicken and Potatoes with Garlic

Serves 4

THE AMISH HAVE ALWAYS raised their chickens in the free-range manner, and now their deliciously succulent birds are popping up on fashionable menus in cities across the country, where they are prized for their superior flavor. Late one afternoon, I was interviewing Esther Bontrager in her kitchen about bushel cookies, and she said, "Say, I've got to start supper. I'll talk while I fix the chicken." Then she prepared a version of this dish (without the thyme), and as it cooked and I scribbled, I thought I had never smelled anything more delicious in my whole life. "There's no recipe," she said. "Just throw the potatoes and stuff around the chicken and pour over some butter and broth and fresh lemon." All dinners should be so simple. And this one really is.

> 1 fresh free-range roasting chicken,
>   approximately 4 pounds
> 2 handfuls fresh thyme (optional)
> 1 large onion, cut into chunks
> 4 red-skinned potatoes, 2 inches in
>   diameter, sliced ¾ inch thick
> 6 garlic cloves, skin on
> ½ cup (1 stick) butter
> 1 cup chicken stock or canned
>   broth
> ½ lemon, seeded
>   Salt and freshly ground pepper

▪ Preheat the oven to 425°F. Rinse and clean the chicken well and pat dry with a paper towel. Place the chicken breast side up in a shallow 15 × 12-inch greased pan. Separate the skin from the breast meat with your fingers and insert a liberal amount of thyme between the two. Place another handful of thyme inside the cavity.

▪ Scatter the onion chunks, potato slices, and garlic cloves around the chicken. In a measuring cup, heat the butter and chicken stock together in the microwave; pour over the chicken and vegetables. Squeeze the lemon half over the chicken and place the lemon in the cavity of the chicken along with the thyme. Add salt and pepper to the chicken and vegetables to taste.

▪ Bake the chicken for 30 minutes, then turn it over, back side up, and baste with the pan juices. Lower the heat to 350°F. and bake the chicken 20 to 30 minutes longer, basting occasionally, or until a meat thermometer inserted into the thigh registers 180°F. and the potatoes are tender.

▪ Remove the chicken from the oven and, keeping it covered, allow it to rest for 10 minutes. Carve and serve with the vegetables and pan juices.

Soft Orange Frosted Cookies

Makes about 75 cookies

VISITING A KENTUCKY AMISH community is a treat since they are so private and rural. Since some of this group deliberately moved to Kentucky to escape the hurly-burly of the encroaching English world, they have not encouraged tourism in any way. There are no signs in their yards advertising quilts for sale, nor are there roadside stands. This exemplifies the dissimilarities that are allowed, even encouraged, among a people whom we tend to think of as a homogenous group.

Now to cookies. This is a superb cookie—soft, cakelike, and definitely orange! The frosting is really good. When these are sold at a roadside stand, customers flock to buy them.

> 1 6-ounce can orange juice concentrate, thawed
> 1½ cups granulated sugar
> 1 cup (2 sticks) butter, at room temperature
> 1 cup sour cream, at room temperature
> 2 eggs
> 4 cups all-purpose flour
> 1 teaspoon baking powder
> 1 teaspoon baking soda
> ½ teaspoon salt
> 2 tablespoons grated orange zest

ORANGE FROSTING
> 1 3-ounce package cream cheese, at room
>   temperature
> 1 tablespoon butter, at room temperature

2 cups confectioners' sugar
2 tablespoons orange juice concentrate
2 tablespoons milk

■ Preheat the oven to 350°F. Remove 2 table-spoons of juice concentrate for the frosting and set aside.

■ In a large mixer bowl, cream the granulated sugar and butter together for about 2 minutes, then add the sour cream, eggs, and remaining juice concentrate; mix well. In another mixing bowl, whisk together the flour, baking powder, baking soda, and salt. Add the flour mixture and zest to the sugar-butter mixture and beat thoroughly. Using a 1-inch cookie scoop or a tablespoon of dough, drop the cookies onto a nonstick baking sheet or a parchment-lined one, and bake for 10 minutes or until the bottoms are lightly browned. Do not overbake. Remove the cookies to a rack to cool.

■ MAKE THE FROSTING: In a mixer bowl, beat the cream cheese and butter until blended. Add 1 cup of the confectioners' sugar, then the 2 tablespoons of orange juice concentrate and the milk. Add the remaining sugar and beat until smooth.

■ Frost the top of each cookie, allow the frosting to firm up, then transfer to tightly covered tins or plastic containers, placing wax paper between the layers.

Buttered Toffee Apple Pie

Makes one 10-inch pie; serves 8 to 10

THE TOFFEE TOPPING on this delicately flavored apple pie makes it most unusual. Be sure to use a 10-inch pie pan, or the pan juices will run over and really mess up your oven.

Some frugal bakers in this part of the country take the leftover apple peelings and cores, cover them with water, and boil them until tender, then strain it. The juice can be made into jelly and the peelings dried and steeped with tea.

Pastry for a 2-crust 10-inch pie (opposite page)
⅓ cup light corn syrup
3 tablespoons granulated sugar
1 tablespoon melted butter
1 tablespoon quick-cooking tapioca
1 teaspoon ground cinnamon
½ teaspoon grated nutmeg
¼ teaspoon salt
6 apples, such as Gala or Mutsu,
    peeled, cored, and thinly sliced

TOFFEE TOPPING
½ cup plus 2 tablespoons dark brown sugar,
    packed
¼ cup chopped English walnuts
3 tablespoons light corn syrup
3 tablespoons melted butter
1 teaspoon vanilla extract
2 tablespoons all-purpose flour
¼ teaspoon ground cinnamon

■ Preheat the oven to 425°F. Roll out half the pastry thinly on a floured surface and line a 10-inch pan, patting it in firmly. Set aside.

■ In a large mixing bowl, combine the corn syrup, granulated sugar, butter, tapioca, cinnamon, nutmeg, and salt. Allow to stand for 10 minutes. Add the apples and toss lightly to coat. Transfer the filling to the pastry shell.

■ Roll out the top crust, roll onto the top of the apples, and seal the edges; slash the top to let steam escape. Bake for 10 minutes, then reduce the heat to 350°F. and bake for 30 minutes more or until the crust is golden brown and juices are bubbling up through the top crust.

■ MEANWHILE, MAKE THE TOFFEE TOPPING: In a small bowl, combine the brown sugar, walnuts, corn syrup, butter, vanilla, flour, and cinnamon. Remove the pie from the oven, pour the topping over the crust, and immediately return it to the oven to bake 5 minutes longer. Transfer to a rack to cool completely before cutting into wedges and serving.

Perfect Pie Pastry

Makes enough for 2 pies with top crusts

THIS REMAINS MY FAVORITE pie pastry; it never, ever fails. It is prepared with an electric mixer and is ideal for the cook who has always been apprehensive about making pie crust, for it handles beautifully and comes out flavorful and golden every time. Make a double recipe and freeze the extra. One-fourth of this recipe is enough dough for one 8- or 9-inch pie shell; half of this recipe is enough for a 2-crust pie.

4 cups all-purpose flour
1 tablespoon sugar
2 teaspoons salt
1¾ cups butter-flavored solid vegetable shortening
1 egg
1 tablespoon cider vinegar
½ cup water

■ Combine the flour, sugar, salt, and shortening in a large mixer bowl and blend until it has the texture of coarse crumbs. In a small bowl, whisk or beat together the egg, vinegar, and water. Drizzle over the flour mixture and mix thoroughly. Shape the dough into a patty, wrap in plastic wrap, and place in the freezer for 45 minutes, or refrigerate overnight.

■ When chilled, form the dough into a long roll, then divide into fourths. Roll and use immediately, or wrap each portion separately and refrigerate or freeze.

Stews, Bogs & Burgoos

Recipes from the Great American Stewpot

JAMES VILLAS

■ **AUTHOR**

James Villas, longtime *Town & Country* food and wine editor

■ **WHY HE WROTE IT**

"This cookbook . . . is devoted exclusively to American stews—their rich geographical history, their paramount role in the evolution of our cookery, their prodigious diversity, and, indeed, their unique succulence."

■ **WHY IT MADE OUR LIST**

Who knew there were so many versions of the great American stew? Mulls, ragouts, bogs, burgoos, hotpots, pilaus, gumbos—though the name may change with the region, stew is a favorite from coast to coast, and Villas serves up an impressive variety here. The recipes range from hearty and homey to surprisingly stylish. Beef stew, for example, is dressed up with wine, applejack, or stout; ancho chiles, cilantro, or orange zest; quinces, oysters, or blue cheese, depending on which of the many versions you choose.

FROM THE BOOK

■ **FIGHTING WORDS**

"Despite the curious, downright stupid neglect that stews have suffered in recent years thanks mainly to the frenzied ambitions of young superstar chefs oblivious to genuine regional cooking and determined to blindly modernize and fancify all American food, I must say that I've never met anyone anywhere who doesn't love a good stew."

■ **CHAPTERS**

Beef Stews ▪ Pork Stews ▪ Lamb and Veal Stews ▪ Poultry Stews ▪ Game and Variety Meat Stews ▪ Seafood Stews ▪ Vegetable, Bean, and Fruit Stews ▪ Biscuits

■ **PREVIOUS CREDITS**

Villas has authored six cookbooks before this one, including *American Taste* and *My Mother's Southern Kitchen*.

■ **SPECIFICS**

306 pages, more than 150 recipes, $25. Published by William Morrow and Company, Inc.

NEW ENGLAND
PORK AND CLAM STEW

THE PORTUGUESE HAVE ALWAYS been an important ethnic influence in New England, not only because they are responsible for much of the commercial fishing but also because their unusual style of cooking has contributed lots to the region's cuisine. Pork with clams might sound like an odd pairing, but I've loved the exotic combination ever since tasting the great Boston chef Jasper White's pork ribs chops with clams and garlic sauce—the inspiration behind this savory stew. This is one of the rare occasions when I use a relatively expensive boneless pork loin, the rationale being that the clams should not be overpowered by the more aggressive flavor of shoulder or other lesser cuts. Notice that the loin requires a shorter cooking time, and remember when seasoning that the clams provide a good deal of salt. This stew is also delicious when small linguiça sausages (so beloved by the Portuguese) are substituted for the pork.

2½ pounds boneless pork loin, trimmed of excess fat and silverskin
  and cut into 1½-inch cubes
3 tablespoons all-purpose flour
3 tablespoons olive oil
1 large onion, chopped
1 celery rib, chopped
1 garlic clove, minced
½ cup dry white wine
2 large, ripe tomatoes, chopped
5 cloves
1 bay leaf
Salt and freshly ground black pepper to taste
2 cups beef stock or broth
12 to 18 littleneck clams, well scrubbed and rinsed

Dust the pork cubes with the flour, tapping off any excess. In a large, heavy pot, heat the oil over moderately high heat, then brown the pork on all sides and transfer to a plate. Add the onion, celery, and garlic, cook, stirring, till softened, about 2 minutes, and transfer to the plate.

Add the wine to the pot and stir. Return the pork and vegetables to the pot, add the tomatoes, cloves, bay leaf, salt and pepper, and stock, and stir. Bring to a boil, then reduce the heat to a gentle simmer, cover, and cook until the pork is tender, about 45 minutes. Add the clams, increase the heat to moderately high, cover, and cook just till the clams open, about 7 minutes (discard any that do not open).

Serve equal amounts of pork and clams on each plate.

Makes 4 to 6 servings

COLUMBIA COUNTY APPLEJACK BEEF STEW

So MUCH DID I RAVE about this boozy stew the first time my friend Don Erickson served it at his eighteenth-century farmhouse in Clinton Corner, New York, that I could depend on seeing the big pot on the stove every time I visited—especially during the snowy months. Applejack, which is brandy made from apple cider throughout much of New England and upstate New York, dates back in the United States to at least the early nineteenth century and can be traced even further to English "apple john," a variety of apple. Although we are still a major producer, you don't see or hear much about this potent, flavorful spirit outside the Northeast, which is a shame since applejack is not only a delectable restorative and important link with our culinary past but the ideal ingredient for adding new character to any number of meat stews. Don would often marinate his beef overnight, but I've found that a few hours is sufficient.

1 cup applejack (apple brandy)
¼ cup vegetable oil
4 shallots, chopped
2 garlic cloves, minced
Juice of 1 lemon
⅛ teaspoon dried thyme, crumbled
1 bay leaf
Salt and freshly ground black pepper to taste

continued

Tabasco sauce to taste

3 pounds boneless beef chuck, trimmed of excess fat and cut into
1½-inch pieces

2 cups beef stock or broth

2 medium-size carrots, scraped and cut into 1-inch-thick rounds

2 small turnips, peeled and cubed

2 small parsnips, peeled and cubed

In a large bowl, combine the applejack, oil, shallots, garlic, lemon juice, thyme, bay leaf, salt and pepper, and Tabasco and stir well. Add the meat, cover with plastic wrap, and refrigerate 3 hours, turning the meat twice.

Transfer the meat and marinade to a large, heavy pot. Add the stock, bring to a simmer, cover, and cook for 2 hours. Add the carrots, turnips, and parsnips, return the stew to a simmer, and cook till the turnips and parsnips are tender, about 1 hour longer. Remove the top of the pot, increase the heat to moderately high, and cook the sauce down to a fairly thick gravy. Taste for seasoning.

Makes 6 servings

TIGUA GREEN INDIAN CHILI

WHILE IN TUCSON to eat barbecue, I was encouraged by my colleagues Jane and Michael Stern to make the detour down to El Paso just to sample this distinctive and rare chili served at the colorful Tigua Indian Restaurant. They also serve a mean red chili, but it was the fiery green one speckled with pepper seeds (and sometimes made with mutton instead of beef) that taught me what the flavor of Southwestern chili is really all about. Needless to say, nobody at the restaurant was about to part with the exact recipe, but after a lengthy conversation with a group of Indians at the next table, I came up with this version that comes pretty close to the slightly soupy, intensely flavored chili that forced me to gasp (delightfully) for breath after every spoonful. Rice and hearty Indian bread were served with it, but I find that cornbread makes a very acceptable substitute—and helps to placate the heat.

2 tablespoons lard

2 pounds boneless beef shank or chuck, trimmed of excess fat and cut into
1-inch cubes

1 medium-size onion, finely chopped

1 garlic clove, minced

1 ripe tomato, diced

¼ cup ground dried hot peppers (like Anaheims, anchos, or serranos)

2 fresh jalapeño peppers, finely chopped

1 teaspoon ground cumin

½ teaspoon dried oregano, crumbled

1 tablespoon chili powder

1 tablespoon finely ground cornmeal

Salt to taste

2 cups beef stock or broth

1 cup water

1 tablespoon cider vinegar

2 medium-size potatoes, peeled and cut into tiny chunks

In a large, heavy pot, melt the lard over moderately high heat, then add the beef, and brown on all sides. Reduce the heat to moderate, add the onion and garlic, and stir 2 minutes. Add all the remaining ingredients except the potatoes, stir well, and bring to a simmer. Cover and let cook for 2 hours, adding a little more water if necessary. Add the potatoes, stir, and cook till the meat and potatoes are tender, about 30 minutes longer. Serve the chili in deep bowls.

Makes 4 to 6 servings

STEW SAVVY *O*ne of the quickest and neatest ways to mince garlic cloves used in so many stews is to rub them over the tines of a heavy fork.

LATIN AMERICAN

COOKING

ACROSS THE U.S.A.

HIMILCE NOVAS AND ROSEMARY SILVA

■ AUTHORS

Himilce Novas, a novelist and poet who lectures on Latino history and culture, and Rosemary Silva, a teacher and amateur cook who spent eight years researching Latin American cooking in the United States

■ WHY THEY WROTE IT

". . . we realized that it was possible, thanks to recent tides of immigration, to sample the cuisines of all twenty-six sovereign nations in Latin America—namely, Mexico, El Salvador, Nicaragua, Costa Rica, Guatemala, Honduras, Panama, Venezuela, Colombia, Ecuador, Peru, Bolivia, Chile, Argentina, Uruguay, Paraguay, Cuba, Puerto Rico, the Dominican Republic, Jamaica, Haiti, Belize, Suriname, Guyana, French Guiana, and Brazil—without ever leaving the country. The idea for a book exploring Latin American cooking in the continental United States was born."

■ WHY IT MADE OUR LIST

Part of the excellent "Knopf Cooks American" series, this collection provides a fascinating look at how Latino cooking has changed, merged with other traditions, turned into an American hybrid called Nuevo Latino or Nuevo Americano, and become an indelible part of this country's cuisine. At a time in our national life when salsa outsells ketchup and jalapeño bagels are a not-uncommon sight, these recipes should find a welcome audience.

FROM THE BOOK

■ CULINARY OBSERVATION

"Fish and shellfish—always flavored with a vibrant marinade or sauce—must dance the mambo on your tongue. Bare broiled scrod is entirely unacceptable."

■ CHAPTERS

Soups ▪ Appetizers and Salads ▪ Fish and Shellfish ▪ Poultry and Game ▪ Meats ▪ Rice, Beans, and Vegetables ▪ Tamales, Empanadas, and Other Turnovers ▪ Breads ▪ Desserts ▪ Drinks

■ SPECIFICS

334 pages, 200 recipes, approximately 50 black-and-white photographs, $27.50. Published by Alfred A. Knopf, Inc.

TORTILLA SOUP

Sopa de tortilla

When winter winds blow, there is something wonderful about dipping into a steaming bowl of Tortilla Soup with its citrus-and-tomato-laced broth. The broth is only the beginning. Each spoonful reveals tender morsels of chicken, earthy tortilla strips, creamy avocado, and lively cilantro. In the America of yesteryear, Tortilla Soup was relished primarily by Mexican Americans who inherited family recipes that had been passed down from generation to generation. Slowly Tortilla Soup has found a place in the pantheon of American soups, and nowadays there are recipes for it, both classic and adventurous, from Latinos and non-Latinos alike in many of the current magazines and cookbooks.

This soup is hearty enough to be the centerpiece of a casual supper for a small gathering of friends or family. Start with a salad of mixed greens with Gorgonzola cheese and pecans, and finish with warm *sopaipillas* rolled in cinnamon sugar or dribbled with honey for dessert.

FOR THE TORTILLA STRIPS:
4 yellow or blue corn tortillas

Vegetable oil, for frying

FOR THE BROTH:
1 tablespoon olive oil
1/2 cup finely minced yellow onion
2 large cloves garlic, peeled and finely minced
1 teaspoon finely minced jalapeño chile
1/2 teaspoon ground cumin

2 cups canned crushed tomatoes
5 cups homemade or canned chicken broth
1 corn tortilla, cut into 1/4-inch-wide strips
2 tablespoons freshly squeezed lime juice

FOR THE SOUP:
1 cup chicken breast, grilled or poached, and cut on the bias into 1/2-inch dice
1/3 cup grated Monterey Jack cheese

1 1/2 medium ripe Haas avocados, halved, peeled, pitted, and cut into 1/2-inch dice
2 tablespoons finely minced fresh cilantro

Cut the tortillas into strips 1/8-inch wide with a sharp knife or a pair of scissors. Pour enough vegetable oil into a large skillet to coat the bottom generously. Heat the oil over medium heat and fry half of the tortilla strips, turning once, until they are crisp and golden, about 2 minutes per side. Transfer the tortilla strips with a slotted spatula to a large plate lined with paper towels and drain. Fry the second batch, adding more oil, if necessary.

Make the broth: Heat the tablespoon of olive oil in a large pot over medium heat. Sauté the minced onions, garlic, jalapeño, and cumin until the onions are lightly browned, about 4 minutes. Add the crushed tomatoes, chicken broth, and the 1 tortilla cut into strips, and

bring the broth to a boil. Cover, reduce the heat, and simmer for 20 minutes.

Transfer the broth to a food processor, add the lime juice, and process until smooth. Return the broth to the pot and reheat it over medium heat. Pour the broth into 4 bowls. Place one fourth of the chicken, cheese, and avocado, in that order, in the center of each bowl. Garnish with the tortilla strips and cilantro, and serve at once.

Serves 4

MUSSELS IN *SALSA CARIBE* AND WHITE WINE

Mejillones en salsa caribe y vino blanco

"**M**y father, Pedro Rivera, makes the most incredible salsa, which we call *salsa caribe*. It is not a salsa in the Mexican sense, but rather a thick, crimson spread or marinade composed of Puerto Rican *adobo* (an oregano-rich spice rub), tomato, onion, garlic, lemon juice, and olive oil," began Gibrán X. Rivera, a senior majoring in International Studies at Boston College and a Woodrow Wilson Fellow. "We slather it on roasted chicken, grilled steak, and broiled fish during the final minutes of cooking, and on anything that strikes our imagination. My dad perfected the salsa recipe while we were still living in Puerto Rico. I remember that a jar of the *salsita* was always tucked in the picnic basket on our trips to the beach. After we moved to the Boston area, my dad continued to make *salsa caribe* often, especially during the long, snowy winter months, so that we would not forget the island we love. Whenever I go home from college and bring my Sri Lankan and Senegalese roommates or my Arab girlfriend along, my dad is sure to fix a batch of the salsa because he is proud to share a taste of Puerto Rico with the world."

"*Salsa caribe* is a great foundation for steamed mussels, a shellfish I have grown fond of in New England," says Gibrán. "In my recipe the salsa is added to mussels, tomatoes, and white wine to create a kind of Puerto Rican Mussels Marseillaise. I serve the mussels and sauce on a bed of al dente linguine with a heaping plate of my dad's garlic bread. It's just one more way we enjoy *salsa caribe* at my house."

4 dozen large live mussels

FOR THE *ADOBO*:
6 medium cloves garlic, peeled and left whole
1/2 tablespoon dried powdered oregano (not crumbled)
1/2 teaspoon salt, or to taste

1/8 teaspoon freshly ground black pepper, or to taste
2 tablespoons freshly squeezed lemon juice or distilled white vinegar
1 tablespoon olive oil

FOR THE *SALSA CARIBE*:
2 1/2 tablespoons olive oil
2 medium yellow onions, peeled and minced
4 large cloves garlic, peeled and minced

4 tablespoons tomato paste
2 tablespoons freshly squeezed lemon juice or distilled white vinegar
1/2 teaspoon granulated sugar

FOR THE SAUCE:
5 medium ripe tomatoes, or 1 1/2 cups canned peeled tomatoes, chopped
1 1/2 cups dry white wine

1/4 cup finely minced fresh parsley or cilantro, for garnish

Prepare the mussels: Discard any mussels that are not closed or feel much lighter (the mussel is dead) or much heavier (the shells are filled with sand) than the rest. Scrub the mussels under cool running water with a stiff brush to rid them of any dirt or barnacles. Debeard with a knife or scissors by cutting off any threads that protrude from the shells. Place the mussels in a bucket filled with cool water and soak them for 1 hour so they release any sand. Rinse the mussels in a colander and drain.

Make the *adobo*: Process the garlic, oregano, salt, pepper, and lemon juice or distilled white vinegar in a food processor or electric blender until blended. Add the olive oil and blend well.

Make the *salsa caribe*: Heat the olive oil in a large stockpot over medium heat and sauté the onions and garlic, stirring occasionally, until the onions are limp, about 6 minutes. Stir in the tomato paste, lemon juice or distilled white vinegar, sugar, and 2 teaspoons of the reserved *adobo*.

Add the tomatoes and white wine to the *salsa caribe*, and cook, covered, for 10 minutes. Raise the heat to medium-high, add the mussels, and cook, covered, until they open, about 5 minutes. (Discard any mussels that remain shut.)

Divide the mussels among 4 large bowls. Ladle the sauce over each and sprinkle with minced parsley or cilantro. (You may also serve the mussels and sauce on a bed of linguine.) Serve at once with garlic bread or crusty Italian bread and place a large bowl in the center of the table for discarding the mussel shells.

Serves 4

CURRY GOAT OR LAMB

Some of the most tantalizing flavors of Jamaica, like aromatic allspice, spirited curry powder, fiery Scotch bonnet peppers, and creamy coconut, commingle in this rich bronze stew that adorns the table at most festive occasions in traditional Jamaican America. Curry Goat came to be when East Indian indentured laborers descended on Jamaica at the invitation of the British, who recruited them to work the fields after the abolition of African slavery in 1838. The curry recipes the East Indians carried with them called for lamb, but sheep were nonexistent in early-nineteenth-century Jamaica, so they turned to goat instead. Nowadays, kid—a baby goat no more than six months old—is the meat of choice for this Jamaican curry, as mature goats have tough, gamy meat. The scarcity of kid meat in the United States has led Jamaican Americans to come full circle and use lamb. If you are lucky enough to find kid in a specialty meat market, give it a try. It is just as tender as lamb and actually tastes less gamy.

Every Jamaican American family has its own special take on Curry Goat or Lamb, though most agree that the meat should first be marinated in a spice rub. Many insist that allspice, a spice native to Jamaica that comes from the dried berries of the pimiento tree, is a necessary ingredient in the spice rub, but a minority does without it. Some Jamaican Americans prepare a simple curry that hinges on the spices and broth, while others enrich the curry with coconut milk and lime juice, or with tomatoes. Since the flavors of coconut, lime juice, and tomatoes fuse so delightfully, this version of curry goat sidesteps tradition and includes all three. Jamaican Americans serve Curry Goat or Lamb over white rice, sometimes with traditional accompaniments of fried green plantains and mango chutney. Curry Goat or Lamb is also used as a stuffing for *roti*, an East Indian griddle-fried bread that has also found a place in the Jamaican kitchen.

2 pounds boneless goat or lamb, trimmed of all excess fat and cut into 1-inch cubes
1 Scotch bonnet chile, or substitute a 1-inch-long habanero chile, seeded, stems removed, and minced, or to taste
1½ tablespoons curry powder (if you use Madras curry powder, cut the amount of chile in half)
½ teaspoon ground allspice
¼ teaspoon salt, or to taste
⅛ teaspoon freshly ground black pepper, or to taste
1 tablespoon butter

1 tablespoon olive oil
1 large white onion, peeled and minced
1 large clove garlic, peeled and minced
1 medium ripe tomato, finely diced
1 cup canned unsweetened coconut milk
½ cup chicken stock, or substitute water
1 tablespoon freshly squeezed lime or lemon juice
2 medium scallions, root ends removed and minced
1 bay leaf
2 tablespoons finely minced fresh parsley or cilantro, for garnish

Season the goat or lamb with the chile pepper, curry powder, allspice, salt, and black pepper in a large nonreactive mixing bowl. Cover with plastic wrap and allow the meat to marinate in the refrigerator for 1 hour.

Heat the butter and olive oil in a large skillet over medium heat. Sauté the meat in 2 batches until the pieces are browned on all sides, about 7 minutes per batch, removing them to a large plate when they have browned.

Raise the heat to medium-high and sauté the minced onions in the oil remaining in the skillet, stirring often, until the onions are lightly browned, about 4 minutes. Add the garlic and sauté an additional minute. Stir in the diced tomatoes and continue cooking for 2 minutes. Return the meat and its juices to the skillet. Add the coconut milk, chicken stock or water, lime or lemon juice, scallions, and bay leaf. Bring to a boil, then reduce the heat, cover, and simmer until the meat is very tender, 45 minutes to 1 hour. Taste and adjust the seasonings. Serve the dish, garnished with fresh parsley or cilantro, with steamed white rice.

Serves 4

MARY ANN ESPOSITO

Host of PBS's Ciao Italia

WHAT YOU KNEAD

Three Simple Yeast Doughs That Turn into Dozens of Breads, Pizzas, Savory Pies, and Desserts

Mary Ann Esposito, host of PBS's long-running *Ciao Italia*

■ WHY SHE WROTE IT

" 'I am afraid to work with yeast.' So many people said this to me that it became a pleasurable mission of mine to help them see how easy it is to make simple yeast dough."

■ WHY IT MADE OUR LIST

Among the several good bread books published recently, this is the least intimidating. With her down-to-earth style, straightforward text, and step-by-step photos, Esposito makes bread-baking look easy, in fact fun. As you might expect from the host of an Italian cooking show, many of these recipes have an Italian accent; as Esposito says, "it is nearly impossible to move too far from one's roots."

■ CHAPTERS

Bread-Making Basics: What You Need to Know ■ The Straight Dough ■ Nonna's Sponge Dough ■ Simply Sweet Dough ■ Beyond Bread Crumbs ■ Homemade Is Better

■ PREVIOUS CREDITS

Esposito is the author of three books on traditional Italian cooking: *Ciao Italia*, *Nella Cucina*, and *Celebrations Italian Style*.

■ SPECIFICS

152 pages, more than 50 recipes, approximately 175 color photographs, $22. Published by William Morrow and Company, Inc.

FROM THE BOOK

■ WHAT SHE KNEADS

"For me, there is nothing like my own pair of hands when it comes to making dough. Call me old-fashioned, but the time-honored tradition of hand-working dough puts me in tune with the whole process of making bread. It is with my hands that I, the baker, am drawn to and connected with this ancient craft."

Nonna's Sponge Dough

■ MAKES 2 POUNDS, 2 OUNCES DOUGH

MADRE (MOTHER DOUGH)
$1/2$ teaspoon active dry yeast
$3/4$ cup warm (110° to 115°F) potato water
1 cup unbleached all-purpose flour

SECOND DOUGH
$3^1/2$ to 4 cups unbleached all-purpose flour
2 teaspoons salt
$1^1/4$ cups warm (110° to 115°F) potato water
1 teaspoon active dry yeast
1 teaspoon olive oil

In a medium bowl, dissolve the yeast in the water and let it proof for 5 minutes; chalky-looking bubbles will appear on the surface. Stir in the flour and mix well. At this point the *madre* will be the consistency of heavy pancake batter. Cover the bowl tightly with plastic wrap and let the sponge rise for at least 3 hours or even overnight.

When the *madre* is ready, it should smell yeasty, look fluffy and light, and have a myriad of bubbles appearing on the surface. The *madre* is now ready to be combined with the additional yeast, water, flour, olive oil, and salt to make the second dough.

continued

Mixing the yeast and water
into the flour

Showing the pancake consistency

Fully risen sponge

Mixing sponge into
yeast mixture

Adding flour to sponge liquid

Mixing dough by hand

Mixing in olive oil

Turning out the shaggy mass

To make the second dough using a fontana, heap 3½ cups of the flour on a work surface. Add the salt and use your hands to mix the flour and salt together. Make a hole in the center of the flour with your fist.

Pour the water into the center, add the yeast, and stir with your fingers to dissolve the yeast. Let the yeast proof as above, then add the *madre* and the olive oil and mix well with your fingers. Working in a clockwise fashion, begin bringing flour from the inside of the wall into the yeast mixture with your fingers.

When a rough, shaggy mass of dough is formed, begin to knead the dough, adding additional flour as needed to make a smooth ball of dough that does not stick to your hands. Knead the dough for about 5 minutes, then cover the dough with a towel and let it rest for 5 minutes. Repeat the kneading and resting 3 more times. Each time, you will notice that the dough is easier to knead than the previous time. This is because the flour is gradually absorbing the water in the dough and allowing the gluten in the flour to relax. The dough should become soft and no longer sticky, and it should move on the work surface with ease.

Spray a large bowl with olive oil spray or coat with butter. Put the dough in the bowl, turn to coat with the oil or butter, and cover the large bowl tightly with plastic wrap. Let the dough rise for about 1½ hours, or until doubled in size.

The dough is now ready to be used in any of the recipes in this chapter. It can also be frozen, which is useful if you want to use only half the dough. Spray a heavy-duty plastic bag with vegetable oil spray, put the dough in the bag, squeeze out the air, and seal the bag. Freeze for up to 3 months.

To make the second dough in a bowl, dissolve the yeast in the water and let proof as directed above. Stir in the olive oil and the *madre*. Using your hands, mix in 3½ cups of the flour, about 1 cup at a time, until a shaggy dough is formed. Add the salt with the third addition of flour. Turn the dough out onto a floured work surface and begin kneading, adding additional flour as needed until a smooth ball of dough is created that is no longer sticky. Follow the directions above for kneading, resting, and rising.

To make the second dough in an electric mixer, follow the instructions below, then add the olive oil to the water before you begin adding the flour. Once the dough feels soft and smooth, beat it for 5 minutes to knead, then let it rest for 5 minutes. Repeat 3 more times, then turn it out onto a floured work surface and knead by hand about 5 minutes. Let rise as directed above.

How to Make Simple Straight Dough in an Electric Mixer

I rarely use an electric mixer for making the Straight Dough, but each baker approaches tasks differently in the kitchen, so if you want to try making the dough in a mixer, here is how to do it.

My mixer is a heavy-duty KitchenAid stand mixer. It has a dough hook, batter paddle, and whisk attachment. I have found that the batter paddle actually works better at thoroughly mixing the dough than the dough hook, but you be the judge—try making dough with the dough hook and with the batter paddle, and see which you prefer.

Pour the amount of warm water indicated in the recipe for dissolving the yeast into the bowl of the mixer and sprinkle the yeast over the top. Attach the dough hook or batter paddle to the mixer and on low speed, mix the yeast into the water. Let the yeast proof for about 5 minutes, until the mixture has lots of chalky-looking bubbles on the top. Pour the remaining water into the bowl and stir on low speed to blend the yeast and water.

Add the flour 1 cup at a time, stirring on low speed to blend the ingredients. Add the salt with the third addition of flour. Turn the speed to medium-high and add just enough additional flour to create a dough that moves away from the sides of the bowl and clings to the dough hook or batter paddle. Stop the machine and feel the dough. It should be soft, but not sticky or gummy. If it is too sticky, add more flour, a tablespoon at a time, until the right consistency is obtained. If the dough is dry and crumbly, add a little water, about a teaspoon at a time, until the dough becomes soft and smooth.

Remove the bowl from the mixer base and turn the dough out onto a floured surface. With your hands, knead the dough for 3 to 4 minutes as described above, forming it into a ball. Lightly spray a large bowl with vegetable or olive oil spray and place the dough in the bowl. Turn the dough to coat with the oil, cover the bowl tightly with plastic wrap, and let the dough rise until doubled in size.

Straight Dough

■ MAKES 1 POUND, 14 OUNCES DOUGH

1 package active dry yeast (0.25 ounce)
1³/4 cups warm (110° to 115°F) filtered or
*   bottled noncarbonated water*
1 tablespoon extra-virgin olive oil
4 to 4¹/2 cups unbleached all-purpose flour
2 teaspoons fine sea salt

To make the dough using the fontana method, in a small bowl, dissolve the yeast in ¹/2 cup of the water, stirring to mix well. Let the yeast proof for about 5 minutes, or until tiny clusters of chalky-looking bubbles appear on the surface. Stir the remaining 1¹/4 cups water and the olive oil into the proofed yeast.

Mound the flour on a work surface and make a hole in the center of the flour (this is the fontana). Sprinkle the salt over the flour. Carefully pour the yeast mixture into the hole. Using your fingers, begin bringing the flour from the inside wall of the fontana into the liquid, working in a clockwise movement as you incorporate the flour. Be careful not to break through the wall; if any liquid does leak out, catch it with some of the flour. As you continue to incorporate the flour, a shaggy, lumpy mass will form; add just enough flour to make a dough that holds together. Push the excess flour to the side with a bench knife. Now you are ready to knead the dough: Knead until you have a soft ball of dough that is slightly tacky but not sticking to your hands, about 5 minutes. Lightly spray a large bowl with olive oil spray, put the dough in the bowl, and turn to coat it with oil. Cover the bowl tightly with plastic wrap and let the dough rise until almost doubled in size, about 1 hour.

To make the dough by hand in a bowl, dissolve the yeast in the water in a large bowl and proof as directed above, then add the remaining 1¹/4 cups water and the olive oil. Begin adding the flour to the yeast mixture, 1 cup at a time, mixing it in well with your hands. Add the salt with the third cup of flour. Add just enough flour so that the dough comes together in a shaggy mass. Turn the dough out onto a lightly floured surface and follow the directions above for kneading and rising.

To make the dough in an electric mixer, dissolve the yeast in the water in the mixer bowl and proof as directed above, then add the remaining 1¹/4 cups water and the olive oil. Follow the instructions on page 280 for mixing, kneading, and rising.

When the dough has risen and is almost doubled in size, it is ready to be used in any of the recipes in this chapter.

Pumpkin Seed, Sage, and Pancetta Bread

Inspiration for this bread comes from the many breads I have joyfully eaten all over Italy. From craggy-looking loaves of crusty Pugliese olive bread to the airy bread of Ferrara called *manina* (little hand), Italian breads have always held a fascination for me. This bread is studded with toasted pumpkin seeds and cracklings of crispy Italian bacon (*pancetta*), and perfumed with specks of fresh sage. Almost a meal by itself, it complements a bowl of homemade tomato soup perfectly. It is *the* bread to serve on your Thanksgiving table, and it is unmatched in its versatility as a sandwich bread for egg salad, grilled vegetables, cold chicken, or roast beef. ■ MAKES 1 LARGE LOAF

1 cup hulled pumpkin seeds
1/4 pound pancetta or unsmoked bacon, diced (about 1 cup)
1 recipe Nonna's Sponge Dough (page 278)
1/3 cup minced fresh sage

Preheat the oven to 350°F.

Spread the pumpkin seeds on a baking sheet and toast in the oven for about 7 minutes, until they just start to brown; watch carefully so they do not burn. Remove the seeds to a bowl and let them cool.

In a small skillet, sauté the pancetta or bacon over medium heat until nicely browned and crisp. Transfer to a cutting board and let it cool slightly. Mince the pancetta or bacon very fine and transfer it to a small dish.

Line a baker's peel with parchment paper or lightly grease a baking sheet.

Punch down the dough and turn it out onto a lightly floured surface. Knead it for 3 to 4 minutes, until smooth and no longer sticky. Roll the dough out into a 14-inch circle.

Sprinkle the pumpkin seeds, pancetta, and sage over the dough. Starting at the side nearest you, roll the dough up tightly and pinch the seam closed. Fold the dough in half and knead it until the filling bursts through the dough. Continue kneading until the filling ingredients are evenly dispersed throughout the dough (if some ingredients pop out, knead them back into the dough) and the dough feels smooth. Form the dough into a round loaf and place it on the baker's peel or greased baking sheet. Cover the dough with a clean towel and set aside to rise for about 35 minutes, until nearly doubled in size.

If using a baking stone, preheat the oven to 425°F and put the stone on the lowest oven rack to preheat. If using a baking sheet, preheat the oven to 400°F.

Make three short shallow slashes across the top of the dough with a lame, sharp knife, or razor blade. If using a baking stone, slide the bread, with the paper, onto the stone. Or put the baking sheet in the oven. Mist the oven walls with water, then mist again once or twice during the first 10 minutes of baking. Bake the bread for 35 to 40 minutes if using a stone, 40 to 45 minutes if using a baking sheet, until it is golden brown and crusty on the top and bottom and the bottom sounds hollow when tapped. Remove the bread to a cooling rack.

Tangy Tomato Logs

Dried tomatoes have many uses: in sauces, stews, salads, antipasto, and sandwiches. I also add them to half the Straight Dough to make a pair of rustic, crunchy bread logs that are great with cheeses such as Asiago and Taleggio. Or use all the dough and double the amount of dried tomatoes (and olives, if you like) to make four logs. The logs freeze beautifully.

■ MAKES TWO 16-INCH-LONG LOGS

$1/2$ recipe Straight Dough (page 281)
$1/2$ cup diced dried tomatoes in olive oil, drained
$1/4$ cup diced oil-cured black olives (optional)

Lightly spray a baking sheet with olive oil spray.

Punch down the dough and turn it out onto a lightly floured surface. Knead the dough for 3 to 4 minutes, until smooth and no longer sticky. Divide the dough into 2 equal pieces. Work with one piece at a time, keeping the other piece covered with a towel or a bowl.

Roll the dough out into a 10-inch round. Spread half the tomatoes and half the olives, if desired, over the dough. Roll the dough up like a jelly roll, beginning at the side nearest you. Pinch the seam closed.

Fold the dough in half and knead it until the tomatoes and olives burst through the dough. The dough will be wet because of the tomatoes, but will come together as you knead it. If you must, add only enough additional flour to the work surface to keep the dough from sticking. With lightly floured hands, roll the dough into a 16-inch-long log. Place the log on the greased baking sheet. With scissors, make alternating $1/2$-inch-deep diagonal slits 2 inches apart on either side of the log.

Repeat the process with the remaining dough, leaving a 3-inch space between the 2 logs on the baking sheet. Cover the logs with a clean cloth and let rise for 30 minutes.

Preheat the oven to 425°F.

Bake the logs for 30 to 35 minutes, until they are nicely browned on the top and underside. Remove the logs to a rack to cool completely.

Grissini Rustici/Country Breadsticks

When is a breadstick more than a breadstick? When it's a knotty, puffy, shiny, irregular-looking stick flavored with bits of prosciutto, sharp provolone cheese, and zucchini. These are great as an antipasto or snack, or pack a handful for lunch instead of a sandwich! For a party, stand them up in a country crock. Or tie a bunch with a pretty ribbon and give as a gift from your kitchen.

■ MAKES 28 BREADSTICKS

6 ounces aged provolone cheese, minced
1/4 pound prosciutto, minced
1 small zucchini, minced
Fine sea salt to taste
1 recipe Straight Dough (page 281)
2 teaspoons extra-virgin olive oil
1 egg, slightly beaten

Preheat the oven to 375°F. Lightly grease four baking sheets with olive oil spray and set aside.

In a bowl, mix the cheese, prosciutto, zucchini, and salt together. Set aside.

Punch down the risen dough and turn it out onto a lightly floured surface. Knead the dough for 3 to 4 minutes, until smooth and no longer sticky.

Divide the dough in half. Work with one half at a time, keeping the remaining dough covered with a towel or bowl.

On the lightly floured surface, roll one piece of dough out into a rough circle about 14 inches in diameter. Brush the dough with 1 teaspoon of the olive oil. Spread half the filling ingredients evenly over the dough.

Starting from the edge nearest you, roll the dough up like a jelly roll, tucking in the ends as you roll to keep the filling from falling out. Pinch the seam closed.

Stretch the dough into a 14-inch log. Cut the log into 14 pieces with a bench scraper or knife.

On the floured surface, roll each piece under the palms of your hands into a 10-inch-long stick. Don't worry if some of the filling falls out—just press it back into the dough. Place the sticks on the prepared baking sheets, spacing them evenly. Brush the tops of the sticks with some of the beaten egg.

Bake for 20 to 25 minutes, until the breadsticks are golden brown and shiny. Remove the breadsticks to a cooling rack. Meanwhile, repeat the shaping process with the remaining dough, oil, and filling. When the first breadsticks are done, bake the second batch.

GREAT HOMEMADE BREAD USING YOUR FOOD PROCESSOR

Foreword by Jacques Pépin

CHARLES VAN OVER

the Best Bread Ever

Charles Van Over, who baked plenty of bread as the owner of Restaurant du Village and Village Breads in Connecticut.

WHY HE WROTE IT

"Once you try the food processor method, I guarantee it will become your preferred method for making everything from multigrain rolls to crusty baguettes . . . . On your very first try, you'll have a kitchen filled with the earthy smell of flour and yeast and a batch of flavorful, crusty bread."

WHY IT MADE OUR LIST

It seems too good to be true: making bread without proofing the yeast, without kneading, without covering the kitchen with flour. What's more amazing is that the bread comes out just fine, whether it's crusty baguettes, buttery brioche, chewy bagels, or rich nut loaves. We'll leave you to decide if it's really the best bread ever, but it's certainly the *easiest*.

CHAPTERS

Terms and Techniques ▪ The Best Bread Ever ▪ Breads, Rolls, and Bagels ▪ Flatbreads: Pizza, Focaccia, Breadsticks, and Ciabatta ▪ Enriched Breads ▪ Sourdough Breads and Starters ▪ The Second Time Around: Using Leftover Bread ▪ Bread Makes the Meal: Good Things to Eat with Bread

FROM THE BOOK

CULINARY OBSERVATION

"The beauty of bread making is in the simplicity of its ingredients: flour, salt, yeast, and water. The baker's art lies in mastering how to maintain a delicate balance between these basics to make flavorful bread."

SPECIFICS

272 pages, 95 recipes, 80 black-and-white photographs, 8 color photographs, $27.50. Published by Broadway Books.

The Best Bread Ever

Dough that is too dry

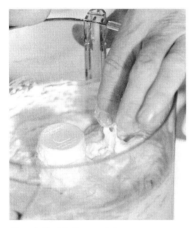

Dough that is too moist

Each step in this recipe is designed to make you feel at ease mixing dough in the food processor. If you've made bread by hand before, then you're accustomed to adding water to the flour as it mixes if the dough feels too firm or flour if the dough feels sticky. When mixing dough in the food processor, you will achieve the same results by holding back a few tablespoons of the water at the beginning of the mixing, adding it if the dough appears to be crumbly or if it is not coming together into a ball in the bowl. Depending on the brand and type of flour you are using, you may not need to add all of the water called for in the recipe. Set out all of your ingredients and have extra flour and a small amount of cool water handy should you need to make adjustments.

The first few times you mix this dough, stop the machine and feel the dough. If it feels very soft and clings to your fingers, add a few tablespoons more flour then resume mixing the dough for the time remaining. Once you have mixed this dough a few times, you'll probably end up throwing the entire amount of water in at the beginning.

Unlike many bread doughs you may be familiar with, this dough does not always double in bulk. In fact, it may seem downright sleepy as it quietly ferments. Once the dough is formed into loaves, it becomes more active. The loaves will puff and swell.

The beauty of this dough is its versatility. Use it to make baguettes or hearty peasant rolls. Make this dough with bread flour as I do or with all-purpose flour for a lighter texture. Once you become adept with this recipe, experiment by adding different blends of flours.

This recipe makes three long baguettes. If you are making baguettes in a home convection oven, try baking them in the convection mode without a pizza stone. You may get better results.

Unbleached bread flour	500 grams	1 pound	3⅓ to 4 cups
Fine sea salt	10 grams	2 teaspoons	2 teaspoons
Instant yeast	1 teaspoon	1 teaspoon	1 teaspoon
Water	315 grams	10 ounces	1¼ cups

Cornmeal for the baking sheet

Three 14-inch loaves

Fermentation:
1½ to 2 hours at room temperature, 70°F to 72°F

Proofing:
35 to 40 minutes at room temperature

1. Place the flour, salt, and yeast in a food processor fitted with the metal blade. Using an instant-read thermometer, adjust the water temperature so that the combined temperatures of the water and the flour give a base temperature of 130°F if using a Cuisinart or KitchenAid or 150°F if using a Braun. With the machine running, pour all but 2 tablespoons of the water through the feed tube. Process for 20 seconds, adding the remaining water if the dough seems crumbly and dry and does not come together into a ball during this time. Continue mixing the dough another 25 seconds, for a total of 45 seconds.

2. Stop the machine and take the temperature of the dough with an instant-read thermometer, which should read between 75°F and 80°F. If the temperature is lower than 75°F, process the dough for an additional 5 seconds. If the temperature of the dough is still lower than 75°F, then process the dough for 5 seconds, up to twice more, until it reaches the desired temperature. If the temperature is higher than 80°F, remove the thermometer, scrape the dough from the food processor into an ungreased bowl, and refrigerate for 5 to 10 minutes. Check the temperature of the dough after 5 minutes; the dough should be 80°F or cooler by that time.

Pour the water through the feed tube

Process the dough for a total of 45 seconds

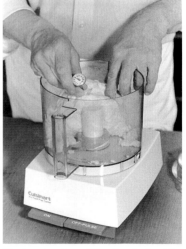
The temperature of the dough should be between 75°F and 80°F

3. Remove the dough from the processor and place it in a large ungreased bowl. Cover the bowl with plastic wrap and allow the dough to ferment for 1½ to 2 hours at room temperature, about 70°F to 72°F. It will increase in volume somewhat, but don't be concerned by how much.

4. Turn the dough onto a lightly floured work surface. With a dough scraper or kitchen knife, divide the dough into 3 equal pieces and shape them into rough balls. Cover them with a sheet of plastic wrap and let rest for 15 to 20 minutes.

5. In preparation for the final proofing, spread a sheet of canvas or a heavy linen cloth on a counter or tabletop and sprinkle it lightly with flour. (If using a baguette pan, spray it with vegetable cooking spray.)

6. Sift a fine coating of flour on the work surface. Place one ball of dough on the surface and gently pat it down to an even thickness of 1 inch. Do not attempt to deflate every air bubble. Using the heels and palms of your hands, flatten the dough into a crude rectangle measuring about 4 x 5 inches and 1 inch thick. Fold the long side farthest from you a little over ⅔ of the way toward you. Using the heel of your hand, gently press the folded edge to seal the dough. Pick up the dough and turn it 180 degrees. Fold over the other long edge of the dough about ⅔ of the way, and seal with the palm of your hand.

7. To make a compact cylinder easy to roll into a baguette shape, use both hands to fold the log in half lengthwise. This time, as you fold, press your thumbs gently inside the fold to create tension on the surface of the log. Using your fingertips, press the edges together to seal the dough into a taut cylinder. This will produce a visible seam running the length of the dough.

8. To roll the dough into a baguette shape, place both hands on the center of the log with your fingers spread apart. Using light uniform pressure, gently roll the dough back and forth into a long snake. Taking care not to stretch the dough, move your hands from the center of the dough to the ends as the loaf begins to lengthen to about 14 inches. If the dough resists rolling, let it rest for 5 minutes before continuing. Repeat steps 6 through 8 with the remaining dough.

9. Using both hands, gently transfer each baguette, seam side up, to the lightly floured cloth. Fold the fabric up to form channels in which each loaf will rise. (Place the baguettes close together so that they rise and don't spread out.) Sprinkle the loaves with flour and cover them loosely with plastic wrap or a kitchen towel. Let the baguettes proof for 30 to 45 minutes, until the dough increases by half its size. It should feel soft but still spring back slightly when poked with your finger.

10. One hour before baking, put the oven rack on the second shelf from the bottom of the oven and place the baking stone on the rack. Place a small pan for water on the oven floor. Preheat the oven to 475°F.

11. Uncover the loaves. Place them seam side down on a peel or on the back of a baking sheet that has been lightly sprinkled with cornmeal. Or place the loaves in greased and lightly floured baguette pans. Sprinkle each loaf lightly with flour, and slash the tops several times diagonally with a razor blade.

12. Carefully pour about 1 cup of warm water into the pan on the oven floor. Slide the baguettes from the peel or the back of the baking sheet onto the baking stone in the oven. Or, place the baguette pan directly on the baking stone. Reduce the heat to 450°F.

13. Bake the loaves for 2 minutes. Open the oven and quickly pour another cup of water into the pan on the oven floor. Continue baking for 20 to 22 minutes until the crust is golden brown. Tap the bottom of the loaves; a hollow sound means they're done. Or, insert an instant-read thermometer into the bread, and if the internal temperature is 205°F to 210°F, the bread is done.

14. Remove the bread from the oven and immediately place the loaves on a wire rack to cool completely before storing.

Store the bread in a paper bag or loosely covered with a towel at room temperature. The bread will remain fresh for up to two days at room temperature when covered with a towel.

For Lighter, Fluffier Bread

When I want a light-textured baguette with a fluffy crumb, I use a slightly different mixing method. Once the dough has come together into a visible ball of dough in the bowl of the food processor (after about 20 seconds of mixing), I stop the machine and let the dough rest in the processor bowl for about 5 to 10 minutes.

As the dough rests, the gluten relaxes and the dough begins to ferment. It softens perceptibly during this brief pause in the mixing. Then I complete the mixing for the remaining 25 seconds and proceed with the recipe.

The Best Bread Ever Dough Makes Classic Bread

Like any classic, it is always good and never goes out of style. By adding simple ingredients to the basic dough, you can create as many variations as your imagination allows, changing the bread to make it your own or adapting it to the type of food you are serving.

Here are some of my favorite additions. Add chopped fresh or dried herbs and spices directly to the flour before mixing the dough in the food processor. Scrape the mixed dough onto a lightly floured work surface and knead in chopped nuts, vegetables, or diced fruits by hand.

Herb Bread—¹/₂ cup chopped fresh parsley, chives, marjoram, tarragon, or any combination

Lemon Pepper Bread—2 tablespoons coarse black pepper and 1 tablespoon grated lemon zest

Sun-dried Tomato and Basil Bread—$^1\!/2$ cup fresh basil leaves, tightly packed, then shredded, and $^1\!/4$ cup sun-dried tomatoes cut into thin strips

Simple Olive Bread—$^1\!/2$ cup each pitted black olives such as kalamata or niçoise and $^1\!/2$ cup pitted green olives

Nut and Fruit Loaf—$^1\!/2$ cup chopped roasted almonds and $^1\!/2$ cup dried cherries, $^1\!/2$ cup raisins, $^1\!/2$ cup dried cranberries, or $^1\!/2$ cup dry currants

Summer Vegetable Bread—$^1\!/2$ cup grated carrots, $^1\!/2$ cup grated zucchini, and $^1\!/4$ cup chopped celery leaves

Autumn Harvest Loaf—$^1\!/2$ cup diced fresh pears, $^1\!/2$ cup diced fresh apples, and $^1\!/2$ cup chopped toasted walnuts

Eight Steps to Making the Best Bread Ever

1. Use the food processor fitted with the metal blade to mix and knead dough

2. Be precise in measuring all ingredients. A scale is best. If you are measuring by volume, be consistent in your measuring.

3. Use instant yeast for ease of handling and superb results.

4. The temperature of the water is neither lukewarm nor ice cold. The water temperature must be calculated based on the temperature of the flour being used. Use the "base temperature," the magic number for mixing dough in the food processor.

5. Mix the dough for 45 seconds. This short mixing time is designed not to overmix the dough.

6. Careful measurement of the finished dough temperature ensures excellent results. An instant-read thermometer is one of the baker's better friends. Use it at every stage of bread making.

7. Time equals taste or fermentation equals flavor. Learn to understand the desirability of a lengthy, cool rise to produce the most flavorful breads.

8. Bake at the recommended oven temperatures and steam the oven to create crackling crust on breads.

The Best Bread Ever

The Secrets
of Cooking
Revealed

NO MORE
FAILED RECIPES

CookWise

*The Hows & Whys of Successful Cooking
with over 230 Great-Tasting Recipes*

Shirley O. Corriher

■ AUTHOR

Well-known culinary problem-solver Shirley O. Corriher

■ WHY SHE WROTE IT

"I find great excitement in this knowledge that allows me to make dishes come out as I want. I hope that you too will find pleasure, not only in becoming a more informed and assured cook but in the amazing inner workings of food and cooking—these hows and whys that enable you to make dishes exactly as *you* want. There is great joy in no more failed recipes!"

■ WHY IT MADE OUR LIST

We love a solution to a mystery, and Corriher solves one after the other: Why do shellfish get tough? Why does sea salt taste so good? Why do some cookies puff up and others fall flat? The answers are here, along with at-a-glance charts for quick reference and recipes that illustrate the principles being discussed. It's a fascinating guide to the way food works.

■ CHAPTERS

The Wonders of Risen Bread ▪ How Rich It Is! ▪ Eggs Unscrambled ▪ Sauce Sense ▪ Treasures of the Earth ▪ Fine Fare from Land, Sea, and Air ▪ Sweet Thoughts and Chocolate Dreams

■ SPECIFICS

524 pages, more than 230 recipes, 16 color photographs, $28.50. Published by William Morrow and Company, Inc.

FROM THE BOOK

■ DISCOVERY

"I am thrilled when I learn something that is a major help in improving a dish. When I first learned how important bubbles in the fat are (the creaming step where you beat the butter and sugar to make a cake), all kinds of things became clearer to me. Baking powder and soda do not make a single new bubble; they only enlarge bubbles that are already there. No wonder I made terrible cakes . . . ."

Chicken Stock

MAKES ABOUT 7 QUARTS (SEE NOTE)

Using a tall pot limits evaporation.

Starting the meat and vegetables in cold water aids in extracting flavor.

Using ripe or overripe vegetables adds flavor since some of their insoluble pectic substances have already changed to soluble pectins.

Keeping stock at a low simmer and skimming it frequently prevents emulsification of the fat.

5 chicken carcasses, including necks, or about 4 pounds chicken necks and backs, no livers

4 onions, quartered

3 carrots, cut into 1-inch slices

2 leeks, white parts only, cut into $\frac{1}{2}$-inch slices

3 ribs celery, leaves included, cut into 1-inch pieces

6 mushroom stems (optional)

$\frac{1}{4}$ white turnip (optional)

8 quarts cold water

10 sprigs fresh thyme

2 bay leaves

10 parsley stems, leaves removed

6 white peppercorns

2 cloves garlic (optional)

2 sprigs fresh rosemary (optional)

1. If there is any blood on the chicken bones, soak them in a large bowl of very cold water for 20 minutes. Place the bones, onions, and carrots in a full 12-quart or larger stockpot. Place the leek slices in a large bowl of cold water and break into rings. Stir to let any dirt settle to the bottom of the bowl, then lift leek slices out and add to stockpot. Add the celery and mushroom stems and turnip if using. Cover with cold water. Bring just to a boil and skim off fat and foam. Reduce heat to simmer. Add thyme, bay leaves, parsley, peppercorns, and garlic and rosemary if using. Simmer, uncovered, for 3 to 5 hours, adding hot water as necessary to keep vegetables covered.

2. Degrease well, first by skimming off fat with a spoon, then a skimmer mop, or by dragging a piece of paper towel over the surface, then strain stock through a fine-mesh strainer into a large saucepan or soup pot. Cool immediately by placing the saucepan in a sink filled with ice water. Store in containers that have lids. Refrigerate immediately, leaving uncovered until completely cold, then seal. Stock will keep for 5 to 7 days in the refrigerator or up to 3 months in the freezer. Boil before using any stored stock.

Note: *Quantities may be halved if desired.*

What to Do	Why
Use a stockpot.	Stockpots are tall and narrow to slow water loss from evaporation.
Start with cold water.	For maximum extraction of flavor components from the bones, meat, and vegetables.
If there is blood on bones, soak them for 20 minutes.	To remove blood and prevent stock from clouding.
Use ripe or overripe vegetables.	They are sweeter, and many of the insoluble pectic substances that hold cells together have changed to soluble pectins, which dissolve and contribute more flavor.
Simmer only.	Boiling the stock causes the fat and stock to emulsify and make a greasy, cloudy stock.
Skim frequently.	Removing the foam as it forms helps prevent a cloudy stock.
Do not cover stock while cooking.	For slow evaporation and intensification of flavor.
Do not stir stock.	Stirring causes emulsification of fat and stock and makes stock cloudy and greasy.
Cool stock as fast as possible.	Bacteria grow most rapidly between 40°F (44°C) and 140°F (60°C).
Never cover hot stock after removing from the heat.	The space between the surface and the lid will remain hot and permit bacterial growth.

FREEZING STOCK

There are so many uses for good chicken stock and brown veal stock that I've given recipes to make a large quantity. It's so handy to have these stocks in the freezer. You can freeze in plastic freezer containers, or you can reduce the stock and freeze in ice cube trays. When the cubes are frozen, dump them into a freezer-type zip-top bag for keeping. It's great to be able to grab a cube or two for a sauce. However, if you don't want to store the stocks, you can easily halve the recipes.

Acknowledgements

CHAPTER 1:
Chefs' Books

■ PAGES 10 THROUGH 15

From *The Food of Campanile* by Mark Peel and Nancy Silverton. Copyright © 1997 by Mark Peel and Nancy Silverton. Reprinted by permission of Villard Books, a division of Random House, Inc.

PHOTOGRAPHS: Steven Rothfeld
BOOK DESIGN: Barbara Marks
JACKET DESIGN: Daniel Rembert

■ PAGES 16 THROUGH 29

From *Alfred Portale's Gotham Bar and Grill Cookbook* by Alfred Portale. Photography by Goren Koshida. Copyright © 1997 by Alfred Portale. Used by permission of Doubleday, a division of Bantam Doubleday Dell Publishing Group, Inc.

TEXT: Andrew Friedman
PHOTOGRAPHS: Goren Koshida
BOOK DESIGN: Marysarah Quinn

■ PAGES 30 THROUGH 37

From *Cooking With Too Hot Tamales* by Mary Sue Milliken and Susan Feniger with Helene Siegel. Copyright © 1997 by Mary Sue Milliken and Susan Feniger. Used by permission of William Morrow and Company, Inc.

BOOK DESIGN: Michele Perez
JACKET PHOTOGRAPHS: Kip Lott

■ PAGES 38 THROUGH 45

From *Emeril's Creole Christmas* by Emeril Lagasse with Marcelle Bienvenu. Copyright © 1997 by Emeril Lagasse. Photographs copyright © 1997 by Christopher Hirsheimer. Used by permission of William Morrow and Company, Inc.

PHOTOGRAPHS: Christopher Hirsheimer
BOOK DESIGN: Jill Armus
JACKET DESIGN: Richard L. Aquan
JACKET PHOTOGRAPHS: Brian Smale

■ PAGES 46 THROUGH 53

From *The New Making of a Cook: The Art, Techniques, and Science of Good Cooking* by Madeleine Kamman. Copyright © 1997 by Madeleine Kamman. Illustrations copyright © 1997 by Jennifer Harper. Used by permission of William Morrow and Company, Inc.

ILLUSTRATIONS: Jennifer Harper
BOOK DESIGN: Laura Hammond Hough
JACKET DESIGN: Iris Jeromnimon
JACKET PHOTOGRAPHS: Faith Echtermeyer

■ PAGES 54 THROUGH 65

From *American Brasserie: 180 Simple, Robust Recipes Inspired by the Rustic Foods of France, Italy, and America* by Rick Tramonto and Gale Gand with Julia Moskin. Photography by Tim Turner. Recipes copyright © 1997 by Dynamic Duo, Inc. Reprinted with permission of Macmillan Publishing USA, a Simon & Schuster Macmillan Company.

PHOTOGRAPHS: Tim Turner
BOOK DESIGN: Amy Trombat

CHAPTER 2:

Italian and Mediterranean Cooking

CHAPTER 3:

Best-Sellers

CHAPTER 4:
Vegetarian and Healthy Cooking

■ **PAGES 200 THROUGH 207**

From *Vegetarian Cooking for Everyone* by Deborah Madison. Recipes copyright © 1997 by Deborah Madison. Photographs copyright © 1997 by Laurie Smith. Used by permission of Broadway Books, a division of Bantam Doubleday Dell Publishing Group.

PHOTOGRAPHS: Laurie Smith
ILLUSTRATIONS: Catherine Kirkwood
DESIGN: Vertigo Design

■ **PAGES 208 THROUGH 215**

From *Mollie Katzen's Vegetable Heaven: Over 200 Recipes for Uncommon Soups, Tasty Bites, Side-by-Side Dishes, and Too Many Desserts* written and illustrated by Mollie Katzen. Text and illustrations copyright © 1997 TANTE MALKA, Inc. Reprinted by permission of Hyperion.

COVER AND BOOK DESIGN: Fifth Street Design, Berkeley CA with Mollie Katzen

■ **PAGES 216 THROUGH 225**

From *The Chinese Way: Healthy Low-Fat Cooking from China's Regions* by Eileen Yin-Fei Lo. Text copyright © 1997 by Eileen Yin-Fei Lo. Illustrations copyright © 1977 by Claudia Karabic Sargent. Reprinted by permission of Macmillan USA, a Simon & Schuster Macmillan Company.

CALLIGRAPHY: San Yan Wong
ILLUSTRATIONS: Claudia Karabic Sargent
BOOK DESIGN: Heather Kern
JACKET DESIGN: George Berrian
JACKET ILLUSTRATION: Marjorie Muns

■ **PAGES 226 THROUGH 231**

From *Martha Stewart's Healthy Quick Cook: Four Seasons of Great Menus to Make Every Day* by Martha Stewart. Copyright © 1997 by Martha Stewart. Published by Clarkson N. Potter, Inc. Used by permission of Martha Stewart.

PHOTOGRAPHS: James Merrell
DESIGN: Claudia Bruno

CHAPTER 5:
Special Topics

■ **PAGES 234 THROUGH 241**

From *Great Fish, Quick* by Leslie Revsin. Copyright © 1997 by Leslie Revsin. Photographs © 1997 by Richard Bowditch. Used by permission of Doubleday, a division of Bantam Doubleday Dell Publishing Group, Inc.

PHOTOGRAPHS: Richard Bowditch
BOOK DESIGN: Bonni Leon-Berman

■ **PAGES 242 THROUGH 249**

From *Quick from Scratch: Fish & Shellfish* edited by Judith Hill. Copyright © 1997 by American Express Publishing Corporation. Reprinted by permission of American Express Publishing Corporation.

PHOTOGRAPHS: Melanie Acevedo
DESIGN: Nina Scerbo

■ **PAGES 250 THROUGH 255**

From *The American Century Cookbook* by Jean Anderson. Copyright © 1997 by Jean Anderson. Published by Clarkson N. Potter, Inc. Used with the permission of Jean Anderson.

BOOK DESIGN: Jill Armus
JACKET DESIGN: Whitney Cookman

Publishers

ALFRED A, KNOPF, INC.
201 East 50th Street
New York, NY 10022
(212) 751-2600

Latin American Cooking Across the U.S.A.
by Himilce Novas and Rosemary Silva;
ISBN 0-679-44408-4

**AMERICAN EXPRESS PUBLISHING
CORPORATION**
1120 Avenue of the Americas
New York, NY 10036
(212) 382-5600

Quick from Scratch: Fish and Shellfish
edited by Judith Hill; ISBN 0-916103-38-2

**ARTISAN (A DIVISION OF WORKMAN
PUBLISHING COMPANY, INC.)**
708 Broadway
New York, NY 10003
(212) 614-7500

*Pierre Franey Cooks with His Friends: With
Recipes from Top Chefs in France, Spain, Italy,
Switzerland, Germany, Belgium & the
Netherlands* by Pierre Franey with Claudia
Franey Jensen; ISBN 1-885183-60-7

**BROADWAY BOOKS (A DIVISION OF
BANTAM DOUBLEDAY DELL PUBLISHING
GROUP, INC.)**
1540 Broadway
New York, NY 10036
(212) 354-6500

*The Best Bread Ever: Great Homemade Bread
Using Your Food Processor* by Charles Van Over
with Priscilla Martel; ISBN 0-7679-0032-4

*Flavors of Puglia: Traditional Recipes from the
Heel of Italy's Boot* by Nancy Harmon Jenkins;
ISBN 0-553-06675-7

*A Fresh Taste of Italy: 250 Authentic Recipes,
Undiscovered Dishes, and New Flavors for Every
Day* by Michele Scicolone; ISBN 0-553-06729-X

Vegetarian Cooking for Everyone by Deborah
Madison; ISBN 0-7679-0014-6

CHRONICLE BOOKS
85 Second Street
San Francisco, CA 94105
(415) 537-3730

The Food and Flavors of Haute Provence
by Georgeanne Brennan; ISBN 0-8118-1235-9

*Matthew Kenney's Mediterranean Cooking:
Great Flavors for the American Kitchen*
by Matthew Kenney and Sam Gugino;
ISBN 0-8118-1443-2

**CLARKSON N. POTTER, INC. (MEMBER OF
THE CROWN PUBLISHING GROUP)**
201 East 50th Street
New York, NY 10022
(212) 751-2600

The American Century Cookbook by Jean
Anderson; ISBN 0-517-70576-1

*Martha Stewart's Healthy Quick Cook: Four
Seasons of Great Menus to Make Every Day*
by Martha Stewart; ISBN 0-517-57702-X

*Recipes from Quilt Country: More Food &
Folkways from the Amish & Mennonites*
by Marcia Adams; ISBN 0-517-70562-1

■ **DOUBLEDAY (A DIVISION AND TRADEMARK OF BANTAM DOUBLEDAY DELL PUBLISHING GROUP, INC.)**
1540 Broadway
New York, NY 10036
(212) 354-6500

Alfred Portale's Gotham Bar and Grill Cookbook by Alfred Portale; ISBN 0-385-48210-8

Great Fish, Quick by Leslie Revsin; ISBN 0-385-48538-7

■ **GT PUBLISHING CORPORATION**
16 East 40th Street
New York, NY 10016
(212) 951-3000

Naomi's Home Companion: A Treasury of Favorite Recipes, Food for Thought, and Kitchen Wit and Wisdom by Naomi Judd; ISBN 1-57719-271-0

Sweetie Pie: The Richard Simmons Private Collection of Dazzling Desserts by Richard Simmons; ISBN 1-57719-276-1

■ **HARPERCOLLINS PUBLISHERS, INC.**
10 East 53rd Street
New York, NY 10022
(212) 207-7000

In Nonna's Kitchen: Recipes and Traditions from Italy's Grandmothers by Carol Field; ISBN 0-06-017184-7

Marcella Cucina by Marcella Hazan; ISBN 0-06-017103-0

■ **HEARST BOOKS (A DIVISION OF WILLIAM MORROW AND COMPANY, INC.)**
1350 Avenue of the Americas
New York, NY 10019
(212) 261-6500

The Good Housekeeping Step-by-Step Cookbook edited by Susan Westmoreland; ISBN 0-688-14716-X

■ **HYPERION**
114 Fifth Avenue
New York, NY 10011
(212) 633-4400

Mollie Katzen's Vegetable Heaven: Over 200 Recipes for Uncommon Soups, Tasty Bites, Side-by-Side Dishes, and Too Many Desserts by Mollie Katsen; ISBN 0-7868-6268-8

■ **MACMILLAN USA (A SIMON & SCHUSTER MACMILLAN COMPANY)**
1633 Broadway
New York, NY 10019-6785
(212) 654-8500

American Brasserie: 180 Simple, Robust Recipes Inspired by the Rustic Foods of France, Italy, and America by Rick Tramonto and Gale Gand with Julia Moskin; ISBN 0-02-861630-8

The Chinese Way: Healthy Low-Fat Cooking from China's Regions by Eileen Yin-Fei Lo; ISBN 0-02-860381-8

■ **RIZZOLI INTERNATIONAL PUBLICATIONS, INC.**
300 Park Avenue South
New York, NY 10010
(212) 387-3400

Invitation to Mediterranean Cooking: 150 Vegetarian and Seafood Recipes by Claudia Roden; ISBN 0-8478-2020-3

■ **SCRIBNER (A DIVISION OF SIMON & SCHUSTER)**
1230 Avenue of the Americas
New York, NY 10020
(212) 698-7000

The Joy of Cooking by Irma S. Rombauer, Marion Rombauer Becker, and Ethan Becker; ISBN 0-684-81870-1

■ **SIMON & SCHUSTER**
Rockefeller Center
1230 Avenue of the Americas
New York, NY 10020
(212) 698-7000

Death by Chocolate Cookies by Marcel
Desaulniers; ISBN 0-684-83197-X

■ **VILLARD BOOKS (A DIVISION AND
REGISTERED TRADEMARK OF RANDOM
HOUSE, INC., NEW YORK)**
201 East 50th Street
New York, NY 10022
(212) 751-2600

The Food of Campanile by Mark Peel and
Nancy Silverton; ISBN 0-679-40906-8

■ **WILLIAM MORROW AND COMPANY, INC.**
1350 Avenue of the Americas
New York, NY 10019
(212) 261-6500

Cooking with Too Hot Tamales by Mary Sue
Milliken and Susan Feniger with Helene Siegel;
ISBN 0-688-15121-3

*Cookwise: The Hows and Whys of Successful
Cooking* by Shirley O. Corriher;
ISBN 0-688-10229-8

Emeril's Creole Christmas by Emeril Lagasse
with Marcelle Bienvenu; ISBN 0-688-14691-0

*Kitchen Conversations: Robust Recipes and
Lessons in Flavor from One of America's Most
Innovative Chefs* by Joyce Goldstein;
ISBN 0-688-13866-7

*Mr. Food® Cool Cravings: Easy Chilled and
Frozen Desserts* by Art Ginsburg;
ISBN 0-688-14579-5

*The New Making of a Cook: The Art,
Techniques, and Science of Good Cooking*
by Madeleine Kamman; ISBN 0-688-15254-6

*Stews, Bogs & Burgoos: Recipes from the
Great American Stewpot* by James Villas;
ISBN 0-688-15253-8

What You Knead by Mary Ann Esposito;
ISBN 0-688-15010-1

■ **WORKMAN PUBLISHING COMPANY, INC.**
708 Broadway
New York, NY 10003
(212) 614-7500

Sheila Lukins U.S.A. Cookbook by Sheila
Lukins; ISBN 0-7611-0775-4 (hardcover);
ISBN 1-56305-807-3 (paperback)

Recipes by Course

HORS D'OEUVRES

▪ Olive Sticks, *page 166*

FIRST COURSES

Salads:

▪ Roasted Beet Salad with Horseradish Vinaigrette, *page 14*
▪ Roquefort and Pear Salad with Grapes and Spiced Pecans, *page 56*
▪ Fennel Salad with Clementines and Moroccan Olives, *page 74*
▪ Turkish Green Tomato Salad with Feta, *page 114*
▪ Salmon Carpaccio, *page 124*
▪ Bulghur Salad with Walnuts, *page 136*
▪ Grilled Ratatouille Salad, *page 161*
▪ Green Salad with Blue Cheese, Walnuts, and Figs, *page 211*
▪ Curly Endive with Citrus Vinaigrette, *page 229*
▪ Avocado and Grapefruit Salad, *page 252*

Soups:

▪ Garlic Soup, *page 12*
▪ Chunky Summer Tomato Soup, *page 48*
▪ Hot and Sour Soup, *page 218*

Pasta, Risotto, and Polenta:

▪ Fettuccine with Lobster Bolognese Sauce, *page 21*
▪ Orange-Ricotta Gnocchi with Broccoli Rabe, *page 58*
▪ Onion Risotto Beaten with Butter and Sage, *page 94*
▪ Spaghetti with Oven-Roasted Tomatoes, *page 105*
▪ Gardner's Risotto, *page 126*

▪ Spaghetti with Herbs and Roasted Cherry Tomatoes, *page 139*
▪ Polenta Layered with Cheeses and Black Pepper, *page 153*
▪ Creamed Mushrooms with Dried Porcini, *page 161*

MAIN DISHES

Soups:

▪ Fish Soup with Saffron and Cream, *page 140*
▪ Tunisian Tomato Soup with Chickpeas and Lentils, *page 212*
▪ Seven-Onion Soup, *page 229*
▪ Thai Hot-and-Sour Fish Soup, *page 245*
▪ French Onion Soup Gratinée, *page 252*
▪ Tortilla Soup, *page 270*

Pasta, Risotto, and Polenta:

▪ Fettuccine with Lobster Bolognese Sauce, *page 21*
▪ Risotto with Mussels, Ouzo, Green Onions, and Hot Pepper, *page 116*
▪ Polenta Layered with Cheeses and Black Pepper, *page 153*
▪ Vivid Parsley and Pea Risotto, *page 203*

Shellfish:

▪ Grilled Jumbo Shrimp with Sage and Pancetta, *page 125*
▪ Grilled Sea Scallops with Olives in Olive Oil, *page 236*
▪ Steamed Mussels with Mustards, *page 238*
▪ Shrimp, Jicama, and Mango Salad, *page 247*
▪ New England Pork and Clam Stew, *page 264*
▪ Mussels in Salsa Caribe and White Wine, *page 272*

Fish:

- Black Cod with Brown Butter Sauce and Fresh Herbs, *page 13*
- Salmon Baked in Salsa Verde, *page 32*
- Wrapped Spicy Snapper, *page 33*
- Steamed Mountain-Style Trout Fillets, *page 50*
- Grilled Tuna with Capers and Tomato Sauce, *page 69*
- Pan-Roasted Cod with Provençal Fava Bean Ragout, *page 77*
- Salt-Baked Snapper, *page 106*
- Roast Fish with Sicilian Sweet-and-Sour Onions, *page 118*
- Grilled Mahimahi with Wilted Escarole, Spinach, and Basil, *page 240*
- Orange Roughy with Gremolada Bread Crumbs, *page 249*

Chicken and Other Birds:

- Duck Breast, Caramelized Endive, Sweet Potatoes, and Green Peppercorn Sauce, *page 27*
- Roasted Chicken with a Papaya Glaze, *page 35*
- Quail and Smoked Sausage Gumbo, *page 41*
- Sautéed Chicken with Wine and Herbs, *page 70*
- Roast Stuffed Chicken, *page 108*
- Chicken Ragout with Black Olives, *page 146*
- Figs Grilled with Roulade and Chicken Livers, *page 148*
- Roast Chicken Stuffed with Black Olives, *page 155*
- Polly's Fried Chicken with Tan Gravy, *page 174*
- Amish Roast Chicken and Potatoes with Garlic, *page 259*

Pork and Veal:

- Sugarcane Baked Ham with Spiced Apples and Pears, *page 42*
- Tramonto's Escarole, Sausage, and White Bean Stew, *page 64*
- Pan-Roasted Veal with Radicchio, *page 96*
- Pulled Pork Sandwiches, *page 162*
- Pulled Pork North Carolina-Style, *page 163*
- Larry Smith's Mother's Pork Chops, *page 186*
- Stir-Fried Sichuan Pork, *page 220*
- New England Pork and Clam Stew, *page 264*

Lamb:

- Butterflied Leg of Lamb in Citrus Marinade, *page 51*
- Medallions of Lamb with Basil, *page 71*
- Easter Lamb with Fresh Green Peas and Parmesan Sauce, *page 110*
- Lamb with Rosemary Sauce, *page 149*
- Sour Cherry Lamb Shanks, *page 186*
- Curry Goat or Lamb, *page 274*

Beef and Venison:

- Loin of Venison in Black Pepper-Pomegranate Marinade, *page 79*
- Carpetbag Steak, *page 255*
- Columbia Country Applejack Beef Stew, *page 265*
- Tigua Green Indian Chili, *page 266*

Meatless:

- Tomato, Basil, and Fresh Ricotta Sandwich with Tapenade, *page 24*
- Savory Tomato Tart, *page 168*
- Macaroni and Cheese Casserole, *page 178*
- Spring Vegetable Stew, *page 206*
- Santa Fe Stew, *page 214*

SIDE DISHES

Vegetables:

- Black Jalapeño Salsa, *page 36*
- Ragout of Peas and Artichokes, *page 48*
- Sautéed Cauliflower with Green Olives and Tomatoes, *page 98*
- Creamed Mushrooms with Dried Porcini, *page 161*
- Braised Fennel with Two Cheeses, *page 167*
- Jamaican Salsa Salad, *page 210*
- Steamed Eggplant with Garlic Sauce, *page 219*

Potatoes, Pasta, and Grains:

- Macaroni and Cheese Casserole, *page 178*
- Cornmeal Mush, *page 181*
- Boarding House Potato Salad, *page 185*

BREADS

- Nonna's Sponge Dough, *page 278*
- Straight Dough, *page 281*
- Pumpkin Seed, Sage, and Pancetta Bread, *page 283*
- Tangy Tomato Logs, *page 284*
- Grissini Rustici Country Breadsticks, *page 285*
- The Best Bread Ever, *page 288*

DESSERTS

Pies and Tarts:

- Apple Lattice Tart, *page 132*
- Sour Cream Pumpkin Pie, *page 163*
- Buttered Toffee Apple Pie, *page 260*

Cakes and Cookies:

- Chocolate Crackups, *page 83*
- Chocolate Boulders, *page 84*
- Chocolate Drop Shortcakes, *page 87*
- Almighty Chocolate Divinity, *page 88*
- Orange Cake, Ancona-Style, *page 100*
- Chocolate Truffle Cake, *page 171*
- "I'm Late, I'm Late" Carrot Cake, *page 190*
- Mississippi Mud Cake, *page 254*
- Soft Orange Frosted Cookies, *page 259*

Fruit Desserts:

- Ginger Crème Brûlée with Warm Plum and Raspberry Compote, *page 18*
- Plum Crostata, *page 65*
- Spiced Figs with Lemon, Fennel, and Cloves, *page 120*
- Roasted Peaches, *page 143*
- Frozen Fruit Salad, *page 196*
- Winter Citrus Compote in Tangerine Syrup, *page 207*
- Prunes Poached in Armagnac with Enlightened Crème Frâiche, *page 230*

Other Desserts:

- Chocolate Bread Pudding with Spiced Cream, *page 45*
- Pink Ice Granita, *page 192*
- Chocolate Malted Pops, *page 197*

Index

Page numbers in **boldface** indicate photographs.

A

Acevedo, Melanie, 301
Adams, Marcia, 256-61, 302
Alfred A. Knopf, Inc., 268-75,
   302, 304
*Alfred Portale's Gotham Bar & Grill
   Cookbook* (Portale), 16-29,
   298, 305
AMARETTO
   Roasted Peaches, **142**, 143
American Brasserie (Tramonto and
   Gand with Moskin), 54-65,
   298, 305
American Century Cookbook, The
   (Anderson), 250-55, 302, 304
American Express Publishing
   Corporation, 242-49, 302, 304
ANCHOVIES, 26
   Tapenade, 26
Anderson, Jean, 250-55, 302
ANISE SEEDS
   Fennel Salad with Clementines and
      Moroccan Olives, 74, **75**
Applejack Beef Stew, Columbia
   County, 265-66
APPLES
   Apple Lattice Tart, **131**, 132-33
   Apple-Walnut Vinaigrette, 57
   Buttered Toffee Apple Pie, 260-61,
      261
   Sugarcane Baked Ham with Spiced
      Apples and Pears, 42, **43**
Aquan, Richard L., 298, 300, 302
Armagnac, Prunes Poached in, 230, **231**
Armus, Jill, 298, 301, 302
Artichokes, Ragout of Peas and, 48-49
Artisan, 66-71, 299, 304
ARUGULA
   Fennel Salad with Clementines and
      Moroccan Olives, 74, **75**
   Roasted Beet Salad with Horseradish
      Vinaigrette, 14-15
   Salmon Carpaccio, 124, **128**

Asian fish sauce, 245
ASPARAGUS
   Spring Vegetable Stew, **204**, 206
Avakian, Alexandra, 302
Avirom, Joel, 299, 300
AVOCADOS
   Avocado and Grapefruit Salad, 252
   Jamaican Salsa Salad, 210
   Tortilla Soup, 270-71

B

BACON
   Steamed Mountain-Style Trout
      Fillets, 50-51
BANANAS
   Frozen Fruit Salad, 196
Bannister, Hallam, 300
Barbecue, Southern Dry Rub for, 162
BASIL
   Fettuccine with Lobster Bolognese
      Sauce, 21-22
   Grilled Mahimahi with Wilted
      Escarole, Spinach, and Basil,
      240-41
   Grilled Tuna with Capers and Tomato
      Sauce, **68**, 69
   Medallions of Lamb with Basil, 71
   Orange-Ricotta Gnocchi with
      Broccoli Rabe, 58-59, **61**
   Pan-Roasted Cod with Provençal
      Fava Bean Ragout, **76**, 77
   Spaghetti with Oven-Roasted
      Tomatoes, 105
   Tomato, Basil, and Fresh Ricotta
      Sandwich with Tapenade,
      24-26, **25**
Batzli, Jeff, 299
BAY LEAVES, 23
   Chicken Ragout with Black Olives,
      146-47
   Chicken Stock, 78, 296
   Quail and Smoked Sausage Christmas
      Gumbo, **40**, 41

Roasted Chicken with a Papaya
   Glaze, 35
Shellfish Stock, 78
Tunisian Tomato Soup with
   Chickpeas and Lentils, 212
White Chicken Stock, 23
BEAN CURD
   Hot and Sour Soup, 218
Beans. *See specific kinds*
Becker, Ethan, 158-63, 300
Beecher, M.T., 302
BEEF
   Columbia County Applejack Beef
      Stew, 265-66
   Louis Diat's Carpet-Bag Steak, 255
   Tigua Green Indian Chili, 266-67
Beet, Roasted, Salad with Horseradish
   Vinaigrette, 14-15
Bell peppers. *See* **Peppers, bell**
Berrian, George, 301
Best Bread Ever, The (Van Over),
   286-93, 303, 304
BEST-SELLERS, 156-197
   *Good Housekeeping Step-by-Step
      Cookbook, The* (ed. Westmoreland),
      164-71, 300, 305
   Joy of Cooking, The (Rombauer,
      Rombauer Becker, and Becker),
      158-63, 300, 306
   Mr. Food® Cool Cravings (Ginsburg),
      194-97, 301, 306
   Naomi's Home Companion (Judd),
      172-81, 300, 305
   Sweetie Pie (Simmons), 188-93,
      301, 305
   Sheila Lukins U.S.A. Cookbook
      (Lukins), 182-87, 301, 306
Bienvenu, Marcelle, 38-45, 298
BISCUITS
   Chocolate Boulders, 84, **85**
   Chocolate Crackups, **82**, 83
   Chocolate Drop Shortcakes, **86**, 87
BITTO CHEESE
   Polenta Concia, 153-54
Black Cod with Brown Butter Sauce
   and Fresh Herbs, 13

Blanching, 206
Blue Cheese, Green Salad with Walnuts, Figs and, 211
Bolognese Sauce, Lobster, Fettuccine with, 21-22
Bowditch, Richard, 301
BREAD
Best Bread Ever, 288-92, **293**
Pumpkin Seed, Sage, and Pancetta Bread, **282**, 283
Tangy Tomato Logs, 284
Bread Crumbs, Gremolada, Orange Roughy with, **248** , 249
Bread Pudding, Chocolate, with Spiced Cream, 45
Breadsticks, Country, 285
Brennan, Georgeanne, 144-49, 300
Brigdale, Martin, 299
Britto, Michael, 300
Broadway Books, 102-11, 122-33, 200-207, 286-93, 299, 300, 301, 303, 304
BROCCOLI
Spring Vegetable Stew, **204**, 206
BROCCOLI RABE. *See also* **Rapini**
Orange-Ricotta Gnocchi with Broccoli Rabe, 58-59, **61**
Broth, Pure Vegetable, 49
Bruno, Claudia, 301
Bulghur Salad with Walnuts, 136, **137**
BUTTER
Black Cod with Brown Butter Sauce and Fresh Herbs, 13
Chocolate Truffle Cake, 171, **171**
Onion Risotto Beaten with Butter and Sage, 94
Pat-in-the-Pan Butter Crust, 163
BUTTERNUT SQUASH
Santa Fe Stew, 214

C

CABBAGE
Cole Slaw, 162
CAKE
Chocolate Drop Shortcakes, **86**, 87
Chocolate Truffle Cake, 171, **171**
"I'm Late, I'm Late" Carrot Cake, 190-91, **190**
Mississippi Mud Cake, 255
Orange Cake, Ancona-Style, 100-101, **101**
CANDY
Almighty Chocolate Divinity, 88, **89**

Cantor, Margery, 300
CAPERS
Grilled Tuna with Capers and Tomato Sauce, **68**, 69
Pan-Roasted Cod with Provençal Fava Bean Ragout, **76**, 77
Tapenade, 26
Carpaccio, Salmon, 124, **128**
Carpetbag steak, 255
Carroll, Susan, 302
CARROTS
Chicken Stock, 78, 296
Columbia County Applejack Beef Stew, 265-66
Gardener's Risotto, 126-27, **130**
Garlic Soup, 12
"I'm Late, I'm Late" Carrot Cake, 190-91, **190**
Pure Vegetable Broth, 49
Sour Cherry Lamb Shanks, 186-87
Spring Vegetable Stew, **204**, 206
Vegetable Stock, 222-23
White Chicken Stock, 23
Casserole, Macaroni and Cheese, 178-79, **179**
Cauliflower, Sautéed with Green Olives and Tomato, 98, **99**
Cazals, Jean, 299
CELERY
Boarding House Potato Salad, 185
Braised Celery with Gruyère, 167
Chicken Stock, 78, 296
Gardener's Risotto, 126-27, **130**
Garlic Soup, 12
Pure Vegetable Broth, 49
Quail and Smoked Sausage Christmas Gumbo, **40**, 41
Shellfish Stock, 78
Vegetable Stock, 222-23
White Chicken Stock, 23
CHEESE. *See also specific kinds*
Braised Celery with Gruyère, 167
Braised Fennel with Two Cheeses, 167, **167**
Chunky Summer Tomato Soup, 48
Easter Lamb with Fresh Green Peas and Parmesan Sauce, 110-11
French Onion Soup Gratinée, 252
Gardener's Risotto, 126-27, **130**
Green Salad with Blue Cheese, Walnuts, and Figs, 211
Lamb with Rosemary Sauce, 149
Macaroni and Cheese Casserole, 178-79, **179**
Olive Sticks, 166, **166**

Onion Risotto Beaten with Butter and Sage, 94
Orange-Ricotta Gnocchi with Broccoli Rabe, 58-59, **61**
Polenta Concia, 153-54
Risotto with Mussels, Ouzo, Green Onions, and Hot Pepper, 116-17
Roquefort and Pear Salad with Grapes and Spiced Pecans, 56-57, **60**
Rustic Gruyère Croutons, 229
in salads, 115
Savory Tomato Tart, 168, **168**
Seven-Onion Soup with Rustic Gruyère Croutons, 229, **230**
Tomato, Basil, and Fresh Ricotta Sandwich with Tapenade, 24-26, **25**
Tramonto's Escarole, Sausage, and White Bean Stew, **62**, 64
Turkish Green Tomato Salad with Feta Cheese, 114-15
Vivid Parsley and Pea Risotto, 203
CHEFS' COOKBOOKS, 8-89
Alfred Portale's Gotham Bar & Grill Cookbook (Portale), 16-29, 298, 305
American Brasserie (Tramonto and Gand with Moskin), 54-65, 298, 305
Cooking with Too Hot Tamales (Milliken and Feniger with Siegel), 30-37, 298, 306
Death by Chocolate Cookies (Desaulniers), 80-89, 299, 306
Emeril's Creole Christmas (Lagasse with Bienvenu), 38-45, 298, 306
Food of Campanile, The (Peel and Silverton), 10-15, 298, 306
Matthew Kenney's Mediterranean Cooking (Kenney and Gugino), 72-79, 299, 304
New Making of a Cook, The (Kamman), 46-53, 298, 306
Pierre Franey Cooks with His Friends (Franey with Jensen), 66-71, 299, 304
CHERRIES
Frozen Fruit Salad, 196
Sour Cherry Lamb Shanks, 186-87
CHERVIL
Black Cod with Brown Butter Sauce and Fresh Herbs, 13
Fettuccine with Lobster Bolognese Sauce, 21-22
Steamed Mountain-Style Trout Fillets, 50-51

CHICKEN
Amish Roast Chicken and Potatoes
with Garlic, 259
Chicken Ragout with Black Olives,
146-47
Chicken Stock, 78, 221-22, 296
Polly's Fried Chicken with Tan Gravy,
174-76, **175**
Roast Chicken Stuffed with Black
Olives, 155
Roasted Chicken with a Papaya
Glaze, 35
Roast Stuffed Chicken, 108-9
Sautéed Chicken with Wine and
Herbs, 70
Tortilla Soup, 270-71
White Chicken Stock, 23
Chicken Livers, Figs Grilled with
Roulade and, 148
Chickpeas, Tunisian Tomato Soup with
Lentils and, 212
CHILES, 37
Anaheim
Black Jalapeño Salsa, 36
Santa Fe Stew, 214
ancho
Wrapped Spicy Snapper, 33
Chipotle Cream, 215
jalapeño
Black Jalapeño Salsa, 36
Thai Hot-and-Sour Fish Soup,
244, 245
Tigua Green Indian Chili, 266-67
poblano
Salmon Baked in Salsa Verde, 32
Santa Fe Stew, 214
Scotch bonnet
Curry Goat or Lamb, 274-75
serrano
Jamaican Salsa Salad, 210
Tigua Green Indian Chili, 266-67
Wrapped Spicy Snapper, 33
Chili, Tigua Green Indian, 266-67
Chinese Way, The (Lo), 216-25, 301, 305
CHIVES
Black Cod with Brown Butter Sauce
and Fresh Herbs, 13
Seven-Onion Soup with Rustic
Gruyère Croutons, 229, **230**
CHOCOLATE
Almighty Chocolate Divinity, 88, **89**
Chocolate Boulders, 84, **85**
Chocolate Bread Pudding with Spiced
Cream, **44,** 45
Chocolate Crackups, **82,** 83
Chocolate Drop Shortcakes, **86,** 87

Chocolate Malted Pops, 197
Chocolate Truffle Cake, 171, **171**
Mississippi Mud Cake, 255
Chronicle Books, 72-79, 144-49, 299,
300, 304
CILANTRO
Salmon Baked in Salsa Verde, 32
Wrapped Spicy Snapper, 33
CITRUS
Butterflied Leg of Lamb in Citrus
Marinade, 51-53, **52, 53**
Citrus Vinaigrette, 230
Curly Endive with Citrus Vinaigrette,
229, **229**
Winter Citrus Compote in Tangerine
Syrup, **205,** 207
Clam and Pork Stew, New England, 267
Clarkson N. Potter, Inc., 226-31, 250-55,
256-61, 302, 304
Clayton, Al, 302
Clementines, Fennel Salad with
Moroccan Olives and, 74, **75**
Cloves, Spiced Figs with Lemon, Fennel
and, 120-21
Cobb Salad, 254
COD
Black Cod with Brown Butter Sauce
and Fresh Herbs, 13
Pan-Roasted Cod with Provençal
Fava Bean Ragout, **76,** 77
Cole Slaw, 162
COMPOTES
Ginger Crème Brûlée with Warm
Plum and Raspberry Compote,
18-20, **19**
Winter Citrus Compote in Tangerine
Syrup, **205,** 207
COOKIES
Chocolate Boulders, 84, **85**
Chocolate Crackups, **82,** 83
Soft Orange Frosted Cookies, 259-60
Cooking with Too Hot Tamales (Milliken
and Feniger with Siegel), 30-37,
298, 306
Cookman, Whitney, 301
Cookwise (Corriher), 294-97, 303, 306
CORIANDER
Chicken Stock, 221-22
Pan-Roasted Cod with Provençal
Fava Bean Ragout, **76,** 77
Vegetable Stock, 222-23
Cornmeal Mush, **180,** 181
Corriher, Shirley O., 294-97, 303
CRANBERRIES
Prunes Poached in Armagnac,
230, **231**

CREAM
Chipotle Cream, 215
Chocolate Bread Pudding with Spiced
Cream, **44,** 45
Enlightened Crème Fraîche, 230
Fish Soup with Saffron and Cream,
140, **141**
Spiced Cream, 45
Creamed Mushrooms with Dried
Porcini, 161
Crème Brûlée, Ginger, with Warm
Plum and Raspberry Compote,
18-20, **19**
Crème Fraîche, Enlightened, 230
Crostata, Plum, **63,** 65
CROUTONS
Rustic Gruyère Croutons, 229
Seven-Onion Soup with Rustic
Gruyère Croutons, 229, **230**
Crust, Pat-in-the-Pan Butter, 161
Curry Goat or Lamb, 274-75

D

Da Costa, Beatriz, 302
Daley, Simon, 300
Dates, Chinese preserved, 222-23
Death by Chocolate Cookies
(Desaulniers), 80-89, 299, 306
Desaulniers, Marcel, 80-89, 299
DESSERTS
Almighty Chocolate Divinity,
88, **89**
Apple Lattice Tart, **131,** 132-33
Buttered Toffee Apple Pie,
260-61, **261**
Chocolate Boulders, 84, **85**
Chocolate Bread Pudding with Spiced
Cream, **44,** 45
Chocolate Crackups, **82,** 83
Chocolate Drop Shortcakes, **86,** 87
Chocolate Malted Pops, 197
Chocolate Truffle Cake, 171, **171**
Frozen Fruit Salad, 196
Ginger Crème Brûlée with Warm
Plum and Raspberry Compote,
18-20, **19**
"I'm Late, I'm Late" Carrot Cake,
190-91, **190**
Mississippi Mud Cake, 255
Orange Cake, Ancona-Style,
100-101, **101**
Pink Ice Granita, 192, **193**
Plum Crostata, **63,** 65

Prunes Poached in Armagnac, 230, **231**
Roasted Peaches, **142**, 143
Soft Orange Frosted Cookies, 259-60
Sour Cream Pumpkin Pie, 163
Spiced Figs with Lemon, Fennel, and
    Cloves, 120-21
Winter Citrus Compote in Tangerine
    Syrup, **205**, 207
de Vicq de Cumptich, Roberto, 299,
    300, 302
DILL
    Black Cod with Brown Butter Sauce
        and Fresh Herbs, 13
Divinity, Almighty Chocolate, 88
Doubleday, 16-29, 234-41, 298, 302, 305
DOUGH
    Nonna's Sponge Dough, 278-80,
        278-79
    Straight Dough, 280-81
Dry Rub, Southern, for Barbecue, 162
Duck Breast, Caramelized Endive, Sweet
    Potatoes, and Green Peppercorn
    Sauce, 27-29, **28**
Duguid, Naomi, 299

E

Echtermeyer, Faith, 298
EGGPLANT
    Grilled Ratatouille Salad, 161-62
    Steamed Eggplant with Garlic
        Sauce, 219
EGGS, 170-71
    Boarding House Potato Salad, 185
    Chocolate Truffle Cake, 171, **171**
    Ginger Crème Brûlée with Warm Plum
        and Raspberry Compote, 18-20, **19**
Emeril's Creole Christmas (Lagasse with
    Bienvenu), 38-45, 298, 306
ENDIVE
    Curly Endive with Citrus Vinaigrette,
        229, **229**
    Duck Breast, Caramelized Endive,
        Sweet Potatoes, and Green
        Peppercorn Sauce, 27-29, **28**
ESCAROLE
    Grilled Mahimahi with Wilted
        Escarole, Spinach, and Basil,
        240-41
    Steamed Mountain-Style Trout
        Fillets, 50-51
    Tramonto's Escarole, Sausage, and
        White Bean Stew, **62**, 64
Esposito, Mary Ann, 276-85, 302

F

Fava Bean Ragout, Provençal,
    Pan-Roasted Cod with, **76**, 77
Feniger, Susan, 30-37, 298
FENNEL
    Braised Fennel with Two Cheeses,
        167, **167**
    Fennel Salad with Clementines and
        Moroccan Olives, 74, **75**
    Grilled Ratatouille Salad, 161-62
    Spiced Figs with Lemon, Fennel,
        and Cloves, 120-21
FETA
    Olive Sticks, 166, **166**
    Risotto with Mussels, Ouzo,
        Green Onions, and Hot Pepper,
        116-17
    Turkish Green Tomato Salad with
        Feta Cheese, 114-15
Fettuccine with Lobster Bolognese
    Sauce, 21-22
Field, Carol, 150-55, 300
Fifth Street Design, 301
FIGS
    Figs Grilled with Roulade and
        Chicken Livers, 148
    Green Salad with Blue Cheese,
        Walnuts, and Figs, 211
    Spiced Figs with Lemon, Fennel, and
        Cloves, 120-21
Filgate, Gus, 299
FISH. *See also* **Shellfish**
    Black Cod with Brown Butter Sauce
        and Fresh Herbs, 13
    Grilled Mahimahi with Wilted
        Escarole, Spinach, and Basil,
        240-41
    Grilled Tuna with Capers and Tomato
        Sauce, **68**, 69
    Orange Roughy with Gremolada
        Bread Crumbs, **248**, 249
    Pan-Roasted Cod with Provençal
        Fava Bean Ragout, **76**, 77
    Roast Fish with Sicilian Sweet-and-
        Sour Onions, 118-19
    Salmon Baked in Salsa Verde, 32
    Salmon Carpaccio, 124, **128**
    Salt-Baked Snapper, 106-7
    Steamed Mountain-Style Trout
        Fillets, 50-51
    Thai Hot-and-Sour Fish Soup,
        244, 245
    Wrapped Spicy Snapper, 33

Fisher, Jeffrey, 300
Flavors of Puglia (Jenkins), 102-11,
    299, 304
Flour, Polly's Toasted, 176
Fontana method, 281
Food and Flavors of Haute Provence, The
    (Brennan), 144-49, 300, 304
Food of Campanile, The (Peel and
    Silverton), 10-15, 298, 306
Franey, Pierre, 66-71, 299
Franz-Moore, Paul, 299
Fresh Taste of Italy, A (Scicolone),
    122-33, 300, 304
Friedman, Andrew, 298
FRISÉE
    Steamed Mountain-Style Trout
        Fillets, 50-51
Fruit Salad, Frozen, 196

G

Gand, Gale, 54-65, 298
Gardener's Risotto, 126-27, **130**
GARLIC
    Amish Roast Chicken and Potatoes
        with Garlic, 259
    Black Jalapeño Salsa, 36
    Chicken Stock, 221-22
    Chunky Summer Tomato
        Soup, 48
    Fettuccine with Lobster
        Bolognese Sauce, 21-22
    Garlic Oil, 223
    Garlic Soup, 12
    Mussels in Salsa Caribe and
        White Wine, 272-73
    Orange-Ricotta Gnocchi with
        Broccoli Rabe, 58-59, **61**
    Roast Chicken Stuffed with
        Black Olives, 155
    Santa Fe Stew, 214
    Sour Cherry Lamb Shanks,
        186-87
    Spaghetti with Herbs and
        Roasted Cherry Tomatoes,
        138, 139
    Spaghetti with Oven-Roasted
        Tomatoes, 105
    Steamed Eggplant with Garlic
        Sauce, 219
    Tramonto's Escarole, Sausage, and
        White Bean Stew, **62**, 64
    White Chicken Stock, 23
    Wrapped Spicy Snapper, 33

GINGER
Butterflied Leg of Lamb in Citrus
Marinade, 51-53, **52, 53**
Chicken Stock, 221-22
Ginger Crème Brûlée with Warm Plum
and Raspberry Compote, 18-20, **19**
Loin of Venison in Black Pepper-
Pomegranate Marinade, 79
Thai Hot-and-Sour Fish Soup, **244,** 245
Vegetable Stock, 222-23
Ginsburg, Art, 194-97, 301
GLAZE
Roasted Chicken with a Papaya Glaze, 35
Spiced Glaze, 42
Gnocchi, Orange-Ricotta, with Broccoli
Rabe, 58-59, **61**
GOAT CHEESE
Lamb with Rosemary Sauce, 149
Savory Tomato Tart, 168, **168**
Goat or Lamb Curry, 274-75
Goldstein, Joyce, 112-21, 299
*Good Housekeeping Step-by-Step
Cookbook, The* (ed. Westmoreland),
164-71, 300, 305
Gottlieb, Dennis, 302
Grand, Michael, 299
Granita, Pink Ice, 192, **193**
GRAPEFRUIT
Avocado and Grapefruit Salad, 252
Citrus Vinaigrette, 230
Pink Ice Granita, 192, **193**
Winter Citrus Compote in Tangerine
Syrup, **205,** 207
Grapes, Roquefort and Pear Salad with
Spiced Pecans and, 56-57, **60**
GRAVY
Polly's Fried Chicken with Tan Gravy,
174-76, **175**
Tan Gravy, 176
Great Fish, Quick (Revsin), 234-41, 302, 305
GREAT NORTHERN BEANS
Chunky Summer Tomato Soup, 48
Green Peppercorn Sauce, 29
Grissini Rustici, 285
GRUYÈRE CHEESE
Braised Celery with Gruyère, 167
French Onion Soup Gratinée, 252
Rustic Gruyère Croutons, 229
Seven-Onion Soup with Rustic
Gruyère Croutons, 229, **230**
GT Publishing Corporation, 172-81,
188-93, 300, 301, 305
Guacamole, 253
Gugino, Sam, 72-79, 299
Gumbo, Quail and Smoked Sausage
Christmas, **40,** 41

H

Ham, Sugarcane Baked, with Spiced
Apples and Pears, 42
Hanson, Paul, 301
HARICOTS VERTS
Roquefort and Pear Salad with Grapes
and Spiced Pecans, 56-57, **60**
HarperCollins Publishers, Inc., 92-101,
150-55, 299, 300, 305
Harper, Jennifer, 298
Harris, Alison, 299
Hazan, Marcella, 92-101, 299
HAZELNUTS
Steamed Mountain-Style Trout
Fillets, 50-51
Hearst Books, 164-71, 300, 305
HERBS
Black Cod with Brown Butter
Sauce and Fresh Herbs, 13
Sautéed Chicken with Wine and
Herbs, 70
Spaghetti with Herbs and Roasted
Cherry Tomatoes, **138,** 139
Hill, Judith, 302
Hirsheimer, Christopher, 298
Hollander, Lisa, 300
Horseradish Vinaigrette, Roasted Beet
Salad with, 14-15
Hough, Laura Hammond, 298
Hyperion, 208-15, 301, 305

I

In Nonna's Kitchen (Field), 150-55, 300, 305
Invitation to Mediterranean Cooking
(Roden), 134-43, 300, 306
**ITALIAN AND MEDITERRANEAN
COOKING, 90-155**
Flavors of Puglia (Jenkins), 102-11,
299, 304
*Food and Flavors of Haute Provence,
The* (Brennan), 144-49, 300, 304
Fresh Taste of Italy, A (Scicolone),
122-33, 300, 304
In Nonna's Kitchen (Field), 150-55,
300, 305
Invitation to Mediterranean Cooking
(Roden), 134-43, 300
Kitchen Conversations (Goldstein),
112-21, 299, 306
Marcella Cucina (Hazan), 92-101, 299, 305

J

Jacobson, Jill, 299
Jalapeño peppers. *See* **Chiles, jalapeño**
James, Janet, 299
Jenkins, Nancy Harmon, 102-11, 299
Jensen, Claudia Franey, 66-71, 299
Jeromnimon, Iris, 298
JICAMA
Jamaican Salsa Salad, 210
Shrimp, Jicama, and Mango Salad,
246, 247
Joy of Cooking, The (Rombauer, Rombauer
Becker, and Becker) 158-63, 300, 306
Judd, Naomi, 172-81, 300

K

Kamman, Madeleine, 46-53, 298
Katzen, Mollie, 208-15, 301
Kenan Books, Inc., 299
Kenney, Matthew, 72-79, 299
Kern, Heather, 301
Kerner, Deborah, 302
Kirkwood, Catherine, 301
Kitchen Conversations (Goldstein),
112-21, 299, 306
Koshida, Goren, 298
KUMQUATS
Winter Citrus Compote in Tangerine
Syrup, **205,** 207

L

Lagasse, Emeril, 38-45, 298
LAMB, 187
Butterflied Leg of Lamb in Citrus
Marinade, 51-53, **52, 53**
Curry Goat or Lamb, 274-75
Easter Lamb with Fresh Green Peas
and Parmesan Sauce, 110-11
Lamb with Rosemary Sauce, 149
Medallions of Lamb with Basil, 71
Sour Cherry Lamb Shanks, 186-87
*Latin American Cooking Across the
U.S.A.* (Novas and Silva), 268-75,
302, 304
LEEKS
Chicken Stock, 78, 296
Chunky Summer Tomato Soup, 48

Pure Vegetable Broth, 49
Seven-Onion Soup with Rustic
    Gruyère Croutons, 229, **230**
LEMONS
    Black Cod with Brown Butter Sauce
        and Fresh Herbs, 13
    Butterflied Leg of Lamb in Citrus
        Marinade, 51-53, **52**, **53**
    Spiced Figs with Lemon, Fennel, and
        Cloves, 120-21
Lentils, Tunisian Tomato Soup with
    Chickpeas and, 212
Leon-Berman, Bonni, 301
Levine, Barbara, 302
LIMA BEANS
    Gardener's Risotto, 126-27, **130**
LIMES
    Black Jalapeño Salsa, 36
    Jamaican Salsa Salad, 210
    Santa Fe Stew, 214
    Thai Hot-and-Sour Fish Soup, **244**, 245
    Wrapped Spicy Snapper, 33
Lo, Eileen Yin-Fei, 216-25, 301
Lobster Bolognese Sauce, Fettuccine
    with, 21-22
Lott, Kip, 298
Louis Diat's Carpet-Bag Steak, 255
LOVAGE
    Vivid Parsley and Pea Risotto, 203
Lukins, Shiela, 182-87, 301
Lynch, Kathleen, 302

M

Macaroni and Cheese Casserole,
    178-79, **179**
Macmillan Publishing USA, 54-65,
    216-25, 298, 301, 305
Madison, Deborah, 200-207, 301
Maestro, Laura Hartman, 300
Mahimahi, Grilled, with Wilted
    Escarole, Spinach, and Basil, 240-41
Malkin, Lori S., 300
Malted Chocolate Pops, 197
MANGO
    Jamaican Salsa Salad, 210
    Shrimp, Jicama, and Mango Salad,
        246, 247
Marcella Cucina (Hazan), 92-101, 299, 305
MARINADE
    Butterflied Leg of Lamb in Citrus
        Marinade, 51-53, **52**, **53**
    Loin of Venison in Black Pepper-
        Pomegranate Marinade, 79

Marks, Barbara, 298, 300
Martha Stewart's Healthy Quick Cook
    (Stewart), 227-31, 302, 305
Matthew Kenney's Mediterranean Cooking
    (Kenney and Gugino), 72-79, 299, 304
McDonald, Jock, 299
Medallions of Lamb with Basil, 71
Mendelsohn, Mike, 300
Merrell, James, 301
Milliken, Mary Sue, 30-37, 298
MINT
    Roast Fish with Sicilian Sweet-and-
        Sour Onions, 118-19
MM Design 2000, Inc., 300
Mollie Katzen's Vegetable Heaven
    (Katzen), 208-15, 301, 305
Moskin, Julia, 54-65, 298
MOZZARELLA
    Braised Fennel with Two Cheeses,
        167, **167**
Mr. Food® Cool Cravings (Ginsburg),
    194-97, 301, 306
Muns, Marjorie, 301
Murray, David, 300
Mush, Cornmeal, **180**, 181
MUSHROOMS, 160-61, 161
    Creamed Mushrooms with Dried
        Porcini, 161
    Gardener's Risotto, 126-27, **130**
    Thai Hot-and-Sour Fish Soup,
        244, 245
    Vegetable Stock, 222-23
MUSSELS
    Mussels in Salsa Caribe and White
        Wine, 272-73
    Risotto with Mussels, Ouzo, Green
        Onions, and Hot Peppers, 116-17
    Steamed Mussels with Mustards,
        238-39
Mustards, Steamed Mussels with,
    238-39

N

Naomi's Home Companion (Judd),
    172-81, 300, 305
Needham, Steven Mark, 300
New Making of a Cook, The (Kamman),
    46-53, 298, 306
New Recipes from Quilt Country
    (Adams), 256-61, 302, 305
Nonna's Sponge Dough, 278-80,
    278-79
Novas, Himilce, 268-75, 302

O

OIL
    Garlic Oil, 223
    Grilled Sea Scallops with Olives in
        Olive Oil, 236-37
    Hot Pepper Oil, 224
    Scallion Oil, 223
Olive Oil, Grilled Sea Scallops with
    Olives in, 236-37
Olive paste, 166
OLIVES
    Chicken Ragout with Black Olives,
        146-47
    Fennel Salad with Clementines and
        Moroccan Olives, 74, **75**
    Green Olives with Tomato and
        Sautéed Cauliflower, 98, **99**
    Grilled Sea Scallops with Olives in
        Olive Oil, 236-37
    Olive Sticks, 166, **166**
    Pan-Roasted Cod with Provençal
        Fava Bean Ragout, **76**, 77
    Roast Chicken Stuffed with Black
        Olives, 155
    Tapenade, 26
ONIONS
    Chicken Stock, 78, 221-22, 296
    French Onion Soup Gratinée, 252
    Gardener's Risotto, 126-27, **130**
    Garlic Soup, 12
    Larry Smith's Mother's Pork
        Chops, 186
    Loin of Venison in Black Pepper-
        Pomegranate Marinade, 79
    Mussels in Salsa Caribe and White
        Wine, 272-73
    Onion Risotto Beaten with Butter
        and Sage, 94
    Pure Vegetable Broth, 49
    Quail and Smoked Sausage
        Christmas Gumbo, **40**, 41
    Risotto with Mussels, Ouzo, Hot
        Pepper and Green Onions,
        116-17
    Roast Fish with Sicilian Sweet-and-
        Sour Onions, 118-19
    Santa Fe Stew, 214
    Savory Tomato Tart, 168, **168**
    Seven-Onion Soup with Rustic
        Gruyère Croutons, 229, **230**
    Shellfish Stock, 78
    Tunisian Tomato Soup with
        Chickpeas and Lentils, 212

Turkish Green Tomato Salad with
Feta Cheese, 114-15
Vegetable Stock, 222-23
White Chicken Stock, 23
Orange Roughy with Gremolada Bread
Crumbs, **248**, 249

ORANGES
Butterflied Leg of Lamb in Citrus
Marinade, 51-53, **52**, **53**
Fennel with Clementines and
Moroccan Olives, 74, **75**
Orange Cake, Ancona-Style,
100-101, **101**
Orange-Ricotta Gnocchi with
Broccoli Rabe, 58-59, **61**
Roasted Chicken with a Papaya
Glaze, 35
Soft Orange Frosted Cookies, 259-60
Winter Citrus Compote in Tangerine
Syrup, **205**, 207

OREGANO
Mexican
Black Jalapeño Salsa, 36
Salmon Baked in Salsa Verde, 32
Wrapped Spicy Snapper, 33
Oriolo, Richard, 299, 302
Ouellette, Ed, 300
Ouzo, Risotto with Mussels, Green
Onions, Hot Pepper and, 116-17

OYSTERS
Louis Diat's Carpet-Bag Steak, 255

P

PANCETTA
Easter Lamb with Fresh Green
Peas and Parmesan Cheese,
110-11
Figs Grilled with Roulade and
Chicken Livers, 148
Grilled Jumbo Shrimp with Sage and
Pancetta, 125, **129**
Pumpkin Seed, Sage, and Pancetta
Bread, **282**, 283
Papaya Glaze, Roasted Chicken
with a, 35

PARMESAN
Braised Fennel with Two Cheeses,
167, **167**
Easter Lamb with Fresh Green Peas
and Parmesan Sauce, 110-11
French Onion Soup Gratinée, 252
Orange-Ricotta Gnocchi with
Broccoli Rabe, 58-59, **61**

Tramonto's Escarole, Sausage, and
White Bean Stew, **62**, 64
Vivid Parsley and Pea Risotto, 203

PARMIGIANO-REGGIANO
Gardener's Risotto, 126-27, **130**
Onion Risotto Beaten with Butter
and Sage, 94

PARSLEY
Black Cod with Brown Butter
Sauce and Fresh Herbs, 13
Chicken Stock, 78, 296
Chunky Summer Tomato Soup, 48
Easter Lamb with Fresh Green
Peas and Parmesan Sauce,
110-11
Fettuccine with Lobster Bolognese
Sauce, 21-22
Quail and Smoked Sausage Christmas
Gumbo, **40**, 41
Risotto with Mussels, Ouzo,
Green Onions, and Hot Pepper,
116-17
Roasted Beet Salad with
Horseradish Vinaigrette, 14-15
Salmon Baked in Salsa Verde, 32
Sour Cherry Lamb Shanks,
186-87
Spaghetti with Oven-Roasted
Tomatoes, 105
Vivid Parsley and Pea Risotto, 203

PARSNIPS
Columbia County Applejack Beef
Stew, 265-66
Garlic Soup, 12

PASTA
Fettuccine with Lobster Bolognese
Sauce, 21-22
Macaroni and Cheese Casserole,
178-79, **179**
Spaghetti with Herbs and Roasted
Cherry Tomatoes, **138**, 139
Spaghetti with Oven-Roasted
Tomatoes, 105
Peaches, Roasted, **142**, 143

PEARS
Roquefort and Pear Salad with
Grapes and Spiced Pecans,
56-57, **60**
Sugarcane Baked Ham with Spiced
Apples and Pears, 42, **43**

PEAS, 202-03
Easter Ham with Fresh Green Peas
and Parmesan Sauce, 110-11
Ragout of Peas and Artichokes,
48-49
Vivid Parsley and Pea Risotto, 203

PECANS
Chocolate Boulders, 84, **85**
Mississippi Mud Cake, 255
Roquefort and Pear Salad with
Grapes and Spiced Pecans,
56-57, **60**
Peel, Mark, 10-15, 298
Pentagram, 299, 300
Pepper, Black, -Pomegranate Marinade,
Loin of Venison with, 79
Pepper, Hot, Oil, 224
Pepper, Hot, Risotto with Mussels,
Ouzo, Green Onions and,
116-17

PEPPERCORN, GREEN
Duck Breast, Caramelized Endive,
Sweet Potatoes, and Green
Peppercorn Sauce, 27-29, **28**
Green Peppercorn Sauce, 29

PEPPERS, BELL
Boarding House Potato Salad, 185
Quail and Smoked Sausage Christmas
Gumbo, **40**, 41
Stir-Fried Sichuan Pork, 220-21
Perez, Michele, 298

PIE CRUSTS, 169
Pastry for 11-Inch Tart, 169
Pastry for 9-Inch Tart, 169
Pastry for 1-Crust Pie, 169
Pastry for 2-Crust Pie, 169
Pat-in-the-Pan Butter Crust, 163
Perfect Pie Pastry, 261
Pierre Franey Cooks with His Friends
(Franey with Jensen), 66-71,
299, 304

PIES
Buttered Toffee Apple Pie,
260-61, **261**
Sour Cream Pumpkin Pie, 163

PINEAPPLE
Frozen Fruit Salad, 196
Jamaican Salsa Salad, 210

PINTO BEANS
Santa Fe Stew, 214

PLUMS
Ginger Crème Brûlée with Warm
Plum and Raspberry Compote,
18-20, **19**
Plum Crostata, **63**, 65

POLENTA, 152
Polenta Concia, 153-54
Pollo con le Olive, 155
Polly's Fried Chicken with Tan Gravy,
174-76, **175**
Pomegranate-Black Pepper Marinade,
Loin of Venison in, 79

Pops, Chocolate Malted, 197
Porcini, Dried, Creamed Mushrooms
with, 161
PORK
Hot and Sour Soup, 218
Larry Smith's Mother's Pork Chops, 186
New England Pork and Clam Stew,
264-65
Pulled Pork, North Carolina-Style, 163
Pulled Pork Sandwiches, 162
Stir-Fried Sichuan Pork, 220-21
Sugarcane Baked Ham with Spiced
Apples and Pears, 42, **43**
Portale, Alfred, 16-29
POTATOES, 184
Amish Roast Chicken and Potatoes
with Garlic, 259
Boarding House Potato Salad, 185
Garlic Soup, 12
Orange-Ricotta Gnocchi with
Broccoli Rabe, 58-59, **61**
Tigua Green Indian Chili, 266-67
POULTRY. *See also* **Chicken**
Secondary Stock, 50
Powell, Chip, 300
Prunes Poached in Armagnac, 230, **231**
Pudding, Chocolate Bread, with Spiced
Cream, **44**, 45
Puff pastry, 166
Pumpkin Pie, Sour Cream, 161
Pumpkin Seed, Sage, and Pancetta
Bread, **282**, 283

Q

Quail and Smoked Sausage Christmas
Gumbo, **40**, 41
Quick from Scratch: Fish & Shellfish
(ed. Hill), 242-49, 302, 304
Quinn, Marysarah, 298

R

Radicchio, Pan-Roasted Veal with, 96-97
RADISHES
Spring Vegetable Stew, **204**, 206
RAGOUT
Chicken Ragout with Black Olives,
146-47
Pan-Roasted Cod with Provençal
Fava Bean Ragout, **76**, 77
Ragout of Peas and Artichokes, 48-49

RAISINS, GOLDEN
Apple Lattice Tart, **131**, 132-33
RAPINI
Garlic Soup, 12
RASPBERRIES
Ginger Crème Brûlée with Warm Plum
and Raspberry Compote, 18-20, **19**
Plum Crostata, **63**, 65
Ratatouille, Grilled, Salad, 160
Rayman, James, 302
Rembert, Daniel, 298
Revsin, Leslie, 234-41, 302
Rice varieties, risotto, 95
RICOTTA
Orange-Ricotta Gnocchi with
Broccoli Rabe, 58-59, **61**
Tomato, Basil, and Fresh Ricotta
Sandwich with Tapenade, 24-26, **25**
RISOTTO
Gardener's Risotto, 126-27, **130**
Onion Risotto Beaten with Butter
and Sage, 94
rice varieties, 95
Risotto with Mussels, Ouzo, Green
Onions, and Hot Pepper, 116-17
Vivid Parsley and Pea Risotto, 203
Rizzoli International Publications, Inc.,
134-43, 300, 305
Roden, Claudia, 134-43, 300
Rombauer, Irma S., 158-63, 300
Rombauer Becker, Marion, 158-63,
300
Roquefort and Pear Salad with Grapes
and Spiced Pecans, 56-57, **60**
Rosemary Sauce, Lamb with, 149
Rosenthal, Howard, 300
Rothfeld, Steven, 298
Roulade, Figs Grilled with Chicken
Livers and, 148
Rub, Dry, Southern, for Barbecue, 162

S

Saffron, Fish Soup with Cream and,
140, **141**
SAGE
Grilled Jumbo Shrimp with Sage and
Pancetta, 125, **129**
Larry Smith's Mother's Pork Chops,
186
Onion Risotto Beaten with Butter
and Sage, 94
Pumpkin Seed, Sage, and Pancetta
Bread, **282**, 283

SALADS
Avocado and Grapefruit Salad, 252
Boarding House Potato Salad, 185
Bulghur Salad with Walnuts, 136, **137**
cheese in, 115
Cobb Salad, 254
Curly Endive with Citrus Vinaigrette,
229, **229**
dressing, 185
Fennel Salad with Clementines and
Moroccan Olives, 74, **75**
Frozen Fruit Salad, 196
Green Salad with Blue Cheese,
Walnuts, and Figs, 211
Grilled Ratatouille Salad, 161-62
Jamaican Salsa Salad, 210
Roasted Beet Salad with Horseradish
Vinaigrette, 14-15
Roquefort and Pear Salad with Grapes
and Spiced Pecans, 56-57, **60**
Salmon Carpaccio, 124, **128**
Shrimp, Jicama, and Mango Salad,
246, 247
Turkish Green Tomato Salad with
Feta Cheese, 114-15
SALMON
Salmon Baked in Salsa Verde, 32
Salmon Carpaccio, 124, **128**
SALSAS
Black Jalapeño Salsa, 36
Jamaican Salsa Salad, 210
Mussels in Salsa Caribe and White
Wine, 272-73
Salmon Baked in Salsa Verde, 32
SANDWICHES
Pulled Pork, North Carolina-Style,
163
Pulled Pork Sandwiches, 162
Tomato, Basil, and Fresh Ricotta
Sandwich with Tapenade, 24-26, **25**
Sargent, Claudia Karabic, 301
SAUCES
Black Cod with Brown Butter Sauce
and Fresh Herbs, 13
Duck Breast, Caramelized Endive,
Sweet Potatoes, and Green
Peppercorn Sauce, 27-29, **28**
Easter Lamb with Fresh Green Peas
and Parmesan Sauce, 110-11
Fettuccine with Lobster Bolognese
Sauce, 21-22
Green Peppercorn Sauce, 29
Grilled Tuna with Capers and Tomato
Sauce, **68**, 69
Lamb with Rosemary Sauce, 149
Steamed Eggplant with Garlic Sauce, 219

SAUSAGE
  Quail and Smoked Sausage Christmas
    Gumbo, **40**, 41
  Tramonto's Escarole, Sausage, and
    White Bean Stew, **62**, 64
SCALLIONS
  Chicken Stock, 221-22
  Pure Vegetable Broth, 49
  Quail and Smoked Sausage Christmas
    Gumbo, **40**, 41
  Salmon Baked in Salsa Verde, 32
  Scallion Oil, 223
  Spring Vegetable Stew, **204**, 206
  Vegetable Stock, 222-23
Scallops, Sea, Grilled, with Olives in
    Olive Oil, 240-41
Scerbo, Nina, 301
Scher, Paula, 300
Scheuer, Philip A., 300
Scicolone, Michele, 122-33, 300
Scoble, Gretchen, 300
Scribner, 158-63, 300, 306
Secondary Stock, 50
Selmes, Jules, 300
SHALLOTS
  Seven-Onion Soup with Rustic
    Gruyère Croutons, 229, **230**
Sheila Lukins U.S.A. Cookbook (Lukins),
    182-87, 301, 306
SHELLFISH
  Fettuccine with Lobster Bolognese
    Sauce, 21-22
  Grilled Jumbo Shrimp with Sage and
    Pancetta, 125, **129**
  Grilled Sea Scallops with Olives in
    Olive Oil, 236-37
  Louis Diat's Carpet-Bag Steak, 255
  Mussels in Salsa Caribe and White
    Wine, 272-73
  New England Pork and Clam Stew,
    264-65
  Risotto with Mussels, Ouzo, Green
    Onions, and Hot Pepper, 116-17
  Shellfish Stock, 78
  Shrimp, Jicama, and Mango Salad,
    246, 247
  Steamed Mussels with Mustards,
    238-39
Shortcakes, Chocolate Drop, **86**, 87
SHRIMP
  Grilled Jumbo Shrimp with Sage and
    Pancetta, 125, **129**
  Shrimp, Jicama, and Mango Salad,
    246, 247
Siegel, Helene, 30-37, 298
Silva, Rosemary, 268-75, 302

Silverman, Ellen, 299,
Silverton, Nancy, 10-15, 298
Simmons, Richard, 188-93, 301
Simon & Schuster, 80-89, 299, 306
Smale, Brian, 298
Smith, Laurie, 301
SNAPPER
  Salt-Baked Snapper, 106-7
  Wrapped Spicy Snapper, 33
SNOW PEAS
  Spring Vegetable Stew, **204**, 206
Snyder, Jason, 300
SOUPS. *See also* **Stews**
  Chunky Summer Tomato Soup, 48
  Fish Soup with Saffron and Cream,
    140, **141**
  French Onion Soup Gratinée, 252
  Garlic Soup, 12
  Hot and Sour Soup, 218
  Quail and Smoked Sausage Christmas
    Gumbo, **40**, 41
  Seven-Onion Soup with Rustic
    Gruyère Croutons, 229, **230**
  Thai Hot-and-Sour Fish Soup, **244**, 245
  Tortilla Soup, 270-71
  Tunisian Tomato Soup with
    Chickpeas and Lentils, 212
SOUR CREAM
  Chipotle Cream, 215
  Sour Cream Pumpkin Pie, 163
SPAGHETTI
  Spaghetti with Herbs and Roasted
    Cherry Tomatoes, **138**, 139
  Spaghetti with Oven-Roasted
    Tomatoes, 105
SPECIAL TOPICS, 232-297
  American Century Cookbook, The
    (Anderson), 250-55, 302, 304
  Best Bread Ever, The (Van Over),
    286-93, 303, 304
  Cookwise (Corriher), 294-97, 303, 306
  Great Fish, Quick (Revsin), 234-41,
    302, 305
  *Latin American Cooking Across the
    U.S.A.* (Novas and Silva), 268-75,
    302, 304
  New Recipes from Quilt Country
    (Adams), 256-61, 302, 305
  Quick from Scratch: Fish & Shellfish
    (ed. Hill), 242-49, 302, 304
  Stews, Bogs & Burgoos (Villas),
    262-67, 302, 306
  What You Knead (Esposito), 276-85,
    302, 306
Spinach, Grilled Mahimahi with Wilted
    Escarole, Basil and, 240-41

Sponge Dough, Nonna's, 279-81,
    279-80
STEAK
  Carpetbag Steak, 255
  Louis Diat's Carpet-Bag Steak, 255
Stern, Cynthia, 302
Stewart, Martha, 227-31, 302
Stews, Bogs & Burgoos (Villas), 262-67,
    302, 306
STEWS, 262-67. *See also* **Soups**
  Columbia County Applejack Beef
    Stew, 265-66
  New England Pork and Clam Stew,
    264-65
  Santa Fe Stew, 214
  Spring Vegetable Stew, **204**, 206
  Tramonto's Escarole, Sausage,
    and White Bean Stew,
    62, 64
Stir Frying, Techniques, 224-25
STOCK AND BROTH
  Chicken Stock, 78, 221-22, 296
    making, 297
  Pure Vegetable Broth, 49
  Secondary Stock, 50
  Shellfish Stock, 78
  Vegetable Stock, 222-23
  White Chicken Stock, 23
Storage of fruits and vegetables, 34
Stradling, Paul, 300
Straight Dough, 280-81
Sugarcane Baked Ham with Spiced
    Apples and Pears, 42, **43**
Sweetie Pie (Simmons), 188-93, 301, 305
Sweet Potatoes, Duck Breast, Caramelized
    Endive, Green Peppercorn Sauce and,
    27-29, **28**
SWORDFISH
  Thai Hot-and-Sour Fish Soup,
    244, 245

T

Tangerine Syrup, Winter Citrus
    Compote in, **205**, 207
Tangy Tomato Logs, 284
TAPENADE, 26, 166
  Tomato, Basil, and Fresh Ricotta
    Sandwich with Tapenade, 24-26, **25**
TART
  Apple Lattice Tart, **131**, 132-33
  Pastry for 11-Inch Tart, 169
  Pastry for 9-Inch Tart, 169
  Savory Tomato Tart, 168, **168**

Thomas, Mark, 300

THYME
Roasted Beet Salad with Horseradish Vinaigrette, 14-15
Roasted Chicken with a Papaya Glaze, 35
Wrapped Spicy Snapper, 33

Tigua Green Indian Chili, 266-67

Toffee Apple Pie, Buttered, 260

TOMATOES
Bulghur Salad with Walnuts, 136, **137**
Chicken Ragout with Black Olives, 146-47
Chunky Summer Tomato Soup, 48
Mussels in Salsa Caribe and White Wine, 272-73
New England Pork and Clam Stew, 264-65
plum
Gardener's Risotto, 126-27, **130**
Grilled Ratatouille Salad, 161-62
Grilled Tuna with Capers and Tomato Sauce, **68**, 69
Medallions of Lamb with Basil, 71
Orange-Ricotta Gnocchi with Broccoli Rabe, 58-59, **61**
Sour Cherry Lamb Shanks, 186-87
Tramonto's Escarole, Sausage, and White Bean Stew, **62**, 64
Roma
Salmon Baked in Salsa Verde, 32
Sautéed Cauliflower with Green Olives and Tomato, 98, **99**
Savory Tomato Tart, 168, **168**
Shellfish Stock, 78
Spaghetti with Herbs and Roasted Cherry Tomatoes, **138**, 139
Spaghetti with Oven-Roasted Tomatoes, 105
Tangy Tomato Logs, 284
Thai Hot-and-Sour Fish Soup, **244**, 245
Tomato, Basil, and Fresh Ricotta Sandwich with Tapenade, 24-26, **25**
Tortilla Soup, 270-71
Tunisian Tomato Soup with Chickpeas and Lentils, 212
Turkish Green Tomato Salad with Feta Cheese, 114-15

Tortilla Soup, 270-71

Tramonto, Rick, 54-65, 298

Tramonto's Escarole, Sausage, and White Bean Stew **62**, 64

Trombat, Amy, 298

Trout Fillets, Steamed Mountain-Style, 50-51

Truffle Cake, Chocolate, 171

Truslow, Bill, 302

Tuna, Grilled, with Capers and Tomato Sauce, 69

Turner, Tim, 298

TURNIPS
Columbia County Applejack Beef Stew, 265-66
Spring Vegetable Stew, **204**, 206

V

Van Over, Charles, 286-93, 303

VEAL
Pan-Roasted Veal with Radicchio, 96-97
Secondary Stock, 50

VEGETABLES. *See also specific kinds*
Pure Vegetable Broth, 49
Spring Vegetable Stew, **204**, 206
Vegetable Stock, 222-23

VEGETARIAN AND HEALTHY COOKING, 198-231
Chinese Way, The (Lo), 216-25, 301, 305
Martha Stewart's Healthy Quick Cook (Stewart), 227-31, 302, 305
Mollie Katzen's Vegetable Heaven (Katzen), 208-15, 301, 305
Vegetarian Cooking for Everyone (Madison), 200-207, 301, 304
Vegetarian Cooking for Everyone (Madison), 200-207, 301, 304

Venison, Loin of, in Black Pepper-Pomegranate Marinade, 79

Vertigo Design, 299, 301

Vertigo, NYC, 302

Vibbert, Carol, 300

Villard Books, 10-15, 298, 306

Villas, James, 262-67, 302

VINAIGRETTE, 185
Apple-Walnut Vinaigrette, 57
Citrus Vinaigrette, 230
Curly Endive with Citrus Vinaigrette, 229, **229**
Roasted Beet Salad with Horseradish Vinaigrette, 14-15

W

WALNUTS
Almighty Chocolate Divinity, 88, **89**
Apple-Walnut Vinaigrette, 57
Bulghur Salad with Walnuts, 136, **137**
Frozen Fruit Salad, 196
Green Salad with Blue Cheese, Walnuts, and Figs, 211

Waxberg, Richard, 302

Westmoreland, Susan, 164-71, 300

What You Knead (Esposito), 276-85, 302, 306

White Bean Stew, Tramonto's Escarole, Sausage and, **62**, 64

William Morrow and Company, Inc., 30-37, 38-45, 46-53, 112-21, 194-97, 262-267, 276-285, 294-297, 298, 299, 301, 302, 303, 304, 306

WINE, RED
Green Peppercorn Sauce, 29

WINE, WHITE
Easter Lamb with Fresh Green Peas and Parmesan Sauce, 110-11
Fettuccine with Lobster Bolognese Sauce, 21-22
Lamb with Rosemary Sauce, 149
Mussels in Salsa Caribe and White Wine, 272-73
Risotto with Mussels, Ouzo, Green Onions, and Hot Pepper, 116-17
Roast Stuffed Chicken, 108-9
Sautéed Chicken with Wine and Herbs, 70
Shellfish Stock, 78
Sour Cherry Lamb Shanks, 186-87

Wong, San Yan, 301

Workman Publishing Company, Inc. 182-87, 301, 306

Wrapped Spicy Snapper, 33

Y

YOGURT
Chipotle Cream, 215

Z

ZUCCHINI
Gardener's Risotto, 126-27, **130**
Grilled Ratatouille Salad, 161-62